DANTE GABRIEL ROSSETTI AND THE GAME THAT MUST BE LOST

Dante Gabriel Rossetti

and the Game That Must Be Lost

JEROME
McGANN

YALE UNIVERSITY PRESS / NEW HAVEN & LONDON

Designed by Mary Valencia
Set in Galliard Old Style and Rennie Mackintosh type by
The Composing Room of Michigan, Inc.
Printed in the United States of America by Sheridan Books, Chelsea, Michigan.

Library of Congress Cataloging-in-Publication Data

McGann, Jerome J.
Dante Gabriel Rossetti and the game that must be lost / Jerome McGann.
p. cm.
Includes bibliographical references (p.   ) and index.
ISBN 0-300-08023-9 (cloth : alk. paper)
1. Rossetti, Dante Gabriel, 1828–1882 — Criticism and interpretation. 2. Art
and literature — England — History — 19th century. 3. Rossetti, Dante Gabriel,
1828–1882 — Aesthetics. 4. England — Civilization — 19th century.
5. Aesthetics, Modern — 19th century. 6. Aesthetics, British.
PR5247.M37 2000
759.2 — dc21   99-053380

A catalogue record for this book is available from the British Library.

10 9 8 7 6 5 4 3 2 1

To the Rossetti Archivists,
my students
my colleagues
at the University of Virginia

To follow knowledge like a sinking star
Beyond the utmost bounds of human thought.

Tennyson, "Ulysses"

In play, there are two pleasures for your choosing,
The one is winning, and the other losing.

Byron, *Don Juan*

CONTENTS

ILLUSTRATIONS

The illustrations for this book are somewhat unusual and require a word of explanation. All the black-and-white figures are taken from engravings or photographs made during or shortly after Rossetti's lifetime. Of the figures in color, half reproduce photographs or mezzotints from the same period, and had similar contemporary reproductions been available for any of the other color illustrations needed for this book, they would have been included as well.

These early reproductions of Rossetti's work are important for a number of reasons. First, the color reproductions — most of them the work of Rossetti's friend Frederick Hollyer — are rarely seen and not well known. These pictures of Rossetti's pictures constitute a significant body of graphic arts work in their own right. Furthermore, these early reproductions remind us of Rossetti's great interest in early photography and of how deliberately he used the new technology to disseminate and advertise his paintings and drawings. To look at Rossetti's pictures in reproductions by Hollyer, Prinsep, Mansell, and others is to see them as they were regularly seen — in many case, exclusively seen — by many who lived before the coming of the Armory or the Postimpressionist shows that inaugurated the Modernist turn.

Unless otherwise indicated in the captions, these reproductions are made from digital images housed in *The Complete Writings and Pictures of Dante Gabriel Rossetti: A Hypermedia Research Archive*, recently published online by the University of Michigan Press. Not all of these digital images are publicly available yet. The digital images were made with the generous help and permission of the Delaware Museum of Art, which houses an incomparable collection of early reproductions of Pre-Raphaelite pictures.

Black-and-white plates follow page 44

Sibylla Palmifera
Proserpine

Acknowledgments

The Delaware Art Museum and its staff have supported my work on Rossetti, not least of all my work in this book, with continuous help over the past six years, and the same is true of the staffs of the Alderman Library, University of Virginia; the Firestone Library, Princeton University; the British Library; and the Fitzwilliam Museum. Melvin Leffler, Dean of Arts and Sciences at University of Virginia, supplied the funds for the illustrations in this book, and he and George Block, Provost for Research at University of Virginia, have been remarkably generous in helping to fund my recent work. Then there are my friends, my colleagues, and especially my students, whom I cannot thank enough for their encouragement, conversation, and learning: Steve Arata, Paul Barolsky, Nick Frankel, Amanda French, Melissa Kennedy, Cecil Lang, Mark Samuels Lasner, Jan Marsh, Bethany Nowviskie, Deborah Parker, Dan Riess, Lisa Samuels, Heather Seagroat, Patricia Spacks, Andy Stauffer, and John Unsworth. Dick Fredeman, now gone from us and one of the two greatest Rossetti scholars who ever lived, is unforgotten. I have also been singularly fortunate in having Dan Heaton as my manuscript editor at Yale University Press. And finally, it is a pleasure to thank the living members of the Rossetti family who have been so generous and enthusiastic in helping me with my work: Roderic O'Conor, Susan Plowden, Joan Rossetti, Nicholas Rossetti, and Mary Rossetti Rutherford.

INTRODUCTION: ROSSETTI DEGREE ZERO

> When work on certain artistic problems has advanced so far
> that further work in the same direction . . . appears unlikely
> to bear fruit, the result is often a great recoil, . . . abandoning
> what has already been achieved, . . . turning back to appar-
> ently more "primitive" modes of representation.
>
> Erwin Panofsky, *Perspective as Symbolic Form* III

"Modernism begins with the search for a Literature which is no longer
possible." Roland Barthes's famous remark locates that beginning at the
watershed dividing Balzac from Flaubert, the "world of difference . . .
of 1848." That revolutionary year marks an epochal moment when the
bourgeois state shifts from social norm to social disease. The consequence, according to Barthes, is the emergence of the Empire of Signs,
for which *Flaubert* is Barthes's "normative" sign:

> He finalizes the uses of verbal tenses according to a conven-
> tion, so as to make them perform the function of *signs* of Lit-
> erature, in the manner of an art drawing attention to its very
> artificiality; he elaborates a rhythm of the written word which
> . . . appeals to a sixth, purely literary, sense, the private prop-
> erty of the producers and consumers of Literature. . . . The
> art of Flaubert points to its mask as it moves forward. . . . The
> writer then gives to society a self-confessed art, whose rules
> are visible to all, and in exchange society is able to accept the
> writer. Baudelaire, for instance, insisted on tracing the ad-
> mirable prosaicness of his poetry back to Gautier, to a kind of
> fetish of *highly wrought* form, situated no doubt outside prag-
> matic bourgeois activity, but inserted into an order of famil-
> iar tasks. (Barthes 38, 64–65)

Barthes's acute formulation is confirmed if we alter the signs only slightly: for instance, if we change *Literature* to *Art* and *Flaubert* to *Manet*. That is, of course, a translation we are now familiar with. What is startling is how aptly the formula applies to another central nineteenth-century figure, writer and artist both, whose remarkable career began in 1847–1848: Dante Gabriel Rossetti. Every one of Barthes's key critical terms designates an essential feature of Rossetti's work, which began and ended — explicitly — as the quest for an art and a literature that was no longer possible.

How Rossetti executed this pursuit can be seen most clearly if we make an Anglo-American shift of perspective. William James set out to reform philosophy in the late nineteenth century, and his work — which follows and parallels Charles Sanders Peirce's — set a foundation under twentieth-century thought. The structure would be pragmaticist and phenomenological. It held as self-evident that ideas are neither a priori forms nor empirical data but acts of the thinking person. Those acts get undertaken in different forms and media, some rational and conceptual in the traditional sense, but many not. For James, works of art are as much acts and forms of thinking as are scientific experiments. Indeed, science and art were for James specialized cases of our ordinary practices of living. Their peculiar function was to give reflexive clarity to quotidian human behaviors.

Works of imagination hold a central position in James's critique of traditional philosophy because they constitute forms of thought that do not abstract and generalize the experiences they take up. They engage their subjects — which include their own processes of making — from what Rossetti calls "an inner standing point." Artwork in this perspective remains more attentive to the multiple possibilities of phenomena — to varieties of conceptual experience, as it were — than do the constructs of reason, whether theoretical or practical. In the end James and Peirce both argued that an adequate account of human thought will represent it as a process of enlightenment generated through repeated critical exchanges between spontaneous intuition and reflexive analysis.

In making this argument James refuses a hard distinction between thinking and feeling. Affective states are neither intellectually inchoate nor mere instances of sensational events. In a famous passage from the chapter entitled "The Stream of Thought" in his *Principles of Psychology*

(1890) James observes: "We ought to say a feeling of *and*, a feeling of *if,* a feeling of *but,* and a feeling of *by* quite as readily as we say a feeling of *blue* or a feeling of *cold*. Yet we do not. . . . All *dumb* or anonymous psychic states have, owing to this error, been coolly suppressed or, if recognized at all, have been named after the substantive perception they led to, as thoughts 'about' this object or 'about' that, the stolid word *about* engulphing all their delicate idiosyncrasies in its monotonous sound" (James 1: 245–246). An artist of the next generation, Gertrude Stein, in a sense dedicated her whole life's work to demonstrating the deep truth of that passage and its considerable implications. And a crucial part of her work comes to say that an imaginative form of argument, rather than James's rationalist and expository form, will perhaps be most adequate to making that demonstration.

Following the work of his two acknowledged precursors, Dante Alighieri and William Blake, Rossetti set out (like James) to frame an argument for the conceptual function of imaginative work, and (like Stein) to cast his argument in imaginative forms. This book is an attempt to explicate the significance and some of the meanings of what Rossetti was trying to do.

In this respect Rossetti's work — his various projects to demonstrate or enact the sensuous operations of intelligence — anticipates some of the most interesting ideas of Wittgenstein and Merleau-Ponty, as well as the more recent arguments for "embodied mind" developed by Maturana and Varela, Lakoff and Johnson. What should interest us most about Rossetti, however, is what sets his work apart from the schemas of science and philosophy. St. Thomas's *Summa,* impressive as it is, only lifts a candle, as Blake would say, to the sun of Dante. It is the great Florentine who takes the measure of St. Thomas, not vice versa. The thinking enacted in and as artistic practice probes deeper than expository thought precisely because it does not exempt its own processes from the critical studies it undertakes. Driven by conscious and unappeasable desire, the practice of this kind of thinking always loops back on itself. So it is that the audience addressed by such work, or addressed to it, typically discovers a complex affect of bewilderment, sympathy, frustration.

To the extent that this situation characterizes all artistic work, artists pursue what Ford Madox Ford called the game that must be lost. But certain artists — Rossetti is distinctly one of them — make their moves in this pitiless game one of their principal subjects. In this book we will be studying Rossetti's work in order to elucidate those moves — what they are, how they get executed. Ultimately, however, if we wish to understand these moves, we will have to make a correspondent practice of our studies and cross over into Rossetti's world. The law of the inner standing point must be obeyed on both sides of the dialectic of artistic practice.

As we follow the trajectory of his work, we will want to keep in mind the Barthesian critical history that I noted at the outset. That history defines the cultural and ideological framework of Rossetti's "inner standing point." It also sets the starting point of Rossetti's career such that we can appreciate from the beginning the great significance of its particular shape. For it is a commonplace of Rossetti studies that his work divides into two clear phases or periods. The shift arcs around 1860, a year as significant for Rossetti as 1848. It is a year identified with certain signal events: on one hand the painting of *Bocca Baciata,* begun in late 1859 and finished a few months later; on the other the publication of *The Early Italian Poets* at the end of 1860 and the death of Rossetti's wife in February 1861.

Previous to that turn around 1860, Rossetti had been occupied with developing an intellectual and programmatic basis for practices of the imagination. This work begins in 1847–1848 and involves a historicist reconstruction and critique of the history of art, on one hand, and a self-consciously experimental approach to his pictorial and his literary work on the other. A painting like *The Girlhood of Mary Virgin* (1849), a story like "Hand and Soul" (1849), the translations from "the early Italian poets" (1846–1861) are all tour de force polemical performances — works of art not only with a palpable design upon us but permeated with Dantean/Blakean convictions about art as a conceptual practice. With *Bocca Baciata* Rossetti announced that he was raising the stakes on the issues he had undertaken in the late 1840s. Inaugurating as it does a more "worldly" and sensuous imaginative practice, the painting is the first in a series of works — pictorial as well as literary — that seem determined to pursue forbidden or contradictory intellectual limits. "Failure" and loss track Rossetti throughout this long second phase of his career, when his fame and success get secured. From this negative space of his work emerge ghostly subtractions and evanishments tricked out in splendid optical illusions. During the last twelve years of his life Rossetti studies these illusions in his famous and often alarming series of female "portraits." These works, no less than his early Pre-Raphaelite pictures, are programmatic commentaries on the mission of art. But by 1870 Rossetti's views have grown at once more worldly and more severe: views about art, about himself as poet and artist, and about the (late-Victorian) world in which his work was being pursued.

It is perhaps a bad idea to try elucidating Rossetti's work with the blunt instrument of critical prose. Rossetti's translations consciously espoused what is surely a better interpretive model. But given the current invisibility of such a remarkable figure, this book takes its lead from A. C. Swinburne, whose study of Blake remains important to this day. Swinburne was a beginner with Blake, as he well knew, and so now are we all with artists like Rossetti and Moreau, who were placed in a cultural twilight for most of this century. In such circumstances a prose beginning may serve a useful purpose.

I have arranged the first six chapters of this book according to a scheme described in a note Rossetti made for a planned but unexecuted painting: "Venus surrounded by mirrors, reflecting her in different views." Each chapter is a view of Rossetti, more or less complete in itself, but (necessarily) partial as well. The chapters also recur to topics and subjects previously taken up — Barthesian and Jamesian topics that return upon themselves from altered points of view. It goes without saying that these critical mirrors might be shifted indefinitely.

By this manner of proceeding I attempt to develop an approach sympathetic with Rossettian ideas about how and what we can know. The approach also points to the book's larger concern. If Rossetti and his work are subjects of immediate attention, they call us to reconsider the ancient quarrel between art and philosophy (or science generally), and their respective claims to knowledge and cultural authority. Rossetti's work brings that quarrel into sharp relief. Itself engaged in the quarrel, his work proposes forms of truth unfounded by any myth of enlightenment, whether the myth be drawn from the practice of art or from the practice of science and philosophy. Seeing and knowing for Rossetti may or may not bring improvement of our estate, least of all redemption for its delinquencies.

Of the "circumstances" that bear upon our understanding of Rossetti, one predominates: the advent of Modernism, which oversaw the expulsion of Rossetti from cultural memory. Why this happened can be illuminated if we think briefly about a famous moment in the early history of Modernist art: the refusal of Duchamp's urinal by the hanging committee of the Society of Independent Artists in New York in 1917. It was turned down because it was judged not a work of art at all. This book will try to indicate why that event should be seen as an index of what happened to Rossetti's work in the twentieth century. These studies therefore recur to the Modernist refusal of Rossetti, when certain views of his work were instituted. These views replaced the ones passed to the twentieth century by late-Victorian imaginations like Ruskin, Morris, Swinburne, Pater, and the many others influenced by their understandings. One Modernist line, Surrealism, ventured a practice that has much in common with Rossetti's work. But that view of Rossetti never gained a purchase in the English-speaking world, largely because of the movement's Continental focus. To articulate those reception histories in a precise way would be a welcome scholarly development. Here they come only in sketched forms, for I have concentrated my attention on Rossetti's primary materials as these highlight the question of the cultural mission of art.

The book is therefore less an argument than an invitation to look again at certain interesting matters: lines of truth, the edges it makes, its colorations. We might look as well to change what we are seeing, to reimagine what we know and what we don't know about Rossetti and his work. And not to seek a finality of truth but a passage through its doors of perception. Is the mind less sensible, less responsive, than the eyes, the ears, the fingertips; do those fleshed instruments fail in acuity? Yes and no, yes and no. And what about words and pictures and the different vehicles of writers and artists? Is text more ideated than pictorial shape, are elementary linguistic marks less important in imaginative language than they are in graphic forms? Perhaps. These kinds of question arise to our view when we engage with Rossetti's work, and various responses suggest themselves. This book is an arrangement of some of those questions and responses.

Dante Gabriel Rossetti
and the
Game That Must Be Lost

1
A Dynamic of Reflection

Every time philosophy determines art, masters it and encloses
it in the history of meaning or in the ontological encyclope-
dia, it assigns it a job as meaning.
                                        Jacques Derrida, *The Truth in Painting*

I think the way a girl takes off her dress.
                                        Georges Bataille

We organize our sense of British Romanticism in terms of two key
artists, Wordsworth and Byron, the one largely English, the other, like
Goethe, distinctively international. But behind both stands an enabling
figure who measures the historical terms that made Wordsworth and Byron, and their romanticisms possible: Robert Burns. One can't imagine
Wordsworth or even Byron inaugurating such innovations as Burns
introduced into the British cultural scene. Both were far too obliged to
imperious traditional inheritances — the very traditions, indeed, that
supplied their work with range and gravity. But both Byron and Wordsworth plundered Burns, that great innovator, who was licensed to his
role by a fortunate set of alienations: his class, his language, and his fiery,
erotic temperament. Though one can point to certain masterpieces, like
the incomparable *Love and Liberty: A Cantata,* his corpus hardly bears
comparison with the Wordsworthian and Byronic legacies. But seeing
that, we also see how much larger Burns is than his authorized textual remains, magnificent as they are.

So there is Duchamp, on one hand, and Picasso or Balthus on the
other: the one a great intellectual force, the others, masters.

Some such frame of thought is needed to understand both the work
and the cultural importance of Dante Gabriel Rossetti. Turner is a master, Rossetti is not. Tennyson and Browning and Swinburne define the
highest points of Victorian verse, not Rossetti. Yet the age's two most

imposing critics, Ruskin and Pater, both saw Rossetti as the period's central artistic presence. Their judgments are borne out by all the children of Rossetti — those he called from obscurity to attention, like Blake, Poe, Browning, and many others; those he called to self-attention, like Swinburne, Morris, Burne-Jones; and all those from Whistler to Yeats whose imaginations were shifted or shaped by Rossetti's ideas. Though not much now remembered, the truth is that between approximately 1848 and 1912 Rossetti was, in Whistler's final phrase, "a king."[1] And his imperium was very broad. It encompassed the leading intellectuals of the period as well as a popular audience created and nourished by many cultural entrepreneurs.

That contemporary authority is not difficult to understand. More than anyone in his circle and more than almost anyone else in his period, Rossetti possessed two extraordinary gifts: an unusually wide range of tastes and interests, and an absolute confidence in his own aesthetic judgments. Blake or Poe, Browning or Fitzgerald; Holst, Meinhold, Emily Brontë: these people's works fall unknown into his purview and there is no hesitation on his part. Inherited authority is not scorned but it does not set Rossetti's horizon. Or consider his own lack of technical skill when he began to paint in a serious way. His early shortcomings and ignorances, fully apparent to himself, did not prevent him from assuming as if by right the intellectual leadership among a group of extraordinary artists — Ford Madox Brown, John Everett Millais, William Holman Hunt. His remarkable self-confidence is plain in the ease with which he apprenticed himself to Brown and Hunt in 1848, when he wanted technical instruction. He even wrote up this experience as the fictional history of Chiaro dell' Erma, the hero of his tale "Hand and Soul." When Chiaro was nineteen years old — Rossetti was not much older in the real-time equivalent of the story (1848–1849) — he sought out the skilled painter Giunta Pisano to learn the art of painting. "He was received with courtesy and consideration, and soon stood among the works of the famous artist. But the forms he saw there were lifeless and incomplete; and a sudden exultation possessed him as he said within himself, 'I am the master of this man.'" Rossetti could write that — could *think* something equivalent in relation to Brown and Hunt — because he was already possessed by the spiritual idea that would drive him all his life. He could write "The Blessed Damozel" in 1847 and paint *The Girlhood of Mary Vir-*

gin in 1849 for the same reason. Whatever deficiencies one might find in early works like these, verbal or pictorial, are overborne by their evident clarity and intellectual confidence.

Everything he did — and he undertook a wide range of artistic projects in many media — was undertaken with absolute decision on one hand, and as part of a spiritual pursuit on the other. These twin determinations riveted those who came into his orbit.

As with Walter Scott and so many others, his success and influence and popularity eventually counted against Rossetti. Anglo-American Modernists took much from the Aesthetic Movement that they did not always acknowledge, and Rossetti's preeminent status almost demanded that his work be called in question. He was drawn and quartered between the two poles of Modernist self-definition: on one hand, tradition and neoclassical standards; on the other, innovation and "individual talent." Rossetti came to appear lost on both sides of that division. In one perspective he seems too romantic and idiosyncratic, in another he is mired in inherited conventions.

Modernist innovations with pictorial abstraction once seemed far removed from the literary cast of Rossetti's pictures. We now see how illusory that difference actually is. Indeed, a Postmodern vantage has restored our access to the power of artists like Gustave Moreau and Rossetti, where abstraction comes erotically charged in fetishized forms.[2] For most Modernists, and especially for the ideologues of Modernism, these forms proved too difficult to manage, perhaps too dangerous and self-revelatory.

Take that most famous of Rossetti's fetish objects, the Blessed Damozel. Growing to reappear throughout Rossetti's work, she is no simple imagining, and least of all a unitary (or dualistic) creation. Rationalist criticism will organize the fetish-world she represents into the moralized dichotomy "Virgin and Whore," and will arrange Rossetti's visioned creatures accordingly. But if we try to imagine these beings from a Rossettian point of view, we can appreciate how various they are. He tracks their multiple apparitions in a long series of studies and pursuits: Beatrice, Lenore, Fiammetta, Sancta Lilias, Pandora, Lilith, Monna Vanna, Jenny, Aurélia, Mary Magdalene, Veronica Veronese, Guenevere, La Pia, Venus Verticordia, Proserpine, Astarte Syriaca, to name only the most prominent, and those only literary or artistic or mythological. If you format their characters along a psychic grid — as Rossetti's personal demons or angels — they will never appear on independent terms.

To recognize objective truth as an order of artistic practice: this is Rossetti's guiding thought. Poet and artist are responsible to that order, which supervenes them and their work. For Rossetti, as for his masters Dante and Blake, artists come neither to represent real worlds nor to fashion imaginary ones. Art's *poiesis* brings revelation, not creation: not to make things, but to make things happen.[3] That conviction will lead him both in to and out of the movement we call Pre-Raphaelitism.

He is drawn in — indeed, he becomes the movement's early guiding spirit — for two reasons. First, a Pre-Raphaelite vantage validated his sympathy for the "passion and worship" of primitive Italian art, where imaginative intelligence gets subsumed to devotional purposes.[4] Rossetti's early sonnet "St. Luke the Painter" meditates critically on the spiritual loss suffered with the coming of the Renaissance, when art "sought talismans, and turned in vain / To soulless self-reflections of man's skill" (lines 10–11). For Rossetti there are to be no spectacles of virtuosity and technique. Not that art or poetry might not exhibit interesting or important technical features. On the contrary, early Italian art (and poetry) supplied Rossetti with examples of remarkable stylistic achievements — all the more important because these procedures, in Rossetti's day, were hardly credited. He was himself the most innovative poet and artist of the period in England, according to Ruskin, Pater, and nearly everyone else who thought about the matter at the time.

The second important feature of a Pre-Raphaelite attitude was called "truth to Nature." This idea meant different things to different people, and in Rossetti's case it had almost nothing to do with, say, Wordsworthian thought. Rossetti was an urban artist all his life and had virtually no interest in "nature" as such. "Truth to Nature" for Rossetti results when artists translate what they see with absolute fidelity. Measure comes not from any standard laws of either earth or heaven but from the desire of the eyes. Teaching at the Working Men's College, Rossetti (like Ruskin) urged his pupils to "Get rid of . . . academic fribble! draw only what you see."[5] His own procedures seemed "inscrutable" to some, but to others they were a revelation of pictorial sincerity, as if his drawing and coloring were culminant acts in a passion of vision.

Like Blake, however, he had no heart to see Wordsworth's nature, nor the nature of the Impressionists. His indifference to the geo- and biophysical order of things drove Ruskin to distraction, as did his irritated refusal of plein air painting. He was uninterested and unimpressed with the country God made, he wanted the Man-made town, Blake's Jerusalem—the City of God:

> Error or Creation will be Burned Up & then & not till then Truth or Eternity will appear It is Burnt up the moment men cease to behold it. . . . What it will be Questioned When the Sun rises do you not see a round Disk of fire somewhat like a Guinea O no no I see an Innumerable company of the Heavenly host crying Holy Holy Holy is the Lord God Almighty.
> (Blake, "A Vision of the Last Judgment")

The Maids of Elfenmere, the Damsel of the San Graal, Sister Helen: works bearing such names are the evidence of things seen. That they come from irreal orders of being is exactly why they draw Rossetti's attention, which he gives lavishly, as his contemporaries regularly observed. When he spends days in a meticulous rendering of flowers, the result is not a study from "nature." The result is iconic, perhaps even abstract.

The situation is similar in the poetry. His early involvement with what he called "the Art Catholic" is a discipline for studying faithful images, in every sense.[6] Emerging as the work of human minds and hands, these images finally reveal their freedom (they are blessings, not rewards) and their power (they are forms of intelligence). For Rossetti, art—and not least of all poetic art—aspires to the condition of the devotional image. Such images instantiate the elementary laws of form: laws for drawing distinctions as forms of primal desire, and (reciprocally) laws for executing desire as the elementary form of knowing.

All that came to seem less and less interesting as the century moved further past its turning point. The extreme artifice of Rossetti's style, grounded in imitation and pastiche, was rejected in the Modernist verse horizon as merely mannered, at once too weird and too correct. And then there were key moral ideas at stake— "the Definition of Culture," as T. S. Eliot famously put the matter. The fact that Hopkins's spasmodic artifices, but not the artifices of Rossetti or Swinburne, would be taken up by Anglo-American Modernism is telling in several ways.

Hopkins, for example, does not explicitly locate his verse in relation to current social and cultural issues. In this respect he is a far more "aesthetic" poet than either Rossetti or Swinburne, for whom religion, aestheticism, and "art for art's sake" are always programmatic concerns. The contemporary controversies that swirled around both these writers — the shock of Swinburne's *Poems and Ballads* (1866) and the furor that exploded as the "Fleshly School" controversy after the publication of Rossetti's 1870 *Poems* — are only the most apparent witnesses to the continued social nexus of their work. And although scholars have never *not* been aware of these plain truths, the knowledge often fails to inflect understanding or interpretation.

Consider for a moment Rossetti's eroticism, or at any rate one aspect of its pictorial presence in his work. For Rossetti, sexuality is an explicitly social issue. Clothing, jewelry, and an elaborate rhetoric of decoration characteristically locate the spectacular — which is to say, the social — mechanisms of sexual desire represented in the paintings; and the act of the picture is the exposure of the social form of these spectacles, of which Rossetti's own pictures come as primary, self-conscious instances. The early work, up to 1860, is largely devoted to exploring spectacles of sublimation. Dante and his circle and the Matter of Arthur give Rossetti a rich body of cultural material to investigate the problematic relation of spirit and flesh, as well as their means of expression, pursuit, and realization. From 1860, with the completion of the astonishing *Bocca Baciata,* these studies go deeper and grow increasingly troubled (and, as some of his friends thought, troubling). The all but angelic treatment of pleasure and sinfulness in *Bocca Baciata* has only technical brilliance in common with its dialectical other, the *Monna Vanna* portrait of 1868. Through Boccaccio, Rossetti comes to realize an image from an earthly paradise, through Cavalcanti an image drawn from the Inferno of the world. The wonder here — it defines the intellectual character of such work, its "fundamental brainwork," in Rossetti's phrase — is that both images come from the same order of reality, according to the argument that Rossetti is developing.[7] Consciously presented as spectacles of desire, these pictures give back to us advertisements of ourselves and implicitly call our ideas and feelings to our judgment. Or rather, they came to that mission for the world of the late nineteenth century. (Rossetti's current relevance will depend on the degree to which we map the cultural forms of our world — perhaps equally consumerist, imperial, and spectacular — to his.) Whatever the ideology of the Modernisms that had to resist Rossetti, the success of his mission is permanently defined in the character of his contemporary celebrity, where his work developed its many signs of contradiction. Neither Ruskin nor Hunt was "wrong" to hold Rossetti in highest honor, in one frame of reference, or to be appalled by the way he translated Venetian art in another. If their revulsion tells us more about codes of sexual understanding than about the quality of his pictures, we may want to remember that they also saw the "technical" mastery of a work like *Bocca Baciata*. As for the honor of Rossetti, so apparent to his greatest contemporaries, it remains for most of ours an unopened book.[8]

If Rossetti, like Duchamp, is primarily a conceptual artist, his proper subject is the cognitive nature of immediated sensual perception. The abstract form of that subject appears in his proto-Modernist concern to break the truth-spell of pictorial illusionism, to show that realist styles, including perspectivism, are but conventions toward vision and truth. His early studies in Flemish and Italian primitive painting and medieval miniatures are partly explorations of new formal possibilities. But if Rossetti's Victorian mind did not exactly go in fear of abstractions, it did not strip them of their rhetorical and socially determined embodiments. Unlike so many Modernist artists, he set no gulf between figural and abstract painting. All cultural acts are acts of desire, whatever their formal self-representations, and all come belabored with the dreams, nightmarish and otherwise, of the histories they involve. In his secular age Rossetti wondered at the lost presence of devotional art, whose soul is betrayed when it is plundered for formal and academic purposes. In that case, he came to believe, its soul was betrayed, paradoxically, by the betrayal of the total physicality of the pictorial action, the ritual sacramentalism presupposed in the devotional image. His social critique of his world, as devastating as Courbet's or Manet's, slipped between the conscious innocence of the one and the uncertain cynicism of the other. In his sharply muddled middle he gained a unique perspective on the worldliness of the work of culture. Rossetti's is an art laid bare.

Which is also to say it is an archive of cultural paraphernalia.

That paraphernalia comprises various embodiments of knowledge and desire, what Rossetti called "Venus surrounded by mirrors, reflecting her in different views."[9] These multiple views whirl in the vortex polarized in well-known Rossettian terms: Madonna and Circe, Virgin and Whore, "Soul's Beauty" and "Body's Beauty." What supplies Rossetti's version of this ancient dialectic with special force and interest are two things: first, the way he complicates the values of the two poles; and second, the way he relates the dialectical exchange to the contemporary scene. Robert Buchanan attacked Rossetti in his "Fleshly School" review because of the way Rossetti argued the ambiguous character of the dialectic ("Thy soul I know not from thy body, nor / Thee from myself, neither our love from God" ["Heart's Hope," 7–8]). As for the contemporaneity of Rossetti's work, it comes in apparitional forms that seem far removed from the "real world" of late-Victorian England. Rossetti's high-cultural apparatus comprises a literal treatment of phenomena that Marx at that very moment was discussing under the rubric "commodity fetishism."[10] Neither human beings nor their gods cease to exist or function in a commodity culture, they simply mutate into visible forms conscious of their own negotiability. For better and for worse, all things appear to live and move and have their being as a system of exchange values.

To be swept up into such a self-annihilating field of force might be — has been — constructed as ecstasy and redemption. So it is in the discourse of mysticism and even the ideology of religion, the "economy of grace." Rossetti brooded over the cultural materials that argued and developed such ecstasies and redemptions, but his nineteenth-century position altered their valence. What ecstasy, much less redemption, could be sought or found in the secular vortex discovered through work like Rossetti's, where all that is solid melts into tense and decorated air? Cassandra, Proserpine, Astarte Syriaca, the Blessed Damozel: their ideated forms advance and dissipate in that vortex, where Henry Adams discovered at the same time as Rossetti the unequal struggle between Dynamo and Virgin.

Rossetti came close to thinking in those terms in poems like "The Burden of Nineveh" and "Dante at Verona," but he preferred more intimate tropes, where the ambiguities of power were less likely to be cast as misleading antitheses. Or rather, where false antitheses could be better exposed. He wrote few explicitly political poems, but the ones he did write are telling to a degree. Consider that epochal political year, 1848. The February Revolution sends its tremors across Europe, even across the Atlantic. Emerson and Clough leave their comfortable situations and go to Paris in the fall to witness the momentous events firsthand. That same year — as everyone who knows Rossetti knows — brings an *annus mirabilis* in his imaginative life. But the events in France and Europe do not draw much of his attention, least of all the passion of his mind, as similar events sixty years earlier captured the imaginations of Wordsworth, Blake, Coleridge, and a bit later, even the romantics of the Napoleonic years, Shelley and Byron. He writes two sonnets about the revolutions of 1848, both skeptical, the second strong for its very cynicism:

> Not that the earth is changing, O my God!
>   Nor that the seasons totter in their walk, —
>   Not that the virulent ill of act and talk
> Seethes ever as a winepress ever trod, —
> Not therefore are we certain that the rod
>   Weighs in thine hand to smite thy world; though now
>   Beneath thine hand so many nations bow,
> So many kings: — not therefore, O my God! —
>
> But because Man is parcelled out in men
>   Today; because, for any wrongful blow
>   No man not stricken asks, "I would be told
> Why thou dost thus" but his heart whispers then,
>   "He is he, I am I." By this we know
>   That our earth falls asunder, being old.

The refusal of the nations to aid Italy and Hungary against Austria: for Rossetti it seems an old story in every sense, and it is one we ourselves hear retold regularly in places named Palestine, Bosnia, Kosovo, Chiapas — wherever. His sonnet works through its unsurprised and flat tone, which cuts back across its critical judgments. The world depicted here is as lost and helpless as the sonnet telling us so.

That loss, in a sonnet like this, brings no injury to the poetic result. Why not? Because the sonnet does not set itself apart from the judgment it is passing. Like the dramatic monologue "Jenny," it is a perfect example, in a satiric mode, of the "art of the inner standing point" (as Rossetti called it).[11] Of the poems whose subjects are frankly social and public, "Jenny" is preeminent partly because of its scale and partly because the political and economic issues are carefully mapped in an intimate erotic space. The poem leaves no room for doubting the spectacular conditions it discloses because, even more than the sonnet, the poem is not permitted to stand apart from those conditions. Here the art of "the inner standing point" comes with full and devastating force, engulfing the entirety of its world, including the poem or the picture of its revelation. Maurice Merleau-Ponty describes this manner of proceeding in a discussion of pictorial space in his late essay "Eye and Mind": "Space is not . . . a network of relations between objects such as would be seen by a third party, witnessing my vision, or by a geometer looking over it and reconstructing it from outside. It is, rather, a space reckoned starting from me as the null point or degree zero of spatiality. I do not see it according to its exterior envelope; I live in it from the inside; I am immersed in it. After all, the world is around me, not in front of me."[12]

All of Rossetti's art is grounded in that kind of affective relation to experience. For the artist, unlike the philosopher, "lives in fascination. The actions most proper to him . . . seem to emanate from the things themselves, like figures emanating from the constellations."[13] So Rossetti studies Browning's dramatic monologues and Poe's hoaxes and tales in order to rediscover and refashion the romantic lyric of sincerity — not as a device by which the creative imagination might redeem the self or the world but as a procedure to expose both to their fullest presence. The example of Dante, especially Dante's canzone, was equally important. All three showed Rossetti how to dismantle the subject's presumptive privilege of self-identity. Alone of the three, Dante also set the strongest example of how the self would survive such a discipline of extinction.

The discipline is first of all — that is to say, phenomenally — a set of stylistic determinants. Consider the following two sonnets from "The House of Life":

Death-in-Love

There came an image in Life's retinue
  That had Love's wings and bore his gonfalon:
  Fair was the web, and nobly wrought thereon,
O soulsequestered face, thy form and hue!
Bewildering sounds, such as Spring wakens to,
  Shook in its folds; and through my heart its power
  Sped trackless as the immemorable hour
When birth's dark portal groaned and all was new.

But a veiled woman followed, and she caught
  The banner round its staff, to furl and cling,
  Then plucked a feather from the bearer's wing
And held it to his lips that stirred it not,
  And said to me, "Behold, there is no breath:
  I and this Love are one, and I am Death."

Soul's Beauty

Under the arch of Life, where love and death,
  Terror and mystery, guard her shrine, I saw
  Beauty enthroned; and though her gaze struck awe,
I drew it in as simply as my breath.
Hers are the eyes which, over and beneath,
  The sky and sea bend on thee, which can draw,
  By sea or sky or woman, to one law,
The allotted bondman of her palm and wreath.

This is that Lady Beauty, in whose praise
  Thy voice and hand shake still, long known to thee
    By flying hair and fluttering hem, the beat
  Following her daily of thy heart and feet,
How passionately and irretrievably,
In what fond flight, how many ways and days!

To see how these poems function, to appreciate their congruities, we
want to register the differences they themselves call to attention. The
tone, for instance: the first is darkly enigmatic, the second energized by
its apparent endlessness. But each hovers on the brink of the other's vision because both are driven by a transformational code that appears
without bounds. "Death-in-Love" turns simultaneously around an alle-

gorical procession and a dream, and both dream and procession are constructed in the stuff of art. This comprises three distinct orders, each folding into the other and all three folded further into the textual order of the sonnet.

Because all the pronominals in "The House of Life" lie open to repeated shifts, "the sonnet" itself barely maintains its own self-identity, even in a case like "Death-in-Love." (Whose dream is being reported here, if it is a dream, and who is making the report? And does the sonnet lie outside the bounds of its own visionary images, or is it still—as the concluding lines lead us to think—moving within the orbit of the visions?) The local moments of extreme ambiguity—phrases like "soul-sequestered face" and "immemorable hour"—define in the most precise way a poetic set of "trackless" dissolutions.[14] These only multiply through the intratextual connections that the sonnet makes with other sonnets in "The House of Life" sequence: most clearly with the "Introductory Sonnet," "Bridal Birth," and "Stillborn Love," along with the secondary enlacements that spread out from those texts. Finally, if explicit biographical references are read into the textual codes—especially the reference to the stillborn child delivered by Rossetti's wife on 1 May 1861—the sonnet's geography undergoes yet another wholesale remapping. Entering this poem we enter a kind of Lucretian force field raining textual particles, each of which can be seen, depending on the point of view one chooses, as a moment in a larger regularity or as a moment of free swerve.

At the end of the sonnet we can't be certain about the psychic or moral import of the figures we encounter. The text seems ominous because its forms—art, dream, allegory—all solicit interpretation. When the sonnet delivers its interpretations, however, they come in the receding mirrors of further figural forms. The text seems plunged in a depthless vortex. Rossetti developed this stylistic procedure very early, in his first oil painting, *The Girlhood of Mary Virgin,* and the pair of accompanying sonnets. In all three no distinction is preserved between the work of art on one hand and its meaning or interpretation on the other.

"Soul's Beauty" comes in a very different style. The difference is all the more striking because the sonnet's metamorphoses are no less energetic than those in "Death-in-Love." But "Soul's Beauty" is not a "Bewildering" text. Its transformations don't wind down vertiginous paths but unfold and multiply, as complete and self-integrated as cancer or coral. "One law" governs "Soul's Beauty," the rule of Lucretius's "Alma Venus Genetrix": endless production. The splendid play on the word *draw*, so irresistible to Rossetti all his life, locates the dialectical terms of this generative process. It enacts a fusion of the dynamic equations Rossetti's poem calls out: Nature and Art; Love, Life, and Death; Painting and Poetry; the Incarnate and the Ideal.

Rossetti might have allowed his sonnet to unfold a different pattern of the "Terror and Mystery" that play about this scene. Here these figures come to "guard," however, not to threaten, and the text centers itself in figures of harmony and achievement. So the sonnet pivots around two allusions: first, to Dante's *Paradiso* (Canto 13, line 78), which emerges here in line 10; and then (in line 11) to Botticelli (in particular the *Primavera*). The latter functions in a more general way, however, since it means to recall — in the context of the "double work of art" that this sonnet locates — the most famous set of illustrations ever made for the *Commedia*.[15] Dante and Botticelli supply Rossetti with a model for rethinking the relation between imaginative vision and artistic execution; and Rossetti suggests, via the Botticelli allusion, that this relation has to be imagined as a continual pursuit: that its achievement comes in and as the pursuit, which is the perpetual execution of ideal attachments. The god of rule is Eros.

Rossetti's determination to poise this sonnet in a mood of benevolence and praise — to guard its fractal forms from emotional catastrophe — is underscored by the sonnet's well-known paired text, "Body's Beauty." The latter's demonic shapes do not terrorize their textual vehicle, they proliferate and unfold as they do in "Soul's Beauty." Nothing stands separate from the textual "web," as Rossetti emphasizes by once again deploying the word *draws*. Sonnet and picture are both "drawn" to her image and likeness, and Lilith, like the ideal lady encountered elsewhere, "lies apparent" ("Supreme Surrender," 3). Indeed, the ideality of this dynamic *is* complete apparition.

Appearances in Rossetti's world can be deceiving and/or surprising, obscuring and/or revelatory, thrilling and/or terrifying. Everything depends on the frame of reference, the point at which an order of appearances is discovered. "Who" or what is Lilith? A figure for late nineteenth-century emancipated woman, as a friend of Rossetti's suggested?[16] La

Belle Dame Sans Merci? The demon expelled from patriarchal Judaeo-Christian ideology? The "body" that a voice in "Heart's Hope" could not distinguish from soul, God, self, or beloved? When questions like these arise in the context of a sonnet like "Death-in-Love," they come under the sign of a troubled understanding; though even there — by the law of transformation that governs throughout Rossetti's work — all the forms can be turned to other, undarkened directions. "Body's Beauty" raises similar questions of interpretation because the sonnet organizes itself under a sign long associated with demonic meanings. But here an invitation is made, via the pairing with "Soul's Beauty," to rethink the interpretive field.

Similar ambiguities define the painting, *Lady Lilith,* that doubles this sonnet, as we see right away from the two versions that Rossetti made. The first version, exhibited in 1868, featured Fanny Cornforth as Lilith's model. Of this picture only photographs and reports survive, including Swinburne's remarkable *ekphrasis,* as well as a later watercolor version.[17] A powerful and very sensuous work, it troubled its owner William Leyland. In 1872 Rossetti agreed to remove Lilith's boldly erotic look from the picture, which he did by repainting Fanny's face with Alexa Wilding's. In an important sense the picture lost none of its threatening character by this transformation, for Wilding's face simply drops the temperature of Lilith's look of aggressive indifference.[18] But Wilding's image complicates our reading of the painting because hers is also the face modeling the companion picture to "Soul's Beauty," *Sibylla Palmifera*. Always the question returns of the meaning of these transformations. We accept the determining report Rossetti gives, the famous declaration "Thy soul I know not from thy body, nor / Thee from myself, neither our love from God." But what does that revelation mean, what is the import of its truth?

Rossetti's work never answers that question for good. Instead, he brings forward multiple answers that reflect the question in different views. Far from voiding (or avoiding) the question of meaning, these explorations of meaning's transformations engage the issue on a new ground.

The context here reaches all the way back to Plato, *The Republic,* and the "old . . . quarrel between philosophy and poetry" (Book 10, 607b).

In that foundational moment of Western culture, the poets — by which Plato means image-making artists — are dismissed from the City. The order of expulsion is given reluctantly, for Plato — himself a great poet — appreciates, as he says, the charms of imagination. But in the well-ordered City those charms will be exercised only in "hymns to the gods and praises of good men" (10: 607a). On such matters, for Plato, there is no question of "different views." "Truth" is the property of philosophers, not image makers, exactly because it is determinate, self-identical, and transcendent. Only the rational mind has access to such immutables. Image makers, like lovers, are caught by the surfaces of things.

> Even as men who have fallen in love, if they think that the love is not good for them, hard though it be, nevertheless refrain, so we, owing to the love of this kind of poetry inbred in us by our education in these fine polities of ours, will gladly have the best case made out for her goodness and truth, but so long as she is unable to make good her defense we shall chant over to ourselves as we listen the reasons we have given as a countercharm to her spell, to preserve us from slipping back into the childish loves of the multitude, for we have come to see that we must not take such poetry seriously as a serious thing that lays hold on truth, but that he who lends an ear to it must be on his guard fearing for the polity in his soul and must believe what we have said about poetry. (10: 607e–608b)

Plato's argument carries his celebrated invitation to the poets or their "advocates" to make a case for poetry's place in the City. This invitation comes with an interesting attachment or qualification, however: that the case be made "in prose without meter" (10: 607d). Because the caveat requires poets to address the issues in a philosophical horizon, it clearly begs the issue at the most basic level. For their part, the poets and image makers might as well require philosophers to establish the claims of reason in imaginative forms. Some philosophers have attempted that very thing — Plato first of all, but also Kierkegaard, Wittgenstein, Derrida. In every case the result has been perilous to the idea of Truth as set forth in the *Republic* and its companion text, the *Laws*.

Rossetti's works comprise arguments for the truth-functions of art and poetry. They may not *look like* arguments because they come in forbidden poetical forms (what Plato, thinking such arguments would have to take a verbal guise, called "meter"). We can perhaps see that a story like "Hand and Soul" involves a kind of artistic manifesto, not so much because we could prise a set of Rossettian and Pre-Raphaelite ideas out of the text as because the work's "argument" and philosophical grounds are established as imaginative features. Even some of Rossetti's best students — D. M. R. Bentley, for example — incline to treat the "brainwork" of his art as an extractable set of ideas rather than a process of work, a kind of polemic of the imagination.[19]

In this context we can usefully recall Plato's thinking about the relation of conversation, dialectic, and truth. At the close of the *Phaedrus* (10: 274d–279c) Socrates recounts a myth about the god Theuth's founding of written texts, a deplorable event to Socrates. Written texts, once again "analogous to painting" (10: 275d), stand opposed to conversation and dialectical exchange. In the one we have "living speech" where truth can be pursued; in the other a "dead discourse . . . a kind of image" (10: 276a). Written texts and paintings are mere simulacra which, if questioned, "maintain a majestic silence" (10: 275d).

If we transport these arguments to an epoch when philosophy comes not as dialogue but in elaborated systematic forms, the status of imaginative works undergoes a radical shift. "Majestic silence" looms across systematic philosophy and the one-way streets of its enormous cities. In face of such monumental structures, how different appear the works of imagination — more like the "monument" raised up in Rossetti's "Sonnet on the Sonnet":

> A Sonnet is a moment's monument,
> Memorial from the Soul's eternity
> To one dead deathless hour. . . .

Momentary monuments, dead deathless hours: this is a text that fairly demands response from its readers. Indeed, from such a text we can see how dialectical philosophy was reborn as philology and textual interpretation. Courting radical obscurity, Rossetti's works call special attention to that great shift. They also call special attention to another important feature of dialectics: the demand for immediacy. Texts and pictures come to challenge and confront, thereby developing a rhetoric of unmediated presence entirely analogous to the "human" relationships that Socrates represented in the *Phaedrus* as the ground of philosophic discourse.

That remarkable line in "Soul's Beauty" — "I drew it in as simply as my breath" — describes a process and a field of action into which reader and viewer are also "drawn." Rossetti was to call it, in general, an art of the "inner standing point." The effect can be alarming, as the reception history of Rossetti's work indicates, and the artist seems to have meant *Lady Lilith* to embody (and enact) the "convulsive" force of beauty, as the Surrealists would have called it. Her "strange fascination," Rossetti observed, illustrates a power to "draw others within [her] own circle."[20] Rossetti does not minimize the danger of such encounters, but "fear for the polity of the soul" is no argument to avoid them, as it is for Plato. The mind in peril, which for Rossetti means the embodied mind, is the mind brinked for revelation.

Various perils haunt *Lady Lilith,* starting with the nightmare legends that her name evokes. Painting and poem only increase those perils by complicating the moral issues. Perhaps this figure, re-presented in what Rossetti called a "modern" guise, means more and other than we have grown to think. This was Pater's argument when he interpreted the Rossettian woman under her earlier incarnation as the *Mona Lisa.* But Rossetti does not cast his argument primarily in moral and thematic terms, though these are clearly not avoided either. The argument is painterly.

Three pictorial qualities of the picture are notable: the depthless and crowded space which Lilith dominates; the relatively unmodeled character of her exposed bosom, shoulder, and neck; and the utterly bizarre standing mirror in which we see reflected the candles in Lilith's room, as well as an exterior scene from nature, or perhaps a garden.

First, the pictorial space. Rossetti regulates the extreme frontal plane at the lower right via the left arm of Lilith's chair, and the extreme rear plane via the frontally placed mirror at the upper left. But the painting's representation of the body of Lilith does not allow the eye to make a sharp division of those planes, and least of all to use them as definers of depth. The front of the bureau holding the mirror, color-rhyming with the left chair arm, further shrinks the painting's midspace. Indeed, the white-on-white figure of Lilith overflows the implied space of the seat, and the irreality of the presentation is underscored by the odd angle at which upper and lower torso stand to each other. The white roses that surround the head and shoulders of Lilith further eliminate the illusion of real depth, for they extend from the plane of the chair's left arm *back* to the surface of the mirror. Furthermore, the roses are laid down in a single plane that floats in all the others like some magical and decorative frame, forming a semicoronal around Lilith's upper body.

The white-on-white presentation weakens the distinction between Lilith's body and her clothing, an effect heightened by the relative lack of modeling in the areas of exposed flesh. Because the breasts have almost no definition at all, the firmly realized head and neck seem to dissolve into a lifeless field of undifferentiated skin. This unrealized flesh contrasts sharply with Lilith's hair, which is meticulously detailed and highlighted.

Finally, the garden or natural scene reflected in the mirror is an impossible imagination by any realistic measure. It is as if the mirror in Lilith's enclosed and fantastic realm (or room) magically preserved a memory of the Edenic garden which she fled. The mirror functions, formally speaking, as a window; but its allusion to that typical piece of pictorial symbology is negative and critical, for it does not face (spatially) outward and (temporally) forward, but inward and backward. Furthermore, the mirror's placement suggests that if we are to imagine it reflecting anything actual, it would have to be the world inhabited by the spectator of the painting.

Like the brilliant puzzle-pictures of the 1850s, *Lady Lilith* comes to the viewer as a pictorial enigma, an imperious presence commanding attention and thought. Rossetti's own acts of painting draw him into their gravity field, leading him to work and rework the pictures, as he worked and reworked his poems, in a seemingly endless pursuit or act of devotion. We glimpse this process in the repainting that *Lady Lilith* underwent and in Rossetti's production of "replicas" and versions of the same subject (*Beata Beatrix, The Blessed Damozel, Proserpine, The Damsel of the San Graal,* and so on). The direct precursor of *Lady Lilith,* the painting best known under the title *Fazio's Mistress,* offers an especially illuminating example of what is involved in these processes.

More than an act of homage to Titian — though important for that — *Fazio's Mistress* incorporates or calls out three different worlds: Fanny Cornforth, the sitter, is the locus of the picture's modernity; the Titianesque style and the pictorial "bricabrac" (as Rossetti called it) allude to sixteenth-century Venice; and the title references the world of Dante and thirteenth-century Florence.[21] The setting was emphasized in the 1863 version of the picture because the frame then was inscribed with part of the canzone that Fazio degli Uberti had written to his mistress, and that led Rossetti to title the work as he did.

These three perspectives define the three chief points of reference for most of Rossetti's work as a painter (primitive Italian, Venetian, modern). In this respect the picture functions as a kind of allegory of the trajectory of Rossetti's artistic career. When he told George Rae, in 1873, to change the title and remove the text by Uberti from the frame, he was essentially arguing that the picture should be seen only as a Venetian-inspired "piece of colour," which was how he originally described the picture to Ellen Heaton ten years before.[22] Uberti's text introduced a perspective Rossetti later decided to suppress. The new title for the picture would be *Aurélia,* a word that reflects the painting in a different set of multiple views. Now the title comes signaling a color, a woman's name, and a literary allusion to Gérard de Nerval.[23]

That act of reconstituting his work is typical of Rossetti. In this case it also forecasts his effort to establish a dialectic of "soul's beauty" and "body's beauty" for his visionary pursuits between about 1860 and 1875. The phrases represent poles of a single idealizing process. Rossetti's turn to Venetian models in 1859 inaugurates a new exploration of idealized forms of embodiment. He had been using the figure of Mary Magdalene for a number of years before 1860 as a christological trope for his eroticized ideal. The image of Fazio's mistress, like *Bocca Baciata,* is a body's form for the same idealizing process. Pictures like these, along with their dialectical counterparts (for example, *Beata Beatrix*), are not representational. Blake called such figures "emanations" — exteriorized projections of an experience of imaginative desire.

It is entirely characteristic that Rossetti would offer an act of pure stylization — this highly ornamental work, this Venetian "piece of colour" — as an emblem of his imaginative ideal. Venetian art was infamous, particularly in English readings of the history of art, as depthless and decorative. When Rossetti deploys the Venetian style as he does in this painting, he is in effect arguing through an act of art making. More, he is arguing that the act of art is in itself meaningful as an idealizing process. By contrast, an art that is representational and anecdotal commits itself, in this way of thinking, to pragmatistic and quotidian meanings — at their highest possibility, to moral meanings.

The argument of this painting can be even more specifically defined. It is framed, so to speak, for Ruskin, the person who more than any other helped Rossetti to realize his understanding of Venetian art. Ruskin's own view of the Venetian School had undergone a major upheaval during the 1850s, and he published his full reconsideration of the subject in the last volume of *Modern Painters,* which came out just after Rossetti finished *Bocca Baciata.* Hunt was quick to see, and to deplore, the sensual and erotic character of this great picture and the series of works that it inaugurated. Ruskin held back from criticism for a number of years, largely because his praise of Venetian art in *Modern Painters* was tied to a polemic on behalf of its spiritual truth, and especially of the relation between Venetian worldliness and religious belief. As Rossetti proceeded with his Venetian-inspired work, however, Ruskin came to decide that Rossetti didn't understand Venetian art — indeed, that his new pictures were only pseudo-Venetian — coarse and merely voluptuous, as Hunt had first thought — and not spiritual at all, in any proper (which is to say, Christian) sense. Eventually Ruskin denounced Rossetti's Venetian work in terms that recall the anathema he pronounced, in the second volume of *Modern Painters,* upon Titian's Pitti Palace *Magdalene.* Ruskin even told Rossetti that he didn't know how to paint.

The argument between the two, which resulted in their famous split in the mid-1860s, went much deeper than a Victorian dispute over the moral message of art. It was a conflict about who understood the truth of art better: the practicing artist or the learned critic and moral philosopher. Ultimately it defined a different approach to a fundamental question: is the "idea" of artistic work an inherent practice or an abstractable conception? Rossetti's pictures raise an argument with *Modern Painters.* The argument is not so much with the *ideas* in that work as with its discursive pretension — as if conceptual forms could be intellectually adequate to artistic ones. By choosing to frame his argument with Ruskin in painterly rather than conceptual terms, Rossetti was in effect mining the ground on which the philosophical critique of art had been resting since Plato.

In this context *Fazio's Mistress, Monna Vanna,* and *Lady Lilith* (1863– 1868) can all be usefully compared with Manet's *Olympia* (1863–1865).

Whereas Manet's treatment of the Venetian style is ironical and self-consciously "modern," there is no irony at all in Rossetti's pictures, whose self-awareness is of another order. As polemical as Manet's, a painting like *Fazio's Mistress* is more an artifice of absorption — almost an act of magic, like a Joseph Cornell collage — than a bold play of conscious wit.[24] Such pictures operate as machines of desire. They come to realize a space extending beyond the picture's framed locality, a space which, if entered, "vivifies" all within it according to the "one law" of desire, dialectical exchange:

Not in thy body is thy life at all
    But in this lady's lips and hands and eyes;
    Through these she yields thee life that vivifies
What else were sorrow's servant and death's thrall. ("Life-in-Love," 1–4)

Life in Love is an action, not a concept or idea, and it is marked by embodied transfers of care and attention. Imagined in purely aesthetic terms, it appears as Rossetti's "double work of art": the creation of a poem to accompany and "interpret" a picture, the creation of a picture to re-realize a poem. Rossetti illustrates the process with his own exemplary works, some of them "double works" in the strictest sense, most of them simply (simply?) arrayed as his numerous "literary" pictures. The most successful "interpretations" of Rossetti's works, of the paintings in particular, therefore come as imaginative forms in their own right: for instance, Pater's displaced Leonardian prose poem that concludes *The Renaissance;* Swinburne's three extraordinary ekphrases of "Soul's Beauty," "Body's Beauty," and "Venus Verticordia"; and — perhaps most remarkable of all — Morris's poetical translations of the great watercolors *The Tune of Seven Towers* and *The Blue Closet.*[25]

    Philosophers like Merleau-Ponty and Derrida have sought to make the case for art against the challenge of Plato.[26] The expository form of their presentations throws into relief the difference that comes when an argument or exposition or interpretation is attempted in a form that is equivalent with its subject: in Rossetti's terms, when a work gets "doubled." Rossetti shows every artist's understanding, that the only adequate interpretation of a work of art is a responsive work of art. Merleau-Ponty's engagement with this same subject assents to the artist's view of the matter, though his argument declares its allegiance in expository form. Taking Descartes as Plato's stand-in, Merleau-Ponty uses the figure of the mirror to illustrate the difference between a philosophic and an artistic way of proceeding. "The Cartesian does not see *himself* in the mirror," Merleau-Ponty says, "The mirror image is in no sense *a part of* him." And again: "As far as the thing and its mirror image are concerned, their resemblance is only an external denomination; the resemblance belongs to thought" alone (131). In the intellectual vision of the artist, by contrast, mirroring involves a wholly different operation: "Mirrors are instruments of a universal magic that converts things into spectacle, spectacle into things, myself into another, and another into myself. . . . This explains why [artists] have so often chosen to draw themselves in the act of painting, . . . adding to what *they* could see of things at that moment, what *things* could see of them — as if to attest to there being a total or absolute vision, leaving nothing outside, including themselves" (130). Thus does Merleau-Ponty argue for what Rossetti, also utilizing expository form, calls "the inner standing point" of an artistic practice. Any meaning situated Elsewhere is merely conceptual meaning, dead on arrival. Merleau-Ponty's struggle to move his own prose within the orbit of an artist's approach to meaning emerges most clearly in those moments when the level of figuration in his prose rises to the point where exposition overflows into a more tropical discourse. In this splendid passage, for example, where Merleau-Ponty is trying to explain "The painter's vision" (141): "Art is not construction," he says, but rather what Hermes Trismegistus called "the voice of the light."

> And once it is present it awakens powers dormant in ordinary vision, a secret of pre-existence. When through the water's thickness I see the tiled bottom of the pool, I do not see it *despite* the water and the reflections; I see it through them and because of them. If there were no distortions, no ripples of sunlight, if it were without that flesh that I saw the geometry of the tiles, then I would cease to see it *as* it is and where it is — which is to say, beyond any identical, specific place. I cannot say that the water itself — the aqueous power, the syrupy and shimmering element — is *in* space; all this is not somewhere else either, but it is not in the pool. It inhabits it, is materialized there, yet it is not contained there; and if I lift my eyes to-

ward the screen of cypresses where the web of reflections plays, I must recognize that the water visits it as well. (142)

The first sentence announces a descriptive passage that here functions not as description but as an elaborate imaginative figure for the vitality of art, the voice of its light. Pushed to try to explain the call of that voice, Merleau-Ponty's text simply escapes its informational conventions and gropes through an imaginative equivalent that hopes to mirror — in no Cartesian or Platonic sense — its subject. The effectiveness of this move is underscored in the final sentence, when the aqueous mirror is suddenly, brilliantly, re-reflected in an aerial one.

In this kind of model, images call out to images and their dialogue is the action of an artistic process of thinking. It is the model that Rossetti will proliferate throughout his work. Texts reflect and open out to each other — "Soul's Beauty," "Body's Beauty" — or they develop other kinds of mirroring relations: *Sibylla Palmifera, Lady Lilith*. Poems by Tennyson, Poe, Allingham get explained in Rossettian equivalents, which mirror their originals as Merleau-Ponty's prose tries to fashion a mirror for his ideas. The same procedure rules Rossetti's way with pictures, his own or those by other artists he admires. Explanatory power rises, paradoxically, from the distance separating the equivalent forms, as Rossetti says more or less explicitly in his sonnet "For an Allegorical Dance of Women, by Andrea Mantegna (In the Louvre)":

Scarcely, I think; yet it indeed *may* be
    The meaning reached him, when this music rang
    Clear through his frame, a sweet possessive pang,
And he beheld these rocks and that ridged sea.

Scarcely thinking in any usual expository sense, Rossetti puts before us an affective equivalent for Mantegna and his painting. Key wordplays in the text create mini-mirrors that serve as images for the reciprocal action taking place here: *frame,* with its doubled perspective signifying both a picture frame and a body; and all the pronouns, for instance *this* and *these,* which reference simultaneously figures in the sonnet and figures in the picture. The first three words themselves involve a kind of wordplay, establishing a figural relation — identity at a distance — between "Rossetti"

and "Mantegna." And that scarcely visible *it* lies in wait for a revelation
of its hidden vitalities that comes when the sonnet turns toward its close:

> It is bitter glad
> Even unto tears. Its meaning filleth it,
>   A secret of the wells of Life: to wit: —
> The heart's each pulse shall keep the sense it had
> With all, though the mind's labour run to nought.

The abstraction of the initial *it* grows through the sonnet to a figural
form for the labor and presence of artistic thinking, the "wit" of Rossetti's eloquent images. "It" is the poem's central emblem for each of the
text's faceted words and phrases, which reflect and transform themselves
in their processes of reflection.

Such transformations are possible only when clear differentials are
maintained between the various reflecting surfaces. Rossetti's "double
work," the dialectic of a particular picture and a particular text, is the
generic form that the differential assumes. Within that generic horizon,
however, a wide range of reflective processes are set in play — at different scales, of many types. Here are two brief examples.

In 1869, as Rossetti was readying the 1870 *Poems* for print, he discussed
with his brother various changes to the poems he wanted to publish. The
case of the early sonnet, "For a Venetian Pastoral, by Giorgione," produced a disagreement over the final line. William Michael argued that
the line as it appeared in 1850, when it was first published, should be re-
tained — "Silence of heat, and solemn poetry" — and the more recent version discarded ("Life touching lips with Immortality"). Gabriel dis-
agreed. The original line, he said, was "quite bad. 'Solemn poetry'
belongs to the class of phrases absolutely forbidden I think *in* poetry. It
is intellectually incestuous — poetry seeking to beget its emotional
offspring on its own identity. Whereas I see nothing too 'ideal' in the present line. It gives only the momentary contact with the immortal which
results from sensuous culmination and is always a half conscious element
of it."[27] Much could be said of the line and the sonnet, whose manner of
proceeding closely resembles "For an Allegorical Dance of Women,"
with which it was initially published in 1850. But here I want only to point
out how Rossetti's commentary privileges a structure of differentials

"*in*" his poetry. The integrity as well as the relation of "immortal," "sensuous," and "conscious" forms depends upon preserving these kinds of differentials.

The second example comes as the key sonnet in "The House of Life," the notorious "Nuptial Sleep":

> At length their long kiss severed, with sweet smart:
> And as the last slow sudden drops are shed
> From sparkling eaves when all the storm has fled,
> So singly flagged the pulses of each heart.
> Their bosoms sundered, with the opening start
> Of married flowers to either side outspread
> From the knit stem; yet still their mouths, burnt red,
> Fawned on each other where they lay apart.
>
> Sleep sank them lower than the tide of dreams,
> And their dreams watched them sink, and slid away.
> Slowly their souls swam up again, through gleams
> Of watered light and dull drowned waifs of day;
> Till from some wonder of new woods and streams
> He woke, and wondered more: for there she lay.

The sonnet is in the simplest and most profound sense a celebration of difference as the ground at once of knowledge and ravishment, clarity and intensity. The poem's sexual and interpersonal features are themselves particular facets reflecting the light of a much more encompassing system of visionary engagements whose interplay we follow in all kinds of tropic and rhetorical details. The sonnet ultimately provokes the figure of a beloved woman to appear in the wondering view of her lover, and it holds out that reciprocating image — it is ubiquitous in Rossetti, as the case of "The Blessed Damozel" should remind us — as an emblem of dynamic reflection. As the story of Chiaro dell' Erma shows so clearly, the determining model for this central scene is Platonic — is in fact the relation Plato represented in the *Symposium* between Socrates and Diotima. The damozel and her lover comprise an iconographical form for the same dynamic, the relation of love and knowledge, which is further replicated as a relation between the poems and the pictures named "The Blessed Damozel." The dynamism of the relation gets exposed by the multiplication of the mirroring forms, which we see most plainly in the different "versions" that Rossetti fashions of both text and picture.[28] As for the vehicle of the relation, it hardly needs decoding. It is art — more particularly, an art practiced as a rite of secular — which is to say, for Rossetti, interpersonal — devotion.

The most literal house of Rossetti's life, his famous lodgings near the river at 16 Cheyne Walk, emblemizes the machinery of his mind. In its six rooms were no fewer than thirty-four mirrors — ten in the dining room alone. Imagine what it must have been like to sit or move about in such a space. Rossetti also filled the house with paintings and drawings, with elaborate furniture, with decorative china and numerous art objects. Among so many mirrors and reflective forms, persons and objects would continually appear and reappear in different angles and perspectives, multiplying reflections of reflections and avenues of focus. The artworks, those meta-mirrors, regenerated the images from the level of appearances to the level of consciousness, from one set of mirrors to another.

The artworks themselves made few references to sunlit realms. Most of the pictures were portraits or virtual portraits — images of Rossetti's wife, his mother, his sister; of Jane Morris and Fanny Cornforth; perhaps of Ruth Herbert, Annie Miller, and other apparitions from Venusian galleries. Like the House of Usher or medieval illuminations, these images project light from within. No doubt many can find much to be troubled by, even repelled at, in Rossettian space, for it is clearly a palace of art — haunted, unnatural, voluptuous, embrained, with Reflection its presiding deity. Various moral tales have been raised, like specters, from this house, most fashioned to deplore, sympathetically or otherwise, a more or less ruined existence. But the truth is that Rossetti thrived in close interpersonal relations to the end of his life, as the devotion of family and friends clearly shows. Nor did addiction to chloral make beasts of either Coleridge or Rossetti. And if 16 Cheyne Walk was in one respect a hall of mirrors, it was not — like the Crystal Palace, say — a museum of Victorian deceptions wearing masks of social improvement. Sixteen Cheyne Walk is an image of an intense and private world, full of pleasure and guilt. Its secrets all lie in the open, in those strange mirrored surfaces that will hide, like Rossetti's art, only what one might choose to fear to see.

2

INTELLIGENCE IN LOVE

Medieval v. Victorian v. Modern

As if we were afraid to conceive of the other in the time of our
own thought.

Michel Foucault, *The Archaeology of Knowledge*

Ever since modernists like T. S. Eliot misrepresented (or perhaps mis-
comprehended) Rossetti's work, the intellectual structure of his art —
both painting and poetry — has been seriously obscured. The problem is
sharply focused in Rossetti's connection to Dante and his circle. According to Eliot and those who took up Eliot's way of thinking, Rossetti
had a weak understanding of stilnovista poetry, and almost no understanding of Dante. Rossetti's mind was too sentimental, his emotions
too fleshly, his language too loose and Victorian.

The judgment that Rossetti lacks intellectual rigor, widespread in the
Modernist academy, runs against earlier views. Indeed, the argument
was mounted specifically to challenge the programmatic authority of
Rossetti's work, and to undermine the force of his famous commitment
to "fundamental brainwork" in imaginative practice. The challenge gains
a certain immediate plausibility because, as everyone has always known,
Rossetti's is — spectacularly — an art of the body. Before 1920 or so people were able to negotiate that basic paradox in Rossetti's work. After-
ward not.

We shall have to turn back across the divide opened by Eliot — back
to the cultural moment when Rossetti's work centered the movement
that ushered in Modernism proper. This reconsideration will ultimately
allow us to make a critical return to the subject of Modernism. The differentials that separate Rossetti from his immediate inheritors can usefully
be seen not as deficiencies in Rossetti or his work but as forecasts of the

critique that Postmodernism would eventually raise against the Modernist project.

My argument will extrapolate that foundational concept of Rossetti (and through him, of the Aesthetic Movement in general): "fundamental brainwork." Drawn from his concern with artistic technique, the word *brainwork* shifts the distinction between idea and act, or theory and method. The "brainwork" of a disciplined artisanal practice organizes the artist's intuitive and emotional insights. As we shall see when we examine Rossetti's crucial connection to Dante, the famous declaration in "Heart's Hope" about soul/body/self/beloved/God expresses exactly what Rossetti has in mind.

His purposes get expressed very clearly in his famous pair of sonnets "Mary's Girlhood," written to accompany his first Pre-Raphaelite picture, *The Girlhood of Mary Virgin*. We should recall that the painting was itself a manifesto about art, as one sees in the heated controversy that followed its exhibition in 1849.

When it was shown at the Free Exhibition, the painting's implicit argument was underscored by the presence of a slip of goldfaced paper Rossetti attached to the frame. Two sonnets were written on the golden slip, as follows:

> This is that blessed Mary, pre-elect
>   God's Virgin. Gone is a great while, and she
>   Was young in Nazareth of Galilee.
> Her kin she cherished with devout respect:
> Her gifts were simpleness of intellect
>   And supreme patience. From her mother's knee
>   Faithful and hopeful; wise in charity;
> Strong in grave peace; in duty circumspect.
>
> So held she through her girlhood; as it were
>   An angel-watered lily, that near God
>   Grows, and is quiet. Till one dawn, at home
> She woke in her white bed, and had no fear
>   At all, yet wept till sunshine, and felt awed;
>   Because the fullness of the time was come.

and

These are the symbols. On that cloth of red
   I' the centre is the Tripoint: perfect each
   Except the second of its points, to teach
   That Christ is not yet born. The books — whose head
Is golden Charity, as Paul hath said —
   Those virtues are wherein the soul is rich:
   Therefore on them the lily standeth, which
Is Innocence, being interpreted.

The seven-thorn'd briar and the palm seven-leaved
   Are her great sorrow and her great reward.
   Until the end be full, the Holy One
Abides without. She soon shall have achieved
   Her perfect purity: yea, God the Lord
   Shall soon vouchsafe His Son to be her Son.

Formally these texts come as a two-handed engine for interpreting the meaning of the painting. Despite their evident symbolic paraphernalia, they are anything but symbolic. The first sonnet identifies the subject, her primitive historical position, her moral and mythological character within the medieval context of Mariolatry. But even as the second sonnet unfolds the Christian iconography of the pictured details, it no more operates as a Christian or symbolic interpretation than the first sonnet. Rather, the second sonnet locates the historicality of all these materials, identifying them as "medieval." This identification comes through the act of stylistic analysis performatively displayed in the poetry's consciously antiqued style.

So the sonnets are not so much an interpretation as the representation of an interpretive field. Attached to the painting's frame, the sonnets label the work itself as "medieval." Their technique appears most dramatically in the mannered self-consciousness of verses like these:

Therefore on them the lily standeth, which
Is Innocence, being interpreted.

The artificial style is a quasi-allegorical signal referencing an idea of the medieval-archaic. In such a context, the symbolistic potential of the imagery gets broken down. The verse turns what might have been (in a medieval context) a symbol into the briefly annotated index of a symbol. Twentieth-century writers and theorists will make much of what Rossetti is doing here; they will call it "laying bare the device." For an agnostic like Rossetti, the critical presentation of Christian materials allows him to construct his contemporary artistic manifesto. The manifesto is performative, coming as the image of a pastiche of an antique set of signs.

This manifesto argues that "meaning" is a function not of concepts and general ideas but of particular (artistic) practices. Highlighting the apparent medievalism of his subject matter, Rossetti historicizes the whole symbolic field. More important still, he forces us to think about those historical materials in specifically artistic terms. So the Christographic symbology appears as a form of artistic expression and style rather than of religious concepts and ideas. Rossetti thereby urges the otherwise Christian symbology to carry purely aesthetic and artisanal significance. Rossetti's sonnets and their associated painting are not about "Catholic" or Christian matters, they are about Art: specifically, about what he called "the Art Catholic," a phrase in which the word "Catholic," self-consciously historicized through an obsolete grammar, gets opened to its root (and secular) meaning.

A brief excursus on the immediate context of Rossetti's work is useful, for it will help to explain why he occupied the programmatic vanguard of the early Pre-Raphaelite movement. The emphasis of the Pre-Raphaelite Brotherhood, the PRB, upon meticulous and accurate rendering of painterly details provoked a novel tension in their work. Whereas the Pre-Raphaelite subject often carried weighty allegorical and religious meanings, those tradition-borne symbolic structures tend to move out of focus as the eye is assaulted from every quarter by all kinds of arresting details, many hardly relevant at all to the apparent or nominal subject. In his treatment of such details Rossetti differs slightly but significantly from both Holman Hunt and John Everett Millais. In *The Girlhood of Mary Virgin,* for example, Rossetti does not load the painting with detail, he formally structures his details so that they carry a general burden of meaning about the significance of painterly detail in itself.[1] This is why his painting is such an effective painterly "statement" about the ability of art to embody and express meaning in nonsymbolic ways. The same kind of ordered formality, as we have seen, governs the presentation of the medieval symbology in the sonnets.

Rossetti's difference from Hunt and Millais is quite instructive. Their early work provoked the hostility of people like Charles Dickens partly because of their remarkable attention to close rendering of physical and historicist detail. Viewers were particularly dismayed at the details in paintings on moral and religious subjects. If these particulars were not "mean, odious, repulsive, and revolting" in themselves, they distracted the attention from the main subject's "religious aspirations . . . elevating thoughts . . . or beautiful associations." Such, at any rate, was the charge.

Ruskin defended Hunt's *The Awakening Conscience* against these objections on two grounds, one general, one particular. The details, he argued, were dramatically appropriate "in this instance" — that is, they represented the realistic figurings "of a mind which has been fevered by violent and excessive excitement." This special pleading, needless to say, scarcely addresses the real issue of "the general propriety of such treatment," as Ruskin called it. That "general propriety" is, of course, a recurrent topic in *Modern Painters;* and Ruskin's argument is that the artist's primary attention must always be directed to the work as such, to the act of painting. The modern painter's true subject is never the nominal subject, it is the artist's own artistic fidelity and devotion. For Ruskin, Hunt is one of those contemporary "poetical" artists bent upon "inventing the story as they painted it" (*Modern Painters* iv.7.18). The nominal subject lives only by virtue of the expressive vigor of the artist and his work.

So if an apparent excess of detail can detract from the painting's nominal subject, it simultaneously urges the viewer to reformulate the subject in other (in aesthetic) terms. Ruskin's defense of the PRB registers his awareness of this pictorial urgency in their work. In this respect, Rossetti's secular and polemical stylistic manner has a clear parallel with the explicitly devotional work of Hunt. The more we focus on the details, the more reflexive (rather than reflective) the works become. The "story" they tell is the act of painterly invention; Ruskin calls such work "poetical" exactly because he reads it in this aesthetic way. In this sense, *The Awakening Conscience* and *The Light of the World* are less the names for subjects in the paintings than they are the names of the paintings themselves. These paintings bring their light to the world, whose aesthetic conscience is meant to be awakened through the experience. The light of the world is art itself, the awakening conscience a redeemed aesthetic sense (whether in the artist or in the viewer).

Of course Pre-Raphaelite art is not Action Painting. But this later vocabulary is useful for calling attention to the decidedly polemical-aesthetic quality of PRB work. If the Pre-Raphaelites did not break completely with representational tradition, they were determined to undermine some of its most fundamental premises. The conceptual character of their work comes not from an aggressive abstraction, as in Modernist art, but from a hyperrealism that anticipates certain Postmodern styles. The Pre-Raphaelite program encouraged artists to handle their traditional subjects with greater imagination. Through their notorious attention to detail, Pre-Raphaelite painters were trying to break into free acts of inventiveness. The sympathetic viewer of the period — in this case, paradigmatically, John Ruskin — responds in kind. In *The Awakening Conscience* Ruskin's conscience is also awakened: "There is not a single object in all that room — common, modern, vulgar (in the vulgar sense, as it may be), but it becomes tragical, if rightly read. . . . Nay, the very hem of the poor girl's dress, at which the painter has laboured so closely, thread by thread, has story in it, if we think how soon its pure whiteness may be soiled with dust and rain, her outcast feet failing in the street." That is criticism in the sentimental style of the period. And if it might be argued that "This [kind of talk] is allowing fancy excessive liberty" with the painter's work, it should also be said that its freedom corresponds to what happens in the painting, which treats its nominal subject in an equally "excessive" fashion.[2] In each case the excess signals a new kind of devotional activity: on one hand a devotion to painterly practice, on the other to the practice of criticism. Both are, in Ruskin's terms, "poetical"; indeed, they are moral and religious precisely because they are, first of all, "poetical."

Rossetti's critical intelligence as an artist lies essentially in this: that he sought a programmatic expression for a new kind of artistic representation. He is extremely self-conscious both as a technician and, in much of his work, as a polemical theorist. More than that, because the polemic is being made on behalf of art as a nonconceptual form of understanding,

Rossetti is most theoretical in his explanations when he expresses himself in artistic (rather than conceptual) terms. So he will interpret a painting by writing a sonnet, or a poem by making a painting. So he will elucidate the poetry of Dante and his circle by translating them into equivalent poems. Rossetti constructs an argument in images for the procedure of arguing by images.

Eliot's celebrated 1929 essay on Dante exorcises Rossetti's translations as "Pre-Raphaelite tapestry" — the phrase being a kind of objective correlative meaning "brainless decoration." The judgment is especially damning, from Eliot's viewpoint, because his essay celebrates Dante's art exactly for its conceptual virtues. Dante's poetry is stronger than Shakespeare's, he argues, because the one works within a coherent conceptual framework, while the other does not.

If we recall Rossetti's general approach to his translations, we can see the problem a reader like Eliot is immediately going to have: "The lifeblood of rhymed translation is this, — that a good poem shall not be turned into a bad one. . . . Poetry not being an exact science, literality of rendering is altogether secondary to this chief aim. I say literality, — not fidelity, which is by no means the same thing."[3] To the polemical Modernist critic, judgment here is all but foregone because Rossetti works in a style — decorative and rhetorical — that was the precise object of Modernist attack. Rossetti's poetry can scarcely not turn good early Italian poems into bad Victorian ones. The subsequent dismissal of Rossetti's translations — like the widespread praise they received before Eliot's essay — reflects a cultural predisposition, not a dependable judgment about the work itself.

Let me observe in passing that Rossetti's translation program implicitly summons some kind of aesthetic value judgment, whether favorable or not. His collection organizes itself around the idea of the "good poem," not just verse that might have some purely historical interest. And his translator's rule lays upon him the obligation to write good poetry in his turn. It is a bold move, and one that Ezra Pound consciously imitated, though most Modernist scholars seem to have forgotten that.[4] But Rossetti's move laid Rossetti open to Eliot's line of attack; for if a serious change in poetic style and taste were to become culturally canonized, as in fact happened in the mid-twentieth century, then Rossetti's work would no longer have even its own ground — artistic fidelity — to stand on.

Despite certain twentieth-century judgments, the scholarly consensus on Rossetti's translations is far more favorable than not.[5] True, the difficulty of translating syllabic into accentual verse is formidable. Furthermore, the cultural distance separating Rossetti's world from Dante's is perhaps even more daunting. First of all, serious medieval thought (like, say, Dante's and Cavalcanti's) and serious Victorian thought (like, say, Rossetti's and Ruskin's) are all but incommensurable. Indeed, it is the absoluteness of the differential here that helps to explain the nineteenth century's (historicist) fascination with the Middle Ages. A second great difficulty is purely linguistic. Stilnovista Italian is refractory in part because its immediate poetical heritage sometimes displays a diction littered with shards of corrupted Latin and early Italian dialectal forms. The so-called Sicilian School, centered at the court of Frederick II in Palermo, began the vernacular move against this linguistic inheritance. The "sweet new style" of the stilnovista movement culminates the effort to purify vernacular poetry of its linguistic crudities. Some of the most spectacular stilnovista moments come when the stylistic and linguistic issues are held in the foreground. Stilnovista verse is commonly far more strict and even stiff in its formalities than the Sicilian and troubadour writings it builds upon. In this respect, the highly polished and often mannered correctness of Rossetti's verse style clearly aims to represent the spirit of the poetry he was translating.

There is no question, I think, that Rossetti understood the problems he was confronting and that he proposed an impressive scheme for addressing the difficulties. Because the scheme is grounded in what Rossetti calls "paraphrase," we are apt to imagine — this was Eliot's imagination — that Rossetti's irreligious (or nonreligious) translation is a travesty of Dante. But this is to misunderstand what Rossetti is trying to "paraphrase." He is not after a contemporary equivalent for the theology or conceptual content of the verse. What he wants is a contemporary equivalent of its form and style, its way of making an argument through images.

Rossetti's procedure is evident in all of his translations, not just the work with Dante. I give one typical but peculiarly salient illustration, a passage from Giacomo Pugliesi, an "early Italian poet" of the Sicilian School:

Lo vostro insegnamento e dond' è miso?
E lo tuo franco cor chi me l' ha priso,
Donna mia?
Ov' è Madonna? e lo suo insegnamento?
La sua bellezza, e la sua canoscianza?

Rossetti renders the passage as follows:

Who hides that smile for which my heart is sore,
And drowns those words that I am longing for,
Lady of mine?
Where is my lady, and the lovely face
She had, and the sweet motion when she walk'd?

In one sense this is deliberate mistranslation. But the move is programmatic and goes to the very heart of what Rossetti believes can and should
be done when a specifically poetical translation is being undertaken for
these kinds of premodern texts. In such cases one's primary obligation
is to seek a "paraphrase" for the poetry-as-such — a paraphrase that holds
strictly to the level of the poetic signifiers. To "paraphrase" this text's conceptual "content," in Rossetti's view, is to seek a conceptual form that
threatens to short circuit any move to formal and sensuous levels of expression.

Criticism inspired by Eliot will therefore deplore translations that
fashion sensuous equivalents for the "moral and spiritual" ideas of medieval verse. Rossetti's sins of omission are said to be even worse. In the
Pugliesi passage, for instance, Elizabeth Gitter argues that Rossetti
"seems to have disliked or been bored by the convention of the lady as
teacher or moral guide."[6] This view arises from the translation's lack of a
literal equivalent for the key word *insegnamento*. But Rossetti hasn't ig-
nored Pugliesi's word, he has "translated" it by distributing its meaning — his understanding of its meaning — across the entire surface of the
passage. Rossetti translates back through the root *(segno)* of the evolved
moral term *(insegnamento)*.

This kind of move, recurrent in Rossetti's translations, defines the
self-conscious physicality of their style. Approaching a word like *insegnamento* as an icon rather than a concept, Rossetti reads it as an allegor-

ical sign whose meaning lies not in what it means but in how it means and in that it means. The procedure is the precise equivalent of what we saw earlier in *The Girlhood of Mary Virgin* and its associated sonnets. In translating, Rossetti always moves toward figurative equivalents. So here he reads Pugliesi in radically formal terms, as if the Italian text were a language of pure signifiers. He therefore transforms the sequence of (what might otherwise be taken for) abstract terms, "insegnamento . . . bellezza . . . canoscianza," into a figural language of seductive gesture: "The lovely face / She had, and the sweet motion when she walked." In Rossetti, what Pugliesi's Donna teaches is an art of embodied practice.

The form of Rossetti's translations implicitly makes an argument about the character of stilnovista poetry. He takes its moral and philosophical terminology as a figural system readable by those who have a Dantean "intelletto d'amore." For him, the stilnovisti poets (and Dante preeminently) harrowed the symbolic order by a root and branch literalizing process. So Dante's Beatrice is for Rossetti a literal form of love: she is a "person" who performs loving acts, and she is a poetical *figura* centering the loving action of Dante's poetry, particularly in the constellation of the *Vita Nuova*. If Dante's ideological horizon translated Beatrice into elaborate conceptual equivalents—and it most certainly did—Rossetti took all the equivalents at face value. They are for him decorative additions to the central (artistic) event: not truths but forms of truth. Exactly the same should be said of any biographical or historical equivalents—Beatrice as Beatrice Portinari, for example. All such forms are "symbolic" and "interpretational" shapes fashioned by the further adventures of an idealizing imagination.

For Rossetti, Dante's importance lies not in his ideology as such, whether philosophical/theological or historical/realistic, whether Catholic or—as his father thought—Masonic. It lies in his art, and in his work's implicit argument that knowledge, expressed in and through the figures of art, gets revealed as a practice:

> Dear Song, I know thou wilt hold gentle speech
> With many ladies when I send thee forth:
> Wherefore (being mindful that thou hadst thy birth
> From Love, and art a modest simple child),
> Whom so thou meetest, say thou this to each:

"Give me good speed! To her I wend along
In whose much strength my weakness is made strong."

Though unspectacular as translation, this verse — Rossetti's rendering of
a passage from the canzone "Donne ch'avete intelletto d'amore" — keeps
faith with Dante's poetic action in its crucial syntactic complexities, and
its faithfulness is perhaps strongest exactly at those moments when it
most departs from the original text's semantic literality, as, for example,
in the final two lines' rendering of Dante's text:

Insegnatemi gir; ch' io son mandata
A quella di cui lauda io so' adornata.

Rossetti leaves behind the semantic meanings of *lauda* and *adornata*, but
he recovers much of the force of their paradoxical relation in the play of
his own text's "strength . . . weakness . . . strong." A complementary
process translates Dante's predominantly assonantal structure into a
largely alliterative one. Rossetti's poetic success as a "translator" depends
upon a random but regular installation of these types of "mistranslation," for in such moments the reader observes with piercing clarity both
the fixed original and the swerving successor, as well as their (literally)
erotic relation. So in this passage we come to realize that Rossetti's text
is primarily a reflection of, and upon, Dante's. Rossetti's *her* is not
Dante's *quella* except in a stunning literal sense. *Quella* is Dante's Beatrice, but Rossetti's *her* is Dante's poem, the poetic practice Rossetti's
poem ventriloquizes for another world and audience, as the example of
Dante's poem had originally enjoined. The order of the verse is an order
of images in interaction — in our contemporary terms, a "play of the signifiers." Love itself, the supreme good, begins when one submits to that
order, which demands performance. Knowledge is a continual process
of knowing, Love of loving; and Art is a continual process of inventing
forms that display those ideal human acts.

We can understand, then, the sharp divergence of opinion about the
quality of Rossetti's translations when they are examined at the level of
the word and the phrase. An aesthetic sensibility will tend to respond fa-
vorably, a moral or philosophical one may not. The issue here is strictly
stylistic — though nonetheless crucial for that very reason, for Rossetti's

translations argue that the meaning of Dante's work is fundamentally a matter of form and style, that its "content" is best taken as a *figura* and image of its performative truth. The Modernist attack on the translations often takes the form of an attack on their style, but Pound's praise and Eliot's critique tell the actual truth: that the work is disparaged for its ideas, for which Pound had more sympathy than Eliot.

Rossetti typically leaves the order of the signifieds to fend for themselves, or treats them as second-order signifiers, as we saw him doing in his sonnets for *The Girlhood of Mary Virgin*. He turned to Dante because he found in his work a renascence of the authority of the signifiers. The stilnovista translations, in this respect, are a series of exercises by which Rossetti trained himself to approach writing in a purely formal and decorative way. This technical approach anticipated the methods of many Modernists, and was all the more dangerous, to a sensibility like Eliot's, for that very reason. For Rossetti's translations are grounded in a profane (Victorian) differential from medieval Catholicism; indeed, they assume that the ideological gulf between the Middle Ages and the nineteenth century is absolute. If religion and morality change, however, the practice of art persists. This practice is what lies open to translation. To be true to Dante and his circle, then, demands aesthetic translation. One good poem deserves another.

To understand Rossetti's poetry in this way is to recognize the mistake in Nicolette Gray's conclusion about Rossetti's way with images. Gray understands that Rossetti learned a "method of images" from Dante.[7] But she goes on to argue that Rossetti lacked a crucial "map" for organizing his intense images. "The place of the particular images must be seen against the background of an order in the abstract ideas in the mind" (Gray 28–29). When Gray looks at Rossetti's surfaces she observes the extreme play of the detail: "The very intensity of the presentation stresses its particularity, its momentariness, Rossetti cannot put it in the clear light of day, like Dante's other illustrator Botticelli" (Gray 29). But Gray is mistaken. Rossetti has simply chosen to "put it in the clear light" of a "day" that is not medieval. Rossetti has a "map," a conceptual scheme for organizing his materials. The map is the critical program of historicist analysis.

This is a strictly formal way of approaching Dante's poetry. It may be disapproved for any number of reasons, of course. What cannot be said is that it lacks either procedural or abstract rigor. And what cannot be gainsaid is that it allowed Rossetti to appropriate one of the most startling and innovative features of Dante's early writing. In this case, we are still dealing with matters of poetic form, but the formalities involve larger procedural operations.[8]

Rossetti's habits of revision are notorious. He worked and reworked both his paintings and his poems obsessively—not as if to refashion them for different audiences and occasions, though he did do this, but as if his efforts might finally achieve some ideal perfection. These localized reworkings replicate his habit of thinking and rethinking the organization of his poems. The case of the 1870 *Poems* is exemplary, as is the centerpiece of that volume and of Rossetti's poetical work as a whole: "The House of Life" sonnet sequence. In 1869–1870 alone Rossetti played with a bewildering series of possible orderings for the poems in the volume, and for the sonnets in the sequence (which formed one section of the volume).

"The House of Life" sonnets are especially important to consider here because the sequence is structured in terms of an implicit narrative. The story involves a young man, an artist, and two (at least two) idealized women. The young man's love for one of the women succeeds to his love for the second. The first woman dies—it is not entirely clear whether her death occurs before or after his second love—and the events radically intensify the man's erotic yearning for perfect love. This new desire is haunted by feelings of guilt and remorse, and dominated by ambiguous images of death and otherworlds.

Now this sequence, like the *Vita Nuova,* has often been read as poetically heightened autobiography. The key historical equivalents—the persons, the dates, the places—are in each instance well known. Indeed, there is little doubt that Rossetti took the *Vita Nuova* as a model and precursor, if not even a forecast, of his sonnet sequence. Each work tells a story of an artist's quest for ideal love. Each quest centers in the image of an ideal woman, and in each case death intervenes in a dramatic and decisive way. Dante has a kind of second love as well, the "screen lady" (or, as in Rossetti, the screen ladies) to whom he addresses some of his poetry. Finally, both works are organized reflexively. Looking back upon past events, both construct an explication of the secret meaning of those events—a meaning both works represent as implicit in the events from the beginning, though at the time the meaning was unknown or unapparent.

For all these similarities, of course, the emotional structure of the two works is very different. This difference is located in the status of each poet's doubled love. Dante's screen lady is never a serious object of his devotion; she is a device, a means by which he can conceal his true love from worldly understandings and curiosities. Rossetti, by contrast, is fully devoted to the beloved and the innominata, and his double attachment defines what it means to be "Lost on Both Sides." So whereas the *Vita Nuova* unfolds an unambiguously redemptive action, "The House of Life" closes in an obscure and troubled "one Hope," "alone." That differential marks the belatedness of Rossetti's work, and the self-consciousness with which he undertakes his Dantean pursuit. Indeed, Dante is important for Rossetti partly because he represents the ideal of an integral imagination.

Nowhere do we see Rossetti following Dante more closely than in the way he (re)organizes his poetry. "The House of Life" (in its first published form) tells a story of events that can be interpreted as falling roughly between 1860 and 1871, its key date being the death of the poet's wife in February 1862. The real-time composition of the sequence as a whole begins in 1869 and is never really completed. Rossetti published two versions, one in 1870, the second in 1881, though he constructed many more.

The *Vita Nuova*'s story has been similarly circumscribed, its key date falling in June 1290, the month of Beatrice Portinari's death. The story it tells begins in 1274, when Dante first sees Beatrice (he is nine years old, she is eight). For nine years—according to the *Vita Nuova*'s retrospective prose account—he haunts her presence, trying to see her whenever he can. Then in 1283 she gives him her famous "salutation." This event throws him wholly under the dominion of love. A year or so after Beatrice's death Dante begins to compose the *Vita Nuova*. He completes the work sometime between 1292 and 1295.

Rossetti clearly understood—and came to understand even more deeply—the key formal innovation of Dante's poetical autobiography. He knew that most of the poems inserted in the *Vita Nuova* narrative were not written for the reasons and with the meanings supplied by the autobiographical interpretation. Indeed, many of the poems—for example, the crucial first sonnet—were written entirely apart from the Beatricean circumstances, not to say the Portinarian circumstances, that dominate the *Vita Nuova*. That interpretive frame is supplied retrospectively—is initiated, in fact, through the *Vita Nuova* itself.

Dante does not conceal this structure of the autobiography, though his revelation is oblique—presumably in order to separate those who have intelligence in love from those who do not. "A ciascun' alma presa" is an explicit request for an interpretive response from others: they are to write back to him ("mi rescrivan") what they make of the dream as it is represented in the poem. The set of answering sonnets is now well-known, the most famous being from Cavalcanti, Cino, and Dante da Maiano. These responses mirror Dante's sonnet, which is the initial interpretive act.

When he narrates all this in the *Vita Nuova,* Dante says that "the true meaning of that vision was not then perceived by anyone, though it be now evident to the least skillful" (*Early Italian Poets,* 228). That is to say, the passage of time has exposed the full structure of events—the Beatricean scheme—that explains the dream. More than this, the Beatricean plot also gives new life and meaning to Dante's poetry. It makes possible not only the work titled *Vita Nuova* but the marvelous new life announced and revealed there. So the *Vita Nuova*'s first sonnet "now" ("ora," ca. 1292) begins to tremble with thoughts Dante did not have when he wrote it in 1283. In this respect the total experience gravitating around this first sonnet defines the *Vita Nuova*'s entire structure of meaning.

So far as Rossetti is concerned, two matters are especially important. The first appears in his translation—or his "mis"translation—of the opening lines of Dante's sonnet:

> To every heart which the sweet pain doth move,
> And unto which these words may now be brought,
> For true interpretation and kind thought . . .
> (*Early Italian Poets,* 227)

The freedom of this rendering gets sharply located in the third line, which corresponds to Dante's "mi rescrivan suo parvente." Rossetti's rendering seems to me brilliant—a perfect example of what he meant by "fidelity" rather than "literality" in translation.[9] When Dante's "mi re-scrivan" becomes "true interpretation," Rossetti is defining interpretive truth—meaning—as poetry. Just as human events are most revealed through poiesis, the "true interpretation" of a poem is another poem.

Secondly, when Rossetti translates the *Vita Nuova* according to this theory of translation, he is explicitly aligning himself with Dante and his circle. Dante says in his autobiography that the dream's meaning is "ora . . . manifestissimo." Rossetti's poetical translation thereby translates Dante's *ora* to the "now" of Rossetti's nineteenth century. In doing so, it implicitly defines the *ora* as an eternal now, a moment in and out of any historical time, a moment that arrives with the arrival of a poetical act.

The act may appear either as vision or revision: dream or text, poem or translation, a new work or a reconstitution. The latter are in certain respects the most dramatic instances of Rossettian art in its vita nuovan mode. In "The House of Life," for example, as in the *Vita Nuova*, many poems were written years before the sequence was even thought about— in certain cases, years before Rossetti had even met Elizabeth Siddal or Jane Burden Morris. A poem like "Lost on Both Sides," written in 1854 but first published in 1869 as part of "The House of Life" project, illus-trates what Rossetti had learned from his study of the *Vita Nuova*. When Dante places his early poems in the interpretive context of his autobi-ography, the meaning of the poems shifts radically. That shift in mean-ing locates one of the central subjects of the sequence as a whole: the rev-elation of a fatality in Dante's life and work, and of secret meanings in his writings that only get exposed when his life's fatalities unfold over time. Rossetti treats his own poetry in the same way. "The House of Life" mixes early poems, from the 1840s and early 1850s, with later ones; and the mixture, as in Dante, forces the early poems to yield up their hidden meanings. Furthermore—and the parallel with Dante is again very clear—the mixture works to suggest that every "present" moment of a poem or work of art is pregnant with unknown futurities. So the poems as they appear in the 1870 "House of Life" will undergo another mean-ing shift when they reappear in the 1881 version.

Those futurities are especially important for Rossetti because his work is tormented by its own desires. Fate in Dante is the revelation of a prevenient benevolence, whereas in Rossetti Fate is ominous precisely because one can't determine the moral value of the signs. One sees only that they have moral value. Rossetti learned from Dante a method for revealing the prophetic power of artistic forms of expression. From that comes the "visionary" quality of his work: the understanding that forms and images possess powers in themselves, powers that cannot be comprehended or even entirely controlled by the artist who is their medium. But Rossetti's visions are not governed by a religious ideology, as Dante's are. He understood Dante's faith, but his understanding was strictly a critical one.

The vision conveyed through Rossetti's work is therefore religious in tone but skeptical in its understanding. Whereas Dante reveals the presence of spiritual forces in the human world, Rossetti's work argues that the world is a kind of incarnate spiritual manifold. This way of thinking is not at all pantheistic because the locus of the spirit is not on the nonhuman plane but exactly on the human one. Inhabiting (and even incarnating) a spiritual state in this way carries a paradoxical consequence: that one cannot establish a fixed perspective on one's condition, whether from below or from above. Every vantage is provisional, relativity is the permanent rule of order. Hence the intensity and particularity of the Pre-Raphaelite images.

And (finally) hence, too, the portentous and even threatening character of so much of Rossetti's work, especially the later work; as if it were declaring, with Hamlet, that "There are more things in heaven and earth, Horatio, / Than are dreamt of in your philosophy."

The Rossetti we have been observing is a figure whose methods closely correspond to many we associate with twentieth-century writing, Modernist as well as Postmodernist. Pater, Wilde, the early Yeats and the early Pound all took Rossetti as a point of departure. Pater's superb "Dante Gabriel Rossetti" (1883, 1889) set Rossetti apart as the most original poet of the age, the one writer who had made truly novel technical and artistic advances. "At a time when poetic originality in England might seem to have had its utmost play," Pater writes, Rossetti came "with a structure and music of verse, a vocabulary, an accent, unmistakably novel."[10] To emphasize the technical basis of Rossetti's originality is in itself to argue Rossetti's "Modernism." But when Pater goes on to elaborate the specific features of that originality, one sees why so many early-twentieth-century writers found Rossetti an important resource.

Three matters are especially significant. First, Pater emphasizes the extreme self-consciousness of Rossetti's work — what Pater calls the "genuine intellectual structure" displayed in his writing. Rossetti makes technique — his artistic practice — a central subject. Second, Rossetti's work invents a whole new vocabulary and method of images. This centers in his "care for minute and definite imagery" derived from his study and translation of the early Italian poets. Here Rossetti anticipates not merely the Imagist movement but the materialist "thing-tradition" that so dominates twentieth-century writing.[11] Third, Rossetti develops what Pater calls a "mythopoeic" method from his study of the Middle Ages: that is, his work unfolds a revelation of "the ideal aspects of common things."

Given these features of his work, we might wonder at Rossetti's virtual disappearance from the discourse of Modernism. The event is explicable when we recall two salient cultural facts of English-language Modernism: first, the centrality of a certain way of reading Joyce's work; second, the dominance that Eliot's Christian reading of Modernism had in the schools.

The Rossetti-Joyce connection is located in the figure of Stephen Daedalus, whose villanelle in *A Portrait of the Artist as a Young Man* establishes his Rossettian credentials. The poem is regularly read as the emblem of a romanticism that imprisons Stephen. In *Ulysses* Joyce will dramatize an artistic method that has escaped the dead end of Stephen's Pre-Raphaelite allegiances. This is a perfectly just reading, although it can license far more problematic interpretations (for example, the unequivocal celebration of Molly and Leopold Bloom over against the tormented and brilliant Stephen). Rossetti's adherence to the Romantic tradition is close and deep, nor does he make any programmatic refusals of that tradition, as certain Modernists, like Eliot, tend to do. From our late-twentieth-century perspective one might want to argue that Rossetti's romantic allegiances — especially his *Sehnsucht* and radical skepticism — begin to reveal features of his work that forecast Postmodern attitudes. The argument would proceed through a total recovery of the Romantic heritage, not just the modernized Romanticism of "strong poets" that was served up in response to early Modernist criticism. Unlike both of the latter, Rossetti's is a contaminated Romanticism, one in which the poet comes to resemble Tennyson's Ulysses, who became a

Sibylla Palmifera (oil on canvas, 1866–70; 37 × 32½ in.: Lady Lever Art Gallery, Port Sunlight). Swan Electric Company Engraving (ca. 1899), reproduction of original oil. Reproduced with permission, Delaware Art Museum, Samuel and Mary R. Bancroft Memorial.

Proserpine (oil on canvas, 1874; 49¾ × 24 in.: Tate Gallery (the "Seventh Version"). Frederick Hollyer photographic reproduction (ca. 1880–85) of the original oil. Reproduced with permission, Delaware Art Museum, Samuel and Mary R. Bancroft Memorial.

The Damsel of the San Graal, late version (oil on canvas, 1874; 36¼ × 22¾ in.: private collection). Autotype Company engraving (ca. 1890), reproduced with permission from a private collection.

Mnemosyne (oil on canvas, 1881; 47½ × 23 in.: Delaware Art Museum). Val Prinsep photographic reproduction (ca. 1890) of original oil. Reproduced with permission, Delaware Art Museum, Samuel and Mary R. Bancroft Memorial.

St. Cecilia (drawing for Moxon's 1857 illustrated edition of Tennyson's *Poems;* 1856–57; 3⅞ × 3¼ in.). Frederick Hollyer photographic reproduction (ca. 1880–85) of the original drawing. Reproduced with permission, Delaware Art Museum, Samuel and Mary R. Bancroft Memorial.

The Salutation of Beatrice, early version (oil on two panels, 1859; each 29½ × 31½ in: National Museum of Canada, Ottawa). Frederick Hollyer photographic reproduction (ca. 1880–85) of the original panels. Reproduced with permission, Delaware Art Museum, Samuel and Mary R. Bancroft Memorial.

The Salutation of Beatrice, late version (oil on canvas, 1880–81; 60¾ × 36 in.: Toledo [Ohio] Museum of Art). Frederick Hollyer photographic reproduction (ca. 1890) of original oil. Reproduced with permission, Delaware Art Museum, Samuel and Mary R. Bancroft Memorial.

Veronica Veronese (oil on canvas, 1872; 43 × 35 in.: Delaware Art Museum).
Swan Electric Company Engraving (ca. 1899), reproduction of original oil.
Reproduced with permission, Delaware Art Museum, Samuel and Mary R.
Bancroft Memorial.

Mary Magdalene at the Door of Simon the Pharisee (pen and india ink, 1858; 21¼ × 18⅜ in.: Fitzwilliam Museum). Reproduced with permission, the Syndics of the Fitzwilliam Museum.

Found (oil on canvas, begun 1854, unfinished; 36 × 31½ in.: Delaware Art Museum). Frederick Hollyer photographic reproduction (ca. 1880–85) of the original oil. Reproduced with permission, Delaware Art Museum, Samuel and Mary R. Bancroft Memorial.

Fair Rosamund (oil on canvas, 1861; 20½ × 16½ in.: National Museum of Wales, Cardiff). Frederick Hollyer photographic reproduction (ca. 1880–85) of the original oil. Reproduced with permission, private collection.

Albions Angel stood beside the Stone
of night, and saw
The terror like a comet, or more like the
planet red
That once inclosd the terrible wandering comets in its sphere
Then Mars thou wast our center & the planets three flew round
Thy crimson disk; so eer the Sun was rent from thy red sphere.
The Spectre glowd his horrid length staining the temple long
With beams of blood & thus a voice came forth and shook the
temple

William Blake, *America*, plate 7, reproduced from a copy of Alexander Gilchrist's *Life of William Blake* (1863) in the library of Jerome McGann, 7¼ × 5 in.

Elizabeth Siddal (watercolor, 1854; 7⅛ × 6⅜ in.: Delaware Art Museum). Frederick Hollyer photographic reproduction (ca. 1880–85) of the original watercolor. Reproduced with permission, Delaware Art Museum, Samuel and Mary R. Bancroft Memorial.

Elizabeth Siddal (pen and brown and black ink, 1855; 4¾ × 4¼ in.: Ashmolean Museum). Frederick Hollyer photographic reproduction (ca. 1880–85) of the original drawing. Reproduced with permission, Delaware Art Museum, Samuel and Mary R. Bancroft Memorial.

Elizabeth Siddal (pencil, n.d.; 4¾ × 4½ in.: Victoria and Albert Museum). Frederick Hollyer photographic reproduction (ca. 1880–85) of the original drawing. Reproduced with permission, Delaware Art Museum, Samuel and Mary R. Bancroft Memorial.

Giotto Painting the Portrait of Dante (watercolor, 1852; 14½ × 18½ in.: Fogg Museum, Harvard University). Frederick Hollyer photographic reproduction (ca. 1880–85) of the original watercolor. Reproduced with permission, private collection.

A Vision of Fiammetta (oil on canvas, 1878; 55 × 36 in.: private collection).
Mansell Company photographic reproduction (ca. 1890) of original oil.
Reproduced with permission, Delaware Art Museum, Samuel and Mary R.
Bancroft Memorial.

A Sea Spell (oil on canvas, 1877; 43 × 35¾ in.: Fogg Museum, Harvard University). Val Prinsep photographic reproduction (ca. 1890) of original oil. Reproduced with permission, Delaware Art Museum, Samuel and Mary R. Bancroft Memorial.

La Bella Mano (oil on canvas, 1875; 62 × 42 in.: Delaware Museum of Art). Mansell Company photographic reproduction (ca. 1890) of original oil. Reproduced with permission, Delaware Art Museum, Samuel and Mary R. Bancroft Memorial.

part of all that he had met: all, the best as well as the worst. Debasement is a self-conscious feature of Rossetti's work from the outset; far from being a sign of artistic failure, however, it is the ground of the originality Pater discerned. It is equally the forecast of his Postmodernism.

Eliot celebrated Joyce's *Ulysses* in a famous review-essay in which he sketched the technical achievement of the book, its "mythic method" whereby art was, he said, once again made possible for the modern world. The argument is especially interesting in light of Pater's celebration of a corresponding mythic method in Rossetti. Eliot's refusal to follow Pater here can and probably should be explained through the special character Eliot assigned to the "myth" represented in the work of Dante. Pater explicitly links Rossetti's "mythopoeic" method to Rossetti's study and understanding of Dante. But for Eliot it is one thing to erect an arbitrary running parallel with a pagan text like the *Odyssey* or with primitive solar myths like those explicated by Sir James Frazer. To treat Dante's work in equivalent ways — which is exactly what Rossetti did — is implicitly to argue that the Christian mythos has no special historic privilege. Rossetti's Dante is a technical resource and inspiration, not a repository of fundamental moral truth. Rossetti therefore treats his "Art Catholic" in purely artistic terms, the way Joyce used Homer. But for Eliot, it is exactly Rossetti's technical approach to Dante and the Christian mythos flowing through him that makes Rossetti a dangerous and finally an impossible model.

3

DANTE AND ROSSETTI

Translation, Pastiche, Ritual, Fate

> Since perception itself is never complete, since our perspectives give us a world to express and think about that envelopes and exceeds those perspectives, . . . why should the expression of the world be subjected to the prose of the *senses* or of the concept? It must be poetry; that is, it must completely awaken and recall our sheer power of expressing beyond things already said or seen. . . . How long it takes . . . before a writer learns to speak with his own voice. Similarly, how long it takes the painter — who does not, as we do, have his work spread out before him, but who creates it — to recognize in his first paintings the features of what will be his completed work.
>
> Maurice Merleau-Ponty,
> "Indirect Language and the Voices of Silence"

Late in February 1870, in the final proof stage for his new book of *Poems,* Rossetti added three sonnets to "The House of Life" sequence. One of these, "Life-in-Love," reflects a profound engagement with the *Vita Nuova,* the single most important work for understanding Rossetti's imaginative goals.

The first version of the sonnet began thus:

> Not in my body is my life at all,
>   But in my lady's lips and hands and eyes

That text did not sustain itself, and with Rossetti's final revisions it became:

> Not in thy body is thy life at all,
>   But in this lady's lips and hands and eyes[1]

46

The changes might seem small enough — a mere alteration of three pronouns. My/my/my become thy/thy/this. But the alteration is major: it cancels the first-person perspective of the original text. The resulting shift exposes a characteristic feature of Rossetti's poetic style. When he turns himself into a second person, as happens here, a certain distantiation enters the verse, as if *the poem* had assumed an identity and had begun speaking of the poet and the lady.

There are plenty of sonnets in "The House of Life" that preserve a first-person rhetoric. Nevertheless, Rossetti (like, say, Wallace Stevens) regularly moves to "sublime" or idealize his rhetoric. Just before publishing his augmented version of "The House of Life" in 1881 he considered printing a "disavowal of personality in the sonnets." He had in mind to print the following prose note as a preface to the sonnet sequence: "To speak in the first person is *often* to speak most vividly; but these emotional poems are in no sense 'occasional.' The 'Life' involved is life representative, as associated with love and death, with aspiration & foreboding, or with ideal art and beauty. Whether the recorded moment exist in the region of fact or of thought is a question indifferent to the Muse, so long only as her touch can quicken it."[2] In the end he decided against publishing this explanatory note. He probably came to think that the "disavowal" might itself be taken as an unneeded personal intervention. So he let the sonnets speak for themselves, as it were.

Rossetti's namesake and master, Dante Alighieri, stands behind this cultivated and idealizing style. Dante and other early Italian poets taught Rossetti how to make poems, as well as their generated textual creatures, speak in their own right. The style culminates in Dante's great canzone "Donne ch'avete intelletto d'amore," in which the poet summons to speech an array of characters including an angel, God, Love, and Dante's very poem, and in a remarkable moment the poet in propria persona quotes a remark that he himself apparently will have made after death. The allegorical theatricalities of Rossetti's great sonnet sequence "The House of Life" trace their origin to the translation work Rossetti began in his late teens.

The importance of this fact about Rossetti's work disappeared when his influential translations came under twentieth-century attack, as we have seen. A gulf seemed to separate Rossetti's erotic style from the conceptual rigors of Dante's work. This view of the matter carries a related and even more significant misconception: that Rossetti's art, both pictorial and verbal, lacks theoretical rigor. Though these critical judgments come in Modernist trappings, they trace themselves back to the notorious "Fleshly School" controversy of the 1870s. The erotic focus of Rossetti's work kept Robert Buchanan from seeing the elaborate argument for Intellectual Beauty that Rossetti was pursuing. F. R. Leavis and T. S. Eliot experienced a similar failure of imagination when they tried to negotiate Shelley and Swinburne.

The truth about Rossetti is not easy to discern in a Modernist neoclassical horizon. For although Rossetti is, as Eliot knew, an erotic and a romantic artist, he cultivates artifice and an impersonal rhetoric. The pictorial and verbal surfaces are alike, and paradoxically, voluptuous in a second-person style, as it were. The aesthetic illusion seeks not a display of sincerity but a form of thought.

Like Kandinsky, Mondrian, and Klee, Rossetti is first and foremost a conceptual artist. His primary idea is to return to the Middle Ages for procedural models in art and poetry. In the case of poetry, Dante is his chief inspiration and the *Vita Nuova* is both point of departure and determining text. Rossetti translated the work in the 1840s and 1850s, along with a large body of poetry by Dante and a related circle of thirteenth- and fourteenth-century Italian poets. When he came finally to publish these translations in 1861, the *Vita Nuova* was made the pivotal work. The pronominal changes that appear in the sonnet "Life-in-Love" reflect Rossetti's desire to carry out for himself a stylistic program that has much in common with the program Dante had defined in his autobiography, particularly in "Donne ch'avete intelletto d'amore," in section 19 of *Vita Nuova*.

According to Dante's argument, the poem emerges from a series of frustrated attempts (recorded in the previous sections of the *Vita Nuova*) to write poems — sonnets in fact — that would express the full truth of his love for Beatrice. These frustrations climax in section 18, where Dante's poetry is severely criticized by one of the ladies to whom he had shown his work. She asks Dante to explain his poetry and its relation to Beatrice, "questa tua beatitudine." When he answers that the function of his poetry is to "praise my lady," the woman bluntly tells him that he has failed — perhaps worse, that he is self-deceived: "If thy speech were true, those words which thou didst write concerning thy condition would have been written with another intent." What she means is that Dante's verse does not so much reveal the glory of Beatrice as the psychic state of the poet. In short, it is merely personal.

Section 19 dramatizes Dante's self-conscious turn to a style that allows the poet's language to become an index — an instantiation — not of himself or his feelings but of "questa tua beatitudine," of Beatrice. Moved by a desire to write more verse, Dante makes the key decision to write "in seconda persona," in the second person, to ladies that have intelligence in love. This decision brings with it a sweet new style: "Allora dico che la mia lingua parlo quasi come per se stessa mossa; e disse: *Donne ch'avete intelletto d'amore*." Rossetti translates this crucial Dante passage thus: "Whereupon I declare that my tongue spake as though by its own impulse, and said, 'Ladies that have intelligence in love.'"

The translation is what Randall McLeod would call a "transformission"; that is to say, it is as much Rossetti as it is Dante. Rendering Dante's "mia lingua parlo" as "my tongue spake" is more Rossettian than Dantean, for it casts Dante's figure of impersonality into physical, even fleshly, terms. It also misses an important literal feature of Dante's word. Dante works the word *lingua* — it isn't exactly a pun — to signify two important matters: first, his poem is grounded in speech, the "mother tongue" that figures so prominently in his decision to write in Italian rather than Latin; and second, the canzone appears to have been authored not by Dante personally but by Dante's language, as if his language were a living Being capable of independent and authorizing acts. Although Dante is a presence in his canzone, none of the first-person pronouns reference himself.

There is no question that Rossetti's translation has altered the sense of Dante's original. The translation is, literally, more "fleshly." On the other hand, there is also no question that Rossetti understood very well what Dante was doing. We realize this from a note Rossetti appended to section 25 of his translation of the *Vita Nuova*. This section comprises an extended explanation of Dante's sweet new style of idealization, its historical origins, and its philosophical purpose. In this discussion Dante implicitly argues how vulgar poetry "during the last hundred and fifty years" acquired true philosophical potential. In that period arose "the writing of rhymes in spoken language corresponding to the writing in metre of Latin verse." This new work "in the vulgar tongue" began,

Dante says, when the poet wanted "to make himself understood of a certain lady, unto whom Latin poetry was difficult. This thing is against such as rhyme concerning other matters than love; that made of speech having been first used for the expression of love alone." Rossetti adds a note to this text: "It strikes me that this curious passage furnishes a reason, hitherto (I believe) overlooked, why Dante put such of his lyrical poems as relate to philosophy into the form of love-poems." Rossetti is trying to make explicit what Dante has left largely to implication. Dante's text is reflecting on the philosophical import of his own early love poetry, all written in Italian. More specifically, the text reaches back to section 19 and the canzone written to those ladies who have intelligence in love — that is, to those who possess and even incarnate true philosophical understanding even though they have no knowledge of Latin. For the key to such intelligence and understanding is not erudition or conceptual skill, it is the actual experience of love.

Rossetti's love poetry takes its intellectual pretensions from Dante's lead. For both, to write of love is to engage a philosophical discourse. For both, however, that discourse must be framed impersonally. The point is to dramatize as clearly as possible the objective dynamic presence of love in the world. It is not to express personal feelings. The latter figure prominently in the dynamic of love, of course, but both poets strive for a style that will reconstruct feelings and other impalpable realities (like ideas and spiritual presences) into an objective — that is (in this case), into a purely linguistic or semiotic — condition. The allegorical figurations so characteristic of both poets locate the philosophical urgency of their styles.

So a sonnet like "Life-in-Love" involves a programmatic nineteenth-century reconstruction of the poetic style Dante evolved and explained when he wrote the *Vita Nuova*. The sonnet appears to address the poet in the second person, as Dante's canzone "Donne ch' avete" appears to address the ladies that have intelligence in love. Throughout "The House of Life" these kinds of distancing effects are produced. The sonnet that follows "Life-in-Love," for example, "The Love Moon," is a textual dialogue between octave and sestet. Personified Love speaks the octave, but the respondent of the sestet is ambiguous: we may take it to be either the voice of the poet or the voice of the poem. In either case it is a voice, not a person, an important distinction that would hardly have been lost on the author of a canzone like "Donne ch' avete." We take it to be the voice of the poem when we negotiate Rossetti's texts as expressions of style, at the rhetorical level. We perceive the voice of the poet when our response registers the constative features of his texts. Rossetti regularly leaves both options open to his readers, for he builds his sequence with a variety of sonnets, some in a personal rhetoric, some in the rhetoric of "Life-in-Love." This diversity replicates Dante's procedure in the *Vita Nuova*.

Because Rossetti's sequence lacks a prose narrative like Dante's *Vita Nuova,* his poems proliferate ambiguities that we don't find in Dante. Rossetti doesn't only construct a style in which poems, ideas, and various spiritual idealities may appear to speak in propriae personae. He constructs a style that appears to have its own identity, including the power to raise up figural presences possessing equivalent self-motivating authority and independent existence. Once again the sonnet "Life-in-Love" exemplifies the situation very well, especially in the context of its placement in 1881 in the more elaborated sequence of "The House of Life." Unlike the poem in the shorter 1870 sequence, the sonnet in 1881 follows a group in which a rhetoric of second-person address envelopes the figure of the poet's beloved. Any reading of "Life-in-Love" in that context comes with the possibility that the second-person address in line 1 — the pair of "thy" pronouns — might not reference the poet, which would probably be our first thought, but might be directed to the woman named "my lady" several sonnets earlier (see especially "Soul-Light," "The Moonstar," and "Venus Victrix"). Or is "this lady" of line 2 in "Life-in-Love" the same person as "my lady" addressed earlier? Or is she someone else altogether? The text raises up all these textual possibilities as iconic forms, figural presences.

These reading complications develop because Rossetti's verse is making a studied use of another distinctive feature of Dante's *Vita Nuova.* He is modifying the Dantean figure of the screen lady ("donna schermo") first introduced in section 5 of Dante's autobiographical treatise. To appreciate what Rossetti is doing we should reconsider some general matters about "The House of Life."

As already observed, a certain narrative, by no means unambiguous, plays out a secret life within and below the elaborate ornamental surface of Rossetti's sonnet sequence. Whatever else may be true of this poetical construction, and leaving aside autobiographical matters for the moment, the drama has at least three key players: the poet plus (at least) two beloved women. Problems arise repeatedly, however, when readers try to identify particular texts with one or another of these women. "Life-in-Love" supplies an excellent instance of such a problem, for it is clear that the sonnet is discussing two women. It is not clear, however, how we are to assign the pronouns' references.

Biographical information helps to elucidate these stylistic problems. Rossetti told his friend Alice Boyd that this sonnet "refers to an actual love with a reminiscence of a former one."[3] He did not say this to encourage a "limitedly personal" reading of the sonnet. And when we read the sonnet in face of his remark we realize that none of the stylistic problems are resolved by what he told Alice Boyd. The pronouns preserve their strange ambiguities. But the remark locates the formal limits of the ambiguous references of the second- and third-person pronouns in the octave. Furthermore, the biographical frame of reference lets us see that the sestet's "poor tress of hair" relates to the "former" love (more specifically, to Rossetti's dead wife, Elizabeth), and once again this information helps to define a formal quality of the sonnet. The vivid hair of the dead woman is a figure of the continuing presence of the dead among the living. As such, it underscores all the haunting and ambiguous presences raised up in the octave.

In the textual event, therefore, the octave realizes precisely the following set of ambiguous imaginations. Taking the text as spoken by the poet, we must negotiate simultaneously these possible readings:

1. My life is not in my body but in the invigorating body of the lady before me, whose presence vivifies my morbid condition, which remains preoccupied with the woman I loved but who is now lost to me — who is in fact dead, as I feel myself to be, etc.
2. Your life, my dead love, is not in your dead body, but lives again in the vivifying body of the woman before me now, etc.
3. [In this reading the text is a set of inner reflections that begin with a recollection of the dead beloved, who becomes the referent of "this lady" just as the woman present to the poet becomes the referent of "thy" in line 1; hence we get:] Your life, my lady, is not a function of your physical being, which is mortal and subject to change and decay,

but of a certain spiritual identity whose living presence remains active among us from a transcendental order of reality.

4. Finally, several variations on these possibilities emerge (*a*) if we take the sonnet to be an impersonal expression, and (*b*) if we disassociate the third-person pronouns in lines 3 and 5 ("she" and "her") from "this lady."

These kinds of ambiguities, recurrent in "The House of Life," clearly recall Dante's special development of the troubadour convention that licensed poets to address fictional lovers in order to conceal the identities of their true loves. In Rossetti the question continually arises: when the poet addresses love to one or the other of the two principal women realized in "The House of Life," does she function as a screen for the other? Or, indeed, are both ultimately screen ladies — perhaps instantiations for "the Muse" Rossetti mentions in the note to the sonnet sequence that he didn't publish with the 1881 text?

To appreciate what is happening in Rossetti's work we want to recall how Dante explains his relation to "questa gentile donna schermo." In section 5 of the *Vita Nuova* Dante sees Beatrice in church, and as he gazes on her he realizes that another woman stands in his line of sight. The latter, believing that Dante is looking at her, "looked round at me many times, marvelling at my continued gaze, which seemed to have *her* for its object. And many perceived that she thus looked; so that, departing thence, I heard it whispered after me, 'Look you to what a pass such a *lady* hath brought him.'" Dante is pleased that this mistaken judgment conceals the true object of his devotion from the public, and "immediately it came to my mind that I might make use of this lady as a screen to the truth; and so well did I play my part that the most of those who had hitherto watched and wondered at me, now imagined they had found me out. By her means I kept my secret concealed till some years were gone over; and for my better security, I even made divers rhymes in her honour." The next five sections of the *Vita Nuova* center in Dante's relations with the screen lady, or rather screen ladies, for he makes another woman a screen lady when the first departs the city. These events culminate in section 10, in which Beatrice refuses Dante her salutation. The refusal is directly related to Dante's use of the screen lady, which has caused evil reports to spread about him.

The focus of all these events is the poetry Dante writes. It has two objects: to express his devotion to Beatrice, his spiritual ideal-love, and to disguise that devotion in poetry which seems to have other objects—specifically, other women—in view. A poem like "O voi che per la via d'Amor passate" (in section 7) is specifically presented as double-faced: in one view it is a lament for the departure of Dante's screen lady, in another it is an expression of his love for Beatrice. Both meanings are of course related, for Dante's commitment to the screen lady has all along been conceived as a device to further his love for Beatrice. The two sonnets of section 8 have a similar doubleness: in one perspective they lament the death of a young woman known to Beatrice, in another they are written to glorify Beatrice, whose goodness shows itself in her grief at her friend's death. In his note to the sonnets in his translation, Rossetti discusses the critical disputes about whether the poems "do not allude to the dead lady, but to Beatrice." He concludes that "Most probably *both* allusions are intended."

Rossetti responded strongly to this kind of elusive and allusive artifice in Dante's work. Disguised and doubled meanings play across the writing, as Dante himself tells us; and while Rossetti did not endorse his father's famous exegeses of Dante, he clearly read the poetry in an analogous way.[4] Discussing the sonnets in section 5, for example, the English poet speculates about various "covert allusion[s] to Beatrice" in different passages. The "donna schermo" device governs the management of the poet's love devotions in "The House of Life," as we see when readers try to identify certain of the sonnets with particular ladies. These critical moves mirror those of the "commentators" Rossetti recollects in his note to section 5.

"Probably *both* allusions are intended": here Rossetti works a distinctive modification upon Dante's coded writing. In simplest terms it might be put thus: that Rossetti's imagined loves can function simultaneously as either Beatricean image or as "donna schermo." What this means is that they are always constructed as images. As such, Dante's figural hierarchy gets leveled and reordered in Rossetti. A sonnet like "The Portrait" illustrates the change very well:

> O Lord of all compassionate control,
>   O Love! let this my lady's picture glow

Under my hand to praise her name, and show
Even of her inner self the perfect whole:
That he who seeks her beauty's furthest goal,
  Beyond the light that the sweet glances throw
  And refluent wave of the sweet smile, may know
The very sky and sea-line of her soul.

Lo! it is done. Above the enthroning throat
The mouth's mould testifies of voice and kiss,
  The shadowed eyes remember and foresee.
Her face is made her shrine. Let all men note
  That in all years (O Love, thy gift is this!)
  They that would look on her must come to me.

The multiple action of this sonnet appears graphically if we ask: is "The Portrait" the sonnet, or does the text reference some picture? That question exposes a whole range of ambiguities that play through the verse. As usual in Rossetti, the pronouns lie open to multiple references, nor do we have a determinate "speaker" of the sonnet. The final "me," for example, simultaneously points to four realized identities: a poet, a painter, and the verbal or pictorial work that one or the other would have created. These four connections then uncover a faint but crucial fifth, "Love," whose presence dominates the poem and who is finally declared to have made of "this" a gift. But what is "this"? The pronoun here locates a complex noun clause—a nominated action involving various figures, each of which is subsumed within the action, each of which fully (if not completely) incarnates the action. In the end we cannot *not* see that the gift is in some important sense (as it were) Love himself (or, in yet another alternative, "herself," for Love and the Beloved, as in Dante, often merge their identities).

Rossetti's poetry, then, does not define and instantiate so much persons (Jane Morris, Elizabeth Siddal, Fanny Cornforth) as the presence and action of Love in the world. Identities, as well as the names and words that signify them, are fluid, dynamic markers of the presence of that action. Love is at once an ideal and a physical experience for Rossetti, as it was for Dante, and both study how the ideal goal can be advanced and/or hindered by Love's mortalities. Whereas Dante represents this psychic drama as a process of growth and enlightenment,

however, Rossetti perceives it as a kind of permanent dialectic of ener-
gizing change. An objective moral order supervenes the action in Dante,
whereas in Rossetti the action supplies its own rationale. It pivots on
what Rossetti called an "inner standing point."[5]

Rossetti appropriates from Dante one other aesthetic procedure of
great importance: both men develop a programmatic attitude toward
poetic revision. In his note to section 25 Rossetti comments on the fact
that the *Vita Nuova* and its embedded poems were not written at the
same time. Rossetti is well aware that the poems were often written — as
the lady of section 18 says to Dante — "con altro intendimento." The first
sonnet in the *Vita Nuova,* for example, is an early composition that gains
its relation to Beatrice only from its inclusion in Dante's programmatic
autobiography. The most famous of Dante's revisionary moves — his interpretation of the *Vita Nuova*'s donna della finestra episode (sections
35–38) as a philosophical allegory — produced one of the great interpretive cruxes in Dantean studies: is the donna a woman who for a time drew
Dante's affections away from Beatrice, or is she rather a figural representation of Lady Philosophy, who would have come to Dante's aid in his
grief at Beatrice's death?

Dante's example of constructing the *Vita Nuova* around materials that
originally had an "altro intendimento," and of reconstructing it later
through radical interpretive revision, had a major impact on the way
Rossetti imagined his own work. The 1870 *Poems,* and "The House of
Life" in particular, use poetic materials that were originally written in
completely different contexts. Signal texts of this kind are the three sonnets "The Landmark," "A Dark Day," and "Autumn Idleness," which were
all written in the early 1850s. When Rossetti decides in 1869–1870 to include such poems in "The House of Life," he forces them to take on
meanings that he could not have consciously intended when he wrote
them many years before. These poetic reimaginings develop an important aesthetic argument: that work written in one context and with certain intentions may contain secret and unrealized meanings that only
emerge over time and through the coming of unimagined events. (Rossetti's thought here has much in common with Surrealist ideas, and especially with the arguments Breton makes in *Les vases communicants.*[6])

If Rossetti follows Dante's lead in thus developing a prophetic view
of imaginative work (both pictorial and verbal, in Rossetti's case), he is

also introducing a fundamental reinterpretation of Dante's aesthetic position as Dante himself represented it in the *Convivio*. There Dante gives his famous interpretation of the *Vita Nuova*'s donna della finestra as Lady Philosophy. He does this through a close reading of his canzone "Voi che 'ntendendo il terzo ciel movete" (*Convivio* 2.2, 12). In a note to his translation of the donna della finestra episode Rossetti argues for "the existence always of the actual events even where the allegorical superstructure has been raised by Dante himself." Like Dante, Rossetti identifies the donna della finestra with Lady Philosophy; unlike Dante, he insists on preserving her as a real woman as well.

The consequence of such a view can be seen in "The House of Life" when Rossetti recapitulates the *Vita Nuova*'s donna della finestra episode in an equivalent sequence. The pivotal text for this act of reconstruction is the sonnet "Life-in-Love," where "we meet for the first time *unmistakeably* in the sequence the New Beloved," as Paull Baum, one of Rossetti's most acute interpreters, has noted.[7] This figure in Rossetti's programmatic autobiography is clearly modeled on Dante's donna della finestra, whose presence in the *Vita Nuova* so strongly affects Dante that his love for Beatrice suffers an eclipse. So the New Beloved enters "The House of Life" to force a complex reimagination of the nature of Love.

Dante's *Convivio* explanation of the episode, which identifies Love with Philosophy, implicitly argues for a nonerotic understanding of Love. Rossetti's thought moves along an exact contrary. Insisting on the "real presence" of the donna della finestra (and of the women invested in his own "Life-in-Love" sonnet), Rossetti is arguing that the identity of Love and Philosophy is grounded in Eros, that is, in incarnate and reciprocal desire. The abstract title of the sonnet — and of so many of the sonnets in "The House of Life" — locates the conceptual orientation of Rossetti's argument. *Idea* functions in his work as figural form, as image, and is assigned no independent conceptual privileges. For Rossetti, Philosophy can be identified with Love only if it functions in a dynamic rather than in a conceptual field, only if it "vivifies," as "Life-in-Love" puts the matter. Explanation comes as apparition, as revelation. The logic of such a view plays itself out in "The House of Life," where understanding is pursued through a series of intense moments, not all of them by any means moments of pleasure or satisfaction. One possesses a "philosophic mind" not as a cherished or anticipated goal but as an immediate determination to imagine what one doesn't know.

"To imagine what one doesn't know": I borrow this phrase from the contemporary poet and critic Lisa Samuels.[8] Consciously revising Shelley's prophetic injunction in the "Defence of Poetry" to "imagine what we know," Samuels asks us to reconsider, as it were, the intelligence quotient of the imagination. Her thinking connects most immediately with works like William Carlos Williams's *The Embodiment of Knowledge*.

I appropriate Samuels's idea in this context because it recalls Rossetti's effort to appropriate Dante and the world of medieval Catholic sensibilities. Rossetti's translations are attempts to imagine something unknowable. If Rossetti could see and otherwise appreciate the splendors of that world — cultural, ideological, aesthetic — the world nonetheless stood beyond his ken, lost for ever. Intellectual and academic attempts to recover it through historicist researches and redactions only emphasized the separating gulf. The *selva oscura* of Rossetti's scholarly father is the point of departure for all his work. And translation becomes the sign under which Rossetti will seek, first, to expose the truth of this gulf, and, second, to cross its void.

The special Rossettian value of translation centers in a key paradox. Rossetti founded his work, and especially his verbal work, on an art of radical imitation. Within a romantic tradition, which is certainly Rossetti's, high values are placed on originality, and the arts of imitation go at a discount. Rossetti's romanticism, however, begins in imitation. A further range of this paradox emerges when we think back to Rossetti through the best single work ever written about his verse: Pater's summatory essay of 1880. Pater saw Rossetti as the most innovative writer of the period, the inventor of a style that would indeed have an overbearing influence on the next generation. Rossetti developed his stylistic resources through his exercises in translation. Nor did he set himself to produce relatively "free" translations in a technical point of view. His goal was not equivalence, it was imitation ("fidelity"). This procedure led him to develop an art of pastiche and ritual form, and to explore the possibility that imaginative work possesses wondrous and terrifying powers of transrational understanding.

The success of these imitations has been measured in several ways. We know how much they were admired in Rossetti's day and beyond, and we know how deeply they impinged on the work of later Modernists like Yeats, Pound, and Eliot. The last of these took Rossetti's translations as a point of departure, a useful antithesis, whereas Yeats and Pound turned to the translations as to useful guides and models. Rossetti himself emerged as a fully developed original writer in the late 1840s largely because of this rigorous and even scholarly linguistic undertaking. The remarkable finish of a work like "The Blessed Damozel" is no happy accident or mere sign of original genius. Then too, certain of these translations are so excellent as poetry in their own right — like Swinburne's translations of Villon — that they force us to engage them as we engage original works.

Beyond all those matters, however, the translations point to something else that may be even more important. They seem an act of extreme linguistic devotion, as resolute as a cultic or ritual performance. We can easily miss this quality of the poems because we usually read works of translation in terms of their scholarly and pedagogical functions. But all of Rossetti's work, not least of all the early work, seems permeated by magical ideas about art and language. At the time he was doing his translations, for example, he also produced the following text. (It has never been printed, and its date is uncertain: early, but probably no earlier than the late 1840s.)

Piangendo star con l'anima smarrita,
Fra se dicendo: già sarà in ciel gita
Beata cosa ch' uom chiamava il nome,
Lasso me, e quando e come
Veder io vi potro visibilmente
Sì che ancora presente
Far io vi possa. Ti conforto vita!
Dunque mi udite ch' io parlo a posta
D'amor, e ai sospir ponendo sosta.

E inver lei parla d'ogni sua virtute.

E, tutta santa omai vostra, innamora
Contemplando nel ciel dov' è locata
Il vostro cor, per cui istà diviso
Che pinto tiene in sì beato viso.[9]

Clumsy as it is — so unlike Rossetti's elegant translations of the same period — the sonnet is a kind of reverse translation made from his involvement with Dante's *Vita Nuova*. Its consciously antiqued style mimics a late-thirteenth- or early-fourteenth-century irregular sonnet that might have been written by one of Dante's circle. The choice of couplet rhymes is notable, being common only to low forms of stilnovista verse, like street songs. Indeed, the broken surface of the text and its obscure linguistic usages may well be studied effects, authenticating signs meant to suggest that this is no invention of Rossetti's but a kind of "found poem" from the fourteenth or fifteenth century.[10]

The texts standing directly behind this act of imitation are clearly from the *Vita Nuova:* the canzoni "Donne ch' avete intelletto d'amore" and especially "Li occhi dolenti per pietà del core," as well as the sonnets associated with those canzoni. Rossetti's imitation all but quotes from the canzone "Li occhi dolenti," which Dante wrote shortly after the death of Beatrice in 1290. The echo is telling not only for this imitation but for Rossetti's work in general, both pictorial and verbal. Dante's poem represents Beatrice as a figure of such inspiring beauty that the heavens themselves desire her presence. At once lost and emparadised in death, Beatrice becomes for Dante the guiding focus of his imaginative and spiritual life.

To pastiche that textual scene from Dante amounts to a magical act, as if Rossetti might call back the dead and become invested with — even possessed by — the soul of Dante. The move is born of an imaginative reaction against the apparent fate of time and history, which throws up, we believe, an uncrossable gulf between disparate cultural scenes like thirteenth-century Italy and nineteenth-century England. Rossetti worked against that secular belief. That his project was impossible is obvious, but that it was a liberating artistic attitude is no less clear. The weight of the Victorian social world and of the empire that sustained it was a powerful, crushing reality. Every English poet of the period either fled it or found some way to evade it (or, like Arnold, abandoned imaginative aspirations altogether). When Rossetti changed his birth name from Gabriel Charles Dante Rossetti to Dante Gabriel Rossetti in 1850, the event was more imperative than symbolic. In changing his name, Rossetti performed a cultic rite, a secular baptism.

Pastiche is the generic sign that dominates Rossetti's early work. Nor

is it a sign of apprenticeship or juvenilia. The latter clearly mark the poems of his early and mid-teens — poems like "Roderick and Rosalba."[11]
By 1845, when he began the project that became *The Early Italian Poets,*
he was brinked at imaginative maturity. This maturity centered in the
translations and all that they entailed. "The Blessed Damozel" is their
most famous outcome, but a poem like "Piangendo star con l'anima
smarrita" is another; and the two have everything in common except
their language. The antique mannerisms of the Italian sonnet are
matched in the more ambitious stanzas of Rossetti's English poem,
which scatters itself with lexical and grammatical archaisms of every
kind. To Pater it seemed "as naively detailed as the pictures of those early
painters contemporary with Dante" — the painters that Rossetti so much
admired. At times it reads like an old translation that Rossetti has discovered, an English text with its own manifest antiquities.

> Circlewise sit they, with bound locks
>   And foreheads garlanded;
> Into the fine cloth white like flame
>   Weaving the golden thread,
> To fashion the birth-robes for them
> Who are just born, being dead.

Like "Piangendo star," "The Blessed Damozel" is a poem with its face set
against the age and culture of the Crystal Palace. It is one of a series of
early works that define a signal characteristic of Rossetti's entire career.
These are the works consciously attempting to resuscitate a gone world.
"Ave," "Madonna Consolata," the two sonnets accompanying his first oil
painting *The Girlhood of Mary Virgin:* all are performative works with
ambitious spiritual aims. The same is true of "Hand and Soul," whose
pastiche style is rarely remarked but crucially important.

   Rossetti undertakes a stylistic regimen on an analogy with the practice of a religious life. A strict observance of the disciplinary forms is
imagined as the means to gain the originary life of the forms. For Rossetti, then, art is a ritual and performative act. Scrupulously practiced in
imitation of models disconnected from worldly objects, the work is to
become what it imitates and beholds. Ultimately this means the ac-
quirement of a kind of transcendental art — an art that will be seen to

have been dictated from Eternity, as Blake, one of Rossetti's masters, saw the matter.[12]

Rossetti's success in this audacious venture came quickly and early, as we know. The results would throw him into contact with beautiful and ecstatic orders of reality, Beatricean orders, as he had hoped. But the realm of the uncanny harbors much that is frightening and terrible, and these too Rossetti came to know. Perhaps most terrifying of all, he had to endure the full brunt of what it might mean to have his art dictated from Eternity.

It began as a literary game in 1848, a kind of automatic writing. To test and stimulate their verse skills, Rossetti and his brother would set a rhyme scheme for each other. The object was to fashion a sonnet to that scheme as quickly as possible. The sonnets were produced in five to ten minutes each.[13]

Fourteen of Dante Gabriel's sonnets survive, though he published none of them. That fact is unsurprising, for they were all stylistic exercises. But if he never published any of these writings, he did set two of them apart in a special way. These two sonnets were included in the book of manuscript poems that Rossetti interred in February 1862 with the body of his wife, Elizabeth. This was the volume, already titled *Dante at Verona and Other Poems,* that Rossetti was planning to issue as a companion volume to his book of translations *The Early Italian Poets.* The collection of original work was announced for publication in an advertising page included in the volume of translations published right at the end of 1861.

But *Dante at Verona and Other Poems* was never published. Rossetti placed his manuscript copy of the book in his wife's coffin — a hieratic gift of the most important original poetical work he had done, most of it unpublished. Rossetti had no copies of the works. The book was meant as a love-sacrifice — some would say a guilt-sacrifice — of his most valued imaginative possessions.

And there the book remained for more than seven years, until Rossetti began to think that he ought to publish some of that poetry after all. But as he gathered together the work of his poetical years 1847–1869, he found that several of his most important works were missing: in particular, "Dante at Verona," "A Last Confession," "Jenny," "The Sea-Limits," and "St. Luke the Painter." All these works lay in Elizabeth's coffin in the manuscript book. Suddenly he regretted his ghastly romantic sacrifice of 1862. Driven by a new remorse, Rossetti had the body exhumed in October 1869 by some friends, who returned the manuscript book to him. He copied out the poems he wanted, revised them, and published them with his other work a few months later.

But not all the works in the manuscript book were published in the 1870 volume. In particular, the two early sonnets were held back. Yet we know that they were part of the exhumed manuscript book because they come down to us on two surviving leaves from that remarkable volume. William Michael Rossetti published both many years after his brother's death, one in 1898, the second in 1911, under titles that he supplied.[14]

Another Love

Of her I thought who now is gone so far:
    And, the thought passing over, to fall thence
    Was like a fall from spirit into sense
Or from the heaven of heavens to sun and star.
None other than Love's self ordained the bar
    'Twixt her and me; so that if, going hence,
    I met her, it could only seem a dense
Film of the brain, — just nought, as phantoms are.

Now when I passed your threshold and came in,
    And glanced where you were sitting, and did see
      Your tresses in these braids and your hands thus, —
I knew that other figure, grieved and thin,
    That seemed there, yea that was there, could not be,
    Though like God's wrath it stood dividing us.

Praise and Prayer

Doubt spake no word in me as there I kneeled.
    Loathing, I could not praise: I could not thank
    God for the cup of evil that I drank:
I dared not cry upon His strength to shield
My soul from weapons it was bent to wield
    Itself against itself. And so I sank
    Into the furnished phrases smooth and blank
Which we all learn in childhood, — and did yield

A barren prayer for life. My voice might mix
With hers, but mingled not. Hers was a full
Grand burst of music, which the crownéd Seven
Must have leaned sideways from their seats to fix
In their calm minds. The seraph-songs fell dull
Doubtless, when heard again, throughout all heaven.

Why didn't Rossetti publish these poems in his 1870 volume? The answer, I think, becomes clear if we make a simple experiment of historical imagination. Think about Rossetti reading these texts in 1862, when he set about copying poems he wanted to include in the manuscript book for his dead wife. The simple verse exercises of 1848 would have become very different poems in February 1862. In that month a sudden death turned these poetical exercises of 1848 uncanny. They became prophetic poems about his wife, whom he had not even met in 1848.

All this brings us back to Dante, who illuminates the most important part of this interesting and untold story. For Rossetti, the *Vita Nuova* was a narrative that exposed the action of spiritual prevenience in works of imagination. Poems have meanings that are "Dictated from Eternity," beyond the knowledge or control of the artist. Dante's spiritual autobiography was for Rossetti a demonstration and proof of that fact about art. In his painting and his writing alike, Rossetti regularly reworked earlier materials in order to reveal their concealed, premonitory significances. In no case, however, is this Dantean inheritance more clear than it is in these sonnets, perhaps especially in "Praise and Prayer." The sestet of the latter distinctly recalls the two major canzoni of *La Vita Nuova,* the "Donne ch'avete intelletto d'amore" and "Donna pietosa e di novelle etate," as well as Rossetti's other Dante-inspired works of 1847–1848, particularly "The Blessed Damozel" and "Piangendo star con l'anima smarrita."

So the answer to our question about why Rossetti held the two sonnets back has to do with their uncanny transformation. With Elizabeth's death in 1862 the poems had become possessed. As such they came to embody one of Rossetti's most cherished convictions: that works of art involve transrational powers of awareness. But Rossetti couldn't bring himself to enlist these works as part of his book's argument for that idea because their evidentiary status was too personal. Though originally the sonnets were in fact among the least personal of his writings, in 1869 they had become intensely, bizarrely personal. How could Rossetti signal for his readers the magical character of these works? He couldn't and he didn't. Nevertheless, he also couldn't bring himself to destroy such precious evidence of the truth of imagination. Of all the original leaves from the inhumed manuscript volume, only these two were saved.

4
THE ICONIC PAGE

There must be, somewhere, primordial figures whose bodies
are nothing but their image. If one could see them one would
discover the link between matter and thought.
Gustave Flaubert, *The Temptation of St. Antony*

Recent literary and cultural studies exhibit a keen interest in the material features of text. Most of this work, however, engages those highly
particular objects — books — at secondary levels. The meanings pursued
are structural and systematic: general insights into various social, political, and cultural patterns and characteristic forms. Rarely do we find a
close study of the poiesis of the specific material artifact, or an effort to
design a general materialist poetics. When readers interpret for local and
immediate meaning, they still find it difficult to get outside the messages
they can decode from the semantic elements of a text. Typefaces, para-
texts, endpapers: these and other bibliographical features of texts still remain largely invisible presences for most interpreters.[1]

In such a situation Rossetti proves a crucial figure, for two reasons.
First, he was preoccupied with the materiality of text and graphic design.
Second, as we have seen, his whole approach to aesthetic practice was
programmatic and self-conscious. These interests drove Rossetti to pursue expression simultaneously in different media, and ultimately to think
at the level of vehicular form.

To appreciate Rossetti's textual ideas and innovations we may usefully
recall the general shape of his early career as an artist. His turn to the Middle Ages and early Renaissance was crucial and centered in three areas:
the study of Italian primitive art, the study of illuminated manuscripts
and printed books, and the study of stained glass. That last subject involved him in rethinking procedures for composition by color fields,
while the other two produced his early intensive studies of line and
plane. It was this work that led Rossetti to reject the authority of sys-

tematic perspective. The studies of line and plane took place between 1848 and approximately 1862, the period when Rossetti also developed a new watercolor technique that permitted a more aggressive treatment of the pictorial surface.[2] At that point he began to move away from Ruskin's influence, he met Whistler, he discovered the remarkable procedures of Japanese art, and he turned to the Venetians to explore the conceptual resources of color.[3]

This set of interests focuses a comprehensive and adventurous imaginative project. Whistler, for example, is famous for the integral design of his paintings, with picture and frame conceived as equally important to the total impression. An extraordinary self-promoter, Whistler said he originated the practice of a totalized approach to the work of art. It is true that he extended this idea of the total work to include interior design and (potentially) the whole architectural space, but it is not true, as he declared, that he invented the idea of completely integrating picture and frame. He learned this after he left Paris and began to live in London in the early 1860s. At that point he saw the work that Madox Brown and especially Rossetti had been doing along these lines since about 1850. In these matters Whistler was Rossetti's student throughout the 1860s, when they were much together and when Rossetti's pictorial experimentation was most active.[4]

Rossetti spent years exploring the expressive potential of the picture frame, and his efforts influenced many besides Whistler. All of his experiments share certain common features. Planarity and gold leaf are striking characteristics. The gold flats of the frames, Byzantine-influenced, undermine spatial recession and extend the pictorial surface, forcing the eye to submit to Rossetti's characteristically shallow spaces and strong planar designs. Equally striking, however, particularly in the present context, are the decorative elements Rossetti invented for his frames. There are two principal kinds: on one hand symbolical devices, typically roundels or emblematic designs placed in formal arrangements on the gold flats; on the other, different kinds of textual materials that relate to the picture in a variety of ways. In each case the frame decorations elucidate and extend conceptual elements of the painting proper. All erode the viewer's inclination to organize perception in illusionistic terms.[5]

Rossetti's frames are thus designed to integrate with his pictures in two respects, pictorially and conceptually. They are in this way doubly

integrated, replicating the dialectical structure of Rossetti's paintings
and drawings themselves. Rossetti's paintings are most interesting because they pursue at once a pair of goals that seem at odds with each
other. In purely painterly terms, his pictures attack or abandon illusionistic space, and they experiment with composition by plane and color
fields. These proto-Modernist moves are grounded in Rossetti's study of
primitive European art and, later, through Whistler, of Japanese art.[6]
But at the same time Rossetti remained committed to the conceptual
powers of pictorial representation: to more narratively based painting
in his early Pre-Raphaelite work, and to more symbolical expression in
his later pictures. It was this second commitment that got Rossetti's
work expelled from school by so many advocates of Modernist Art.

Rossetti's programmatic approach to his specifically artistic work
reappears in his writings as well. In each case he is committed to integrating both iconic and verbal goals. In a genre like painting iconic im-
peratives control the intellectual action. In books the situation is re-
versed. Books are dominantly verbal works, often (even) dominantly
linguistic; but as we know from the history of inscribed materials, they
bear within themselves iconographic powers that can be released and developed. Certain artists — Blake, Klee, Kandinsky, in our own day Johanna Drucker — work on one or the other side of the word/picture divide to exploit the expressive potential of the two media. Rossetti is
emphatically an artist of their sort. His graphics imagination was so original, in fact, that he became a major figure in the modern history of book
design — though his works in the field are not very many.[7] His graphical
inventions were largely confined to the period of the 1860s. As in the case
of his work with picture frames, his efforts were both experimental and
carefully directed. That is to say, very personal goals drove his actions: in
the one case, to develop a totally integrated pictorial field for his visioned
works; in the other, to do the same for his writings. During the 1860s
Rossetti experimented with his ideas about book design largely by car-
rying out design commissions for relatives and friends. All of this work
would culminate, for Rossetti at any rate, in the publication of his own
volume, the famous 1870 *Poems,* which he wrote and designed cover to
cover.[8]

After Rossetti's wife, Elizabeth, committed suicide in 1862, the poet
abandoned his plan to publish *Poems* as a companion to *The Early Ital-*

ian Poets—abandoned, in fact, if only temporarily, the poems themselves, in Elizabeth's coffin. Rossetti's discussion of his publication plans at the time shows very clearly how the books were intended to complement one another.[9] The Dante-centered book of early Italian translations was to rhyme with the collection of original poems, whose announced title underscored the close relation of the two works: *Dante at Verona and Other Poems*. This complementarity would have extended to the design of the volumes, as is quite apparent from the close similarity between the cover design of *The Early Italian Poets* and the designs for his sister's two early books, *Goblin Market and Other Poems* (1862, 1865) and *The Prince's Progress and Other Poems* (1866). It is clear that when Rossetti decided to withdraw his volume of original poetry from publication, he transferred the book design he had worked up for himself to his sister's 1862 volume, her inaugural poetic appearance.

Rossetti's interest in book design was a long-standing one. His illustrations of Poe and other favorite authors began in the 1840s, and in the 1850s he undertook a serious study of the design—graphic, calligraphic, and typographic—of early books and manuscripts. The fruit of these studies appears initially in his watercolors of the period, but his bibliographical passions were never out of sight, as his stunning book illustrations of the period show. We also want to remember that Rossetti kept trying to find a publisher for his book of translations throughout the 1850s and that this project always loomed in his mind as an illustrated volume. Even in 1861, when he finally secured a publisher, he was pressing for a book that would include a series of his accompanying illustrations. The publisher in the end refused the idea because of the expense involved, but we have the evidence of Rossetti's unabated desire to see such a book in the unique copy of the first edition in the Troxell Collection at Princeton, which carries a set of Rossetti's decorative illuminations for several of the translations.

The book designs that Rossetti worked out for his and his sister's books in the 1860s represent his initial thoughts—which is to say his artisanal ideas—about integrating the written word with the decorative possibilities inherent in the book as a physical object, and exclusive of illustration. *The Early Italian Poets* and the two editions of *Goblin Market and Other Poems* illustrate a common and coherent set of design strategies—a chaste use of narrow gold bands and small gold circles stamped on a coarse grained cloth (black in one case, blue in the other). The simple geometric forms carry an allusion to the small handmade fifteenth-century books that influenced the later binding designs of prayer books and hymnals.

Alastair Grieve (Grieve5) has written well about the novel integrity of Rossetti's binding designs, which pull the covers of the book into a close relation with the spine. Had Rossetti published his two projected volumes in 1862, he would have issued a clear public statement about his aesthetic purposes: an integration of translation and original writing; a convergence of verbal text and visual design; a dialogue between dislocated cultural materials, between the world of Dante and his circle and the world of Rossetti and his contemporaries. Appearing alone, the handsome and important 1862 volume of translations lost half its point. But Rossetti continued to experiment with book design for the next several years, and one can see a clear development through each of his next three designs: for his brother's translation of The Inferno (The Comedy of Dante Alighieri: Part I, The Hell [1865]); for his friend Swinburne's Atalanta in Calydon (1865); and for Christina's new volume The Prince's Progress and Other Poems (1866). In each case the design becomes at once more elaborate and more complexly integrated. This set of decorative inventions was also creating a kind of second-order sociocultural sign — what Peirce would call an indexical sign — identifying Rossetti and his artistic circle, and integrating their work.

By the time Rossetti came to plan the publication of a book of his original writing, in 1869–1870, much had changed in his personal and artistic life. The 1870 Poems does not encourage the intimate dialogue with The Early Italian Poets that Rossetti had in mind in 1862.[10] Nonetheless, if much was taken, much remained, and the great 1870 volume is both a record and an incarnation of Rossetti's life and artistic pursuits.

First, the ideas driving Rossetti's plans in 1862 remain in 1870. These plans are now to be executed in a single volume, and some emphases shift, but the basic program remains the same. Most important for my immediate purposes is the continued stress Rossetti places on the idea of the total book, and (correlatively) on the relation between iconic and verbal expression. As far as book design goes, the basic approach is the same: to use inexpensive and commercially available materials, and to construct a book that marries formal simplicity and elegance with a rich texture. Rossetti's book designs of the early 1860s are simple, even to a certain extent severe. By 1870, however, he has evolved ways to enrich the decorative design without sacrificing simplicity of form. The work that signals the turn of Rossetti's new ideas is the exquisite design he makes for Swinburne's *Atalanta in Calydon* in 1865. The line is direct from that book to the design he invented for Swinburne's 1871 *Songs Before Sunrise* and for his own 1870 *Poems*. The design of these two books is similar, though Swinburne's is a more ornate volume. These decorative differences, it seems to me, index the differences between the two poets' styles. They stand as a method of commenting on those differences — indeed, as a method of interpreting and "reading" the differences.

An important issue is at stake in all these materials and events: the extent to which the decorative features of a text can be made to function in conceptual ways. The entire program of the Arts and Crafts Movement, and of the Renaissance in Printing particularly, is grounded in the conviction that ornamental and nonlinguistic forms, including the decorative forms of book design and typography, might embody ideas and conceptual content. The efforts of William Morris, inspired by Rossetti (as he often acknowledged), were to focus mainly on typography and page design. Rossetti concentrated on general book design and decoration.

So we see that as a maker of pictures and as a maker of poems Rossetti, like Wagner, was pursuing an imagination of a total work of art. This synthetic approach realized itself most dramatically in his famous "double works of art," those remarkable marriages of picture and poem that he elaborated all his life, from his first oil painting, *The Girlhood of Mary Virgin* (1849), to his last, *Mnemosyne* (1881). Rossetti often attaches text to his pictures, usually on the frame but sometimes within the picture itself. His inspiration comes from medieval and early Renaissance paintings, which incorporate various texts (usually biblical or religious texts) into the pictorial field. Unlike his master Blake, however, Rossetti pursues a dialectical rather than an organic approach to his doubled works. With the possible exception of the illuminated text for the "Sonnet on the Sonnet," in every case Rossetti is careful to preserve the distinct integrities of picture and text. So in his "Sonnets for Pictures," for instance, we always have to deal with three aesthetic events: the picture itself, the sonnet itself, and the liminal event that emerges from their dialectical relation. The liminal event issues a programmatic call for a heightened response: to the conceptual aspects of the picture and to the iconographical features of the text.

Rossetti's dialectical approach to the relation of image and text defines an aesthetic imagination that replicates itself in each of those artistic venues. To Rossetti's view both "image" (an artist's pictures) and "text" (a poet's works) are equally riven by competing expressive urgencies that can be broadly classified as iconic and linguistic. The distinction explored during the past several years between a text's bibliographical and its linguistic codes represents this double and competing expressive urgency in a text.[11] And the relation that Rossetti promotes in his "double works of art" — to develop the conceptual aspects of the image and the iconographical powers of the text — is also pursued independently in his pictures and in his poems.

Rossetti's texts, then, are always iconic texts, in several senses. One sense comes from the fact that virtually all involve pictorial elements of a more or less explicit kind. In these cases the texts mirror the pictures, which are all in the end "literary" works. The texts are also iconic because Rossetti paid the closest attention to the graphic design of his texted works. Rossetti's poems are to be seen as well as read and heard.

All that being the case, an important question forces itself to attention: how are Rossetti's linguistic codes affected by these powerful graphical and bibliographical urgencies in his textual work? What kind of text do we face when the decorative and apparitional forms of book design and typography are driven to embody ideas and conceptual content?

Although we have yet to frame comprehensive answers to those kinds of questions, many features of Rossetti's works help to explain or illuminate the issues they raise. Let me give two instances. The first centers in a pervasive quality of his writings: that specific works have multiple textual states. "The House of Life," a famous case, has two publicly authorized versions, one issued in 1870, the other in 1881. It also has a number of other versions that were more privately determined, as well as an important "super" version, as it were, that we might reconstruct posthumously from all the versions that Rossetti imagined in his lifetime.[12] One of the privately authorized versions is especially interesting in the present context: the sonnet sequence of twenty-five poems that Rossetti wrote and arranged in a notebook. These particular texts, which were composed at various times in the early 1870s — most of them in 1871 — focus on Jane Morris and Rossetti's love for her. The sequence has been aptly named "The Kelmscott Love Sonnets" because these sonnets celebrate events that took place when the two were together at various times at Kelmscott Manor.[13]

To appreciate the character of "The Kelmscott Love Sonnets" we have to remember that they were not copied into the notebook at the time of their composition. After Rossetti published his 1870 volume of *Poems,* which contained the first published version of "The House of Life" in fifty sonnets and eleven songs, he continued to write sonnets "for 'The House of Life,'" which is the rubric we find on many loose manuscripts of his post-1870 sonnets, including most of those that he eventually organized as the twenty-five-sonnet sequence for Jane Morris.[14] Not all of these loose manuscript poems found their way into the sonnet sequence, and of course none in the sequence carried the rubric "for 'The House of Life'" in their notebook versions. The notebook sonnets are not "for" that transformational work at all, they are "for" Jane Morris.

Inscription rather than composition is the defining feature of the sonnet sequence for Jane Morris. Rossetti fair-copied the sonnets as a deliberately chosen sequence constructed from a larger body of sonnet materials that might have brought different choices of more or fewer sonnets. Indeed, it is clear that the sequence originally had twenty-seven sonnets and not twenty-five, for two leaves have been carefully cut away from the notebook within the sonnet sequence. Choosing and copying the poems in the notebook were acts of poetic gift-making. In point of historical fact, he probably copied the sonnets and gave her the gift of the notebook in the summer of 1874, when he was leaving Kelmscott for what turned out the last time. Perhaps both of them understood that it would be the last time.

The expressive character of these sonnets is clarified when we imagine them in an editorial horizon. Editors typically assemble their documentary materials with the purpose of constructing a stemma of their compositional descent. Each documentary state is a record of some moment in the evolving history of a work's composition and revision. "The Kelmscott Love Sonnets" can and should be imagined in such terms — both the sequence as a whole and the individual sonnets in particular. Nevertheless, that editorial perspective promotes a certain distortion insofar as it asks us to think of the document as part of a calculus of textual variants. We want to remember that "The Kelmscott Love Sonnets" was made as a love-gift — much as the Morgan Library manuscript of "The Blessed Damozel" was made as a gift of friendship for the Brownings, and as Morris made *A Book of Verse* as a gift for Georgiana Burne-Jones. Each of these works possesses an iconic status much like a Blake illuminated work.

These works recall many of Emily Dickinson's poems. She had a habit of recycling her texts in letters written to different correspondents. Different texts of "the same poem" might well vary from each other, but these variances clearly have less to do with an evolving progress toward some "final" textual intention than with a set of different but quasi-absolute intentions. "The same" poem is being sent to different people at different times for different purposes. In this sense, it "means" something very different each time it is sent. One thinks as well, perhaps, of the troubadour and stilnovista traditions which treat poems as if they were independent agents: "Go, little book," "Go, my ballad." In such an imagination a text is being manipulated in an iconic rather than in a linguistic perspective.

What we see in the example of such "purely textual" materials, then, is Rossetti's typical inclination to handle his linguistic works as if they were kinds of objects. A manuscript in the Fitzwilliam Library is exemplary here, but to grasp its full significance requires a somewhat complex unraveling of the relevant documentary information. Titled "Three Songs" by Rossetti, the Fitzwilliam manuscript is a fair copy consisting of three separately numbered and named "songs": "Belcolore"; "Bellebuona"; and "Bocca Baciata." Rossetti scholarship carries no record of any of these (four) titles, though every student of Rossetti will connect the last of the songs with Rossetti's great painting of the same title; and a few will remember that the titles of the first two songs are alternative titles for the well-known paintings *Monna Vanna* and *Il Ramoscello*.

Reading the manuscript text, one sees that if a composite work called "Three Songs" is unknown, each separate text is quite recognizable — but in each case under a different title. Rossetti published all three poems separately, as "A New Year's Burden," "Plighted Promise," and "The Song of the Bower." The poems were written in 1859, 1865, and 1860, respectively, and all three were first published in Rossetti's 1870 *Poems*. In that book the first and the third were grouped among the "Songs" in the section headed "Sonnets and Songs, Towards a Work to be Called 'The House of Life,'" while the second was included in the separate opening section headed "Poems."

What is the point of knowing all this? To see not so much the fluidity of these texts as their malleability. Rossetti's renamings are in effect remakings, and they map a constellation of at least ten different but related works. Three have been imagined by Rossetti as "double works" (the songs as they are connected to the three paintings) while the others are variously reconfigured in terms of different times and different circumstances. The composite work "Three Songs," for instance, was made at a moment (spring/summer 1869) when Rossetti had the model of Petrarch's *Sonnets and Songs* very much in his mind as he was developing his idea for "The House of Life."[15] Rossetti can entertain these kinds of alternative textual embodiments, or reframings, precisely because he is alive to the "objecthood" of his linguistic works, as if they occupied space and could be as readily moved about as moved through. The meanings of Rossetti's works change because he quite literally sees them differently; and he sees them differently because he *can see* his texts as visible things: elementally, as constructions of letters, scripts, typefaces.

My second example goes to a somewhat more particular event in Rossetti's work — the endpapers that he used for his three books of original poetry and that he first designed for his 1870 volume of *Poems*. These endpapers illustrate the depth to which Rossetti carried out his discursive intentions toward the decorative elements of his books. Furthermore, they expose the often recondite character of Rossetti's forms of expression — a fact of his general style, both as artist and as writer, that can't be forgotten if we want to appreciate his work.

Scholars have described and praised these endpapers, noting how well they fit into the total design structure of the book. What has gone unrecorded is the following remarkable fact: the blue floral pattern is a coded act of memorial homage to Rossetti's father, the celebrated Dante scholar who elsewhere figures in important discursive ways in Rossetti's book.[16] The homage is made as a private gesture, unrecognizable by anyone outside the immediate family. We know about this textual event only because Rossetti's brother William registered his awareness in a manuscript note buried away in a set of proofs that he once owned of the 1870 volume: "The flowered paper used in the binding appears to have been brought by my father in 1824 from Malta — perhaps from Naples."[17] That is to say, the endpapers recollect perhaps the most important event in Rossetti's father's life: his forced (and ultimately permanent) exile from Italy to England. For Dante Gabriel, the event served to emblemize the bifurcation of his national identity.

In our day the poet Alan Davies has written some important pages on what he calls the "private enigma in the opened text."[18] Davies thinks that all poetry inclines to produce such moments, much as all poetry can never entirely lose its connection to riddle and nonsense. However that may be, rarely has his thought been so splendidly illustrated as it is in these endpapers, so open to our view as we open Rossetti's book, yet so covetous of expressive privacy. Furthermore, the endpapers function as a veritable index of the book they enclose, which everywhere constructs itself as a compendium of Rossetti's life and works, but at the same time seems to wrap itself in an oblique discourse, as if more were always being said than we could ever be aware of. The famous autobiographical secrecies of *The House of Life,* which receive a first full expression in this volume, only epitomize the style of the book as a whole. Rossetti deliberately organized his book as a poetical account of his life and career from about 1848 to 1870. It tells the story of his personal quest for what his namesake and master, Dante Alighieri, named "l'amor che move il sole e l'altre stelle" (*Paradiso* 33.145).

Readers who do not appreciate or perhaps even approve the startling erotic turn that Rossetti gives to his Dantean inheritance are apt to underestimate the magnitude and coherence of his aesthetic program. But the truth is that as an artist and poet he did nothing without purpose and deliberation. Indeed, his typical aesthetic failures follow not from a slipshod artistic intelligence but from his embrained, self-conscious procedures. He took Keats's famous dictum, to load every rift with ore, to amazing extremes. His project of a totalized work of art has simply reformulated that idea at the largest possible scale; and the effort to exploit and integrate all the expressive features of the text, iconic as well as discursive, executes the program and its driving ideas. More than most, Rossetti pursued the ideal of an Adamic language announced by Coleridge when he reported his dream of Kubla Khan as a vision in which "all the images rose up before him as *things.*"[19] That dream prophesies the coming of Rossetti's literalist style, which Rossetti himself defined in his famous erotic trope: "Thy soul I know not from thy body." Praising his lady, which is to say his muse, Rossetti also gives us his definition of poetical language.

For all its extreme ideality, this is physicalized language. When Ruskin responded to the pictorial ideals of the new Pre-Raphaelite movement in art, he called it a "materialist" art.[20] In each case the goal is to exploit as far as possible the dichotomies of *res/verba*, form/content, and image/text. Rossetti was especially fitted for such a project because he regularly worked in two liminal regions: he was a pictorial and a verbal artist, and he lived in two languages. His visualist practices impinge on his linguistic work, driving his language to find its depths of significance at the surfaces of its actions. The play of letters, morphemes, and phonemes continually holds our attention and resist that final communicating plunge when words die of some meaning, however ambiguous or complex:

Infinite imminent Eternity

one dead deathless hour[21]

Rossetti regularly builds his poems from linguistic units of this kind, which retard and even immobilize conceptual encounters with the texts. His notebooks are littered with this type of phrasal jottings — single words, lists of words, and words-strings that have an immediate, arresting force. Not just assonance and consonance but a choreography of letter-forms creates a scene of absolute verbal immediacy. Such texts do not forbid conceptual translation — on the contrary, they may well encourage the flight of interpretation. But the extreme surface complexity checks these flights, which turn "bewildered" (a favorite Rossetti word that recalls and reworks a key Dantean word, *smarrire*). A simple *thisness* of particular letters in particular linguistic arrangements appears to discover scenes of pure expression. The meticulous, irrelevant details that emerge with such systematic irregularity in Pre-Raphaelite pictures locate analogous moments of pictorial arrest.

The rhetoric that organizes such writing "lies apparent," as Rossetti said of his lover in "Supreme Surrender." We see it clearly in the "Son-

nets for Pictures" and the numerous other "double works of art" that he
constructed:

> O Lord of all compassionate control,
>   O Love! let this my lady's picture glow
>   Under my hand to praise her name. . . .
>   ("The Portrait")

> Scarcely, I think, yet it indeed *may* be
>   The meaning reached him, when this music rang
>   Clear through his frame, a sweet possessive pang,
> And he beheld these rocks and that ridged sea.
> ("For an Allegorical Dance of Women,
>   By Andrea Mantegna [In the Louvre]")

> Mother, is this the darkness of the end,
>   The Shadow of Death? and is that outer sea
> Infinite imminent Eternity?
>   ("For Our Lady of the Rocks, By Leonardo da Vinci")

> Is it this sky's vast vault or ocean's sound
>   That is Life's self and draws my life from me. . . .
>   ("The Monochord")

In each of these passages the word *this* defines the rhetorical action. The
first three texts come from doubled Rossettian works. They evoke an implicit scene of the poet contemplating some pictorial work that may or
may not be famous and that may be either present to his eyes or simply
to his imagination. The poems thus undertake the idea of "looking at a
picture" as an exponent of an act of language that turns pictorial in the
reading, as we are called to watch and contemplate Rossetti's language.
The pronoun's referent becomes at once the absent pictorial image
named in the title and the textual construction that unfolds as we read.

The doubled set of textual/pictorial references in "The Portrait" have
a special clarity just because the implied picture is not named. Like Fazio
degli Uberti's "Canzone. His Portrait of His Lady, Angiola of Verona,"
which is the sonnet's conscious precursor, Rossetti's poem creates "this
my lady's picture" as the textual work of the sonnet itself.[22] It may also

refer to some unnamed painting or drawing — perhaps the famous *Beata Beatrix;* perhaps the now lost painting, once owned by Rossetti's patron L. R. Valpy, that had lines 4 and 8 of the sonnet inscribed on its frame; perhaps the portrait of Jane Morris "in a blue dress," now hanging at Kelmscott Manor. All three pictures have been associated with the poem.[23] Furthermore, Rossetti leaves us free to take the "hand" in line 3 as either the artist's or the poet's, or both. In either case, the textuality of the portrait is emphasized.

In "For an Allegorical Dance of Women, By Andrea Mantegna (In the Louvre)" and "The Monochord," Rossetti elaborates the verse complexities in some important and typical ways. *This* in the sonnet on the Mantegna painting does not reference a visible feature of the painting but the "music" implied in the pictured scene. A characteristic Rossettian play on the word *frame,* as we have seen, then comes to tilt all the textual relations, suggesting that Mantegna may have glimpsed the "meaning" of his painting not as an intention but as an experience: a nonconceptual aesthetic perception gained when the original musical inspiration rose before his eyes in the visible forms created through his painter's desire. The music rings through the frame of the picture and the frame of his body. That primary transformation defines the transformation enacted in Rossetti's sonnet, where Mantegna's musical images are then retranslated into textual forms. The sonnet unfolds a radically metamorphic scene where the presence of a transcendental order gets materialized:

> Scarcely, I think, yet it indeed *may* be
>   The meaning reached him, when this music rang
>   Clear through his frame, a sweet possessive pang,
> And he beheld these rocks and that ridged sea.
>   And I believe that, leaning tow'rds them, he
>   Just felt their hair carried across his face
>   As each girl passed him. . . .

The word *music* draws an equivalence between an immediate responsive thrill and the spheral harmony intimated in the "Allegorical Dance." But that equivalence depends entirely on the equivocal play of the text's pronouns, which refer to painterly images, poetical texts, and the unheard

melodies that both are involved with. The pronouns open every kind of
border and defining limit to the possibility of dissolution, as we see most
dramatically in the ambiguous referents of *these, that,* and *their.*

The important wordplay on *frame* calls attention to the word *draws,*
which is used twice in "The Monochord" (lines 2 and 12). At signal moments in his writing Rossetti invokes this word to create an even more
potent iconic urgency in his texts, and "The Monochord" locates one
such moment: in the 1870 *Poems* the sonnet appears last in the volume,
culminating the book as a whole and the "Sonnets for Pictures" section
in particular. In the 1881 *Ballads and Sonnets* volume it is moved into "The
House of Life" sequence, where it completes the unit of six sonnets that
constitute a summary statement of Rossetti's artistic ideas.

Beginning with the three sonnets "Old and New Art," the unit moves
to the famous "Soul's Beauty," "Body's Beauty," and finally "The Monochord." In each of these sonnets the word *draw* is worked for its iconic
significance:

> Under the arch of Life, where love and death,
> 　　Terror and mystery, guard her shrine, I saw
> 　　Beauty enthroned; and though her gaze struck awe,
> I drew it in as simply as my breath.
> 　　　　　　　　　　　　　　　　　　　　("Soul's Beauty," 1–4)

The startling wordplay in line 4 creates three basic reciprocities: between
art and life; between art as inspiring ideal and art as artisanal practice; and
finally between textual and pictorial artistic figures. The sonnet goes on
to say that the central focus of all these figures, "Beauty enthroned," is
herself an artist whose eyes appear as an impinging, ideal landscape:

> Hers are the eyes which, over and beneath,
> 　　The sky and sea bend on thee, — which can draw,
> 　　By sea or sky or woman, to one law,
> The allotted bondman of her palm and wreath. (lines 5–8)

Anticipating the argument of "The Monochord," the passage elaborates
a representation of the "one law" governing artistic action. Although
this law here constellates around Rossetti's characteristic Beatricean
figure, the text complicates its representation by constructing a palimp-

sest of two pictorial genres, the portrait and the landscape. This type of complexity is one form of what Rossetti calls, in another famous icono-graphical sonnet, "A Superscription."

Soul's Beauty, Beata Beatrix, the Blessed Damozel: the figure has many names and superscripts. One of these, Sancta Lilias, is relevant here because it reappears in the companion sonnet to "Soul's Beauty" as the textual variant Lilith, another artist who "Draws men to watch the bright web she can weave" ("Body's Beauty," line 8). This demonic figure, so harshly judged by Arnoldian imaginations, enters every aspect of Ros-setti's work, as she does of Swinburne's. In the Rossettian economy she corresponds to what Wordsworth called the Ministry of Fear, just as Lil-ias stands for the Ministry of Hope. According to the argument of "The Monochord," "one law" governs both types of Beauty, and the law so functions because the dialectic of the types is unstable. We don't want to forget that the name Lilias — as in *Sancta Lilias,* an explicit version of *The Blessed Damozel* — is a cognate of the name Lilith.[24]

But this discussion begins to open another subject. Let me close by calling attention to one of the most remarkable stylistic consequences of this iconic handling of linguistic materials. "Drawing" explicit analogies between pictorial and textual forms of expression, Rossetti regularly builds poetic works of such notorious density that a common form of explication has always been simple prose paraphrase.[25] Such criticism reflects a poetical discourse that is resisting demands for conceptual defi-nition. In that resistance the texts begin to engage their other resources: phonemes turn acoustic, morphemes are stripped to their letters. The sestet of the iconic sonnet "A Superscription" is eloquent of this process:

> Mark me, how still I am! But should there dart
>   One moment through thy soul the soft surprise
>   Of that winged Peace which lulls the breath of sighs —
> Then shalt thou see me smile, and turn apart
> Thy visage to mine ambush at thy heart
>   Sleepless with cold commemorative eyes.

This passage can (and should) be translated into a statement-form. Hav-ing done so, however, the reader will not find the text much more con-ceptually transparent when a new process of reading is undertaken; for

the realized body of the text does not readily submit to ideational definition. It is as if *at the experiential level* the signifiers were determined to
give their first allegiance to their bodies rather than their souls; as if their
souls might more surely be found by resisting the sublimities of con-
ceptualization, by an adventure among pure physical forms. Here the adventure is located in the figure of the "eyes," as might be expected in such
an iconographical text. Liberated from the urgency for ordinary meanings, these eyes begin to see through the textual superscripts. But not to
deeper things. Look again at the rhymes: in one case there are only "eyes,"
in the other, only "art." And think again: in each case these are meanings
of the body, surface events. We have to hear such eyes before we can see
them; and we have to see that the "art" of this splendid text, in word and
in deed, should not get lost in the verbal illusions created by other letters
and by the other words those letters make: (d)art, (ap)art, (he)art. We
have to *see* that, we have to *see to it*.

Rossetti's decorative books encourage us to those kinds of seeing —
optical as well as deliberative. The loss of the ability to read in these ways
is a relatively recent and decidedly twentieth-century phenomenon,
when grammarians and philosophers replaced rhetoricians and artists as
language authorities. Before this — let us say between 1820 and 1930 —
artists and writers gradually developed a new and extraordinarily so-
phisticated understanding of the expressive character of physical text.[26]
The dates are somewhat arbitrary, but they signal on one end the emergence in England of the literary gift book, and on the other the crack-up
of American Modernism, and of the Harlem Renaissance in particular.
The great precursor of that nineteenth-century movement was William
Blake, whom Rossetti rediscovered and reinvented for the modern
world. From its Ruskinian and Pre-Raphaelite origins in the 1850s, the
next seventy years of literary work brought an amazing reimagination of
language and media resources. These activities were initiated in practical ways — as poetical and artisanal "makings" rather than as philosophical or theoretical reflections. Saussure and his epigones would come
later seeking their generalizations.

If the twentieth century brought the study of language to the center
of all cultural questions, it often did so in the most abstract and formal
ways. Rossetti and Morris, Wilde and Ricketts, do not consider textual
meanings in terms that have much in common with Saussure and Hjelm-

slev, Chomsky or even Jakobson. Breton's argument with Freud about the unconscious — whether it is creative or memorial — locates an analogous intellectual divide: is desire, or what Blake called "Energy," a subject to be studied and controlled, or a set of unrealized functions and potentials?[27] We have set reflective measures upon all kinds of productive enterprise, but one wants to test the critical power that lies in imaginative practices as such. It will make a great difference, for example, to what extent we organize our modern understandings of textuality in artisanal and productive frame of references — in the field of poiesis — or in theoretical and philosophical considerations — in the field of cultural reflection.

Interpretation would do well to turn to the inventors rather than the philosophers when seeking to learn how to explicate poetical work. There are even principles to be learned.

5

ARS NEGATIVA

> I'm interested in objects that try to play up the schism between
> an idealized notion of the object and the failure of the object
> to attain that.
>
> Mike Kelley, "Talking Failure"

There is no dearth of useful commentary on the founding of the Pre-
Raphaelite movement in 1849–1850. Through it all, however, one small
but interesting fact has gone unremarked. Only Rossetti's two pictures,
The Girlhood of Mary Virgin (1849) and *Ecce Ancilla Domini!* (1850), exhibit literally supernatural elements. Flames support the feet of the angel Gabriel in the latter picture, while both paintings represent theo-
phanies of the Holy Ghost.

This kind of literal treatment of ideal and spiritual presences is typical of Rossetti, as it would later be of Burne-Jones and of symbolist art
in general. No effort is made to mediate transcendental orders through
meaningful symbolic codes, which is what Hunt and Millais do. Not that
Rossetti's two pictures aren't laden with symbolic paraphernalia. They
are. But the treatment of these materials is uniformly literalist, and corresponds to the forward flatness of Rossetti's pictures and to the composition by color fields and overlapping planes. All the elements here—
natural and supernatural, symbolic and representational—occupy the
same pictorial manifold. The technical management of Hunt's and Millais's pictures is quite like Rossetti's, but because they admit supernatural
presence only in symbolic form, their total effect is much different and
far less problematic.

Two important issues are at stake for Rossetti, and they will dominate
all his work. The first involves the problem of the historicality of supernatural phenomena, the second the relation of artistic practice to the in-
vocation of such phenomena. We can begin to appreciate his distinctive
concerns if we compare *The Girlhood of Mary Virgin* with, say, Millais's

Christ in the House of His Parents (1850) or Hunt's *A Converted British Family Sheltering a Christian Priest from the Persecution of the Druids* (1850). The composition of the three pictures is quite similar, as has often been noted, and of course all three exemplify the programmatic claims for art that were being promoted by the early PRB. In Rossetti's picture, however, two distinct levels of historicality are being evoked, whereas in the others there is only one. Rossetti's picture involves a kind of palimpsest, with a coherent set of medieval images being laid over a scene drawn from the life of the family of Jesus. The archaic title, typical of Rossetti, replicates this double perspective, as do the self-conscious sonnets he wrote to accompany the painting. When Hunt at the turn of the century gave his version of the founding of the PRB, he clearly defined this difference. Under the influence and encouragement of Ford Madox Brown, Rossetti cultivated what Hunt derisively called his "Quattrocentro Exotic style." Although Rossetti's pictures never look anything like the work of the Nazarenes, Hunt saw an analogy between their aims for art and Rossetti's. Both seemed to him "*antiquarianism or quattrocentism*," and he argued that "Millais and I had set ourselves directly to oppose" this kind of "mannerism" from the beginning.[1]

In these early pictures Hunt and Rossetti — and to a certain extent even Millais — are interested in the spiritual function of art. Only Rossetti's painting grasps that subject as an urgent current problem because only Rossetti's painting engages the problem by making itself an index of the problem's immediacy. These early paintings by Hunt and Millais are historicist exercises promoting certain moral concerns for society and for its artists. The paintings, however, stand apart from the problems they represent for us; they engage their subjects from a position of (apparent) control and authority. By contrast, when Rossetti makes his primary subject medieval discourse and the artistic practice that developed and executed such a symbology, the picture implodes upon itself. For Rossetti knows very well, and he knows that his audience knows, that these archaic signs once carried enormous spiritual power. By 1849 that power has retreated to the museums and to the enlightened art histories that created such depositories. The historical fate of medieval art becomes in Rossetti's painting, as it does also in a work like "Hand and Soul," a premonitory sign to the Future that is Rossetti's world, a prophetic warning and question. Does this art live as a spiritual force or is it already filled with its own death? More deeply: how can any art with serious spiritual pretensions survive *as a spiritual practice* beyond the historical moment of its original conditions? Rossetti poses that question by constructing a picture in which three historical moments call out to each other: a primitive Christian eventual moment, a medieval artistic and imaginative moment, and a mid-nineteenth-century moment in which the relation between the first two has been staged as a problem.

So if Hunt's and Millais's pictures pose questions for the procedures of contemporary art practice, their critique is not directed to the conventions of narrativity as such. In Rossetti's picture, by contrast, narrative turns to pure formality, in both senses. His painting is not retelling the story referenced by its ostensible subject matter. Rather, it raises foundational questions about art and culture by juxtaposing for critical attention three different ways of perceiving a famous mythological event. (The third of these, the contemporary perspective, appears as the painting itself.)

As programmatic an artist as Rossetti, Hunt was well aware of the difference between their aims. His retrospective comments in *Pre-Raphaelitism and the Pre-Raphaelite Brotherhood* are forthright and acute. Pre-Raphaelitism for him was a movement to correct and renew the practice of art, to purge it of certain acquired bad habits. Rossetti's "Revivalism" was a different matter. According to Hunt, it involved commitments to bad artistic models. What Hunt called "the constant negation of medievalism in every point of our work" — his own and Millais's, that is — defined his anti-Rossettian views. Reflecting on the animus against early Pre-Raphaelite work that came from official quarters in 1850 and 1851, Hunt wants to say that so far as it was justified, Rossetti was the problem. "The resolve of Millais and myself in 1848 to join in the search for new possibilities in art was of a strictly peaceful nature. . . . Our new ideals, although distinct, were not intended as an inimical affront to existent artists, . . . we were possessed with a sense of indebtedness to the Academy Schools."[2] Hunt is remembering the early attacks on the PRB, especially the charges of following primitive models. He is saying that he sympathized with certain qualities in the work of pre-Renaissance artists. He doesn't specify what these were, but looking back over the evidence, we can. He sympathized with the purity and startling brightness of their colors, and like the other early Pre-Raphaelites he was inspired toward a greater abstractness and simplicity in his drawing by the work of medieval exemplars. But Rossetti, as Hunt argues, went much further. Rossetti was drawn to the anti-illusionist space cultivated by German, Italian, and Flemish primitives. The edifice of realist conventions constructed and passed on by the Renaissance, and of course taught in "the Academy Schools," was never opposed by Hunt, as he himself insisted. But it was not a house in which Rossetti could live. Nothing shows that set of differences so well as the contrast between their early, programmatic "Pre-Raphaelite" pictures. The figures and represented forms occupy an idea of space rather than an illusion of space in *The Girlhood of Mary Virgin,* and the same is true of the chromatic experiment *Ecce Ancilla Domini!* — a more adventurous but less successful picture. In Hunt's (and of course Millais's) early Pre-Raphaelite pictures the space is fundamentally realistic.[3]

This difference plays itself out in other notable ways. Rossetti, it is said, had no sense of anatomy and could not master the system of perspective. Both statements are in a certain sense true. They are also grossly misleading, at least if we want to understand what is good and what is not good about Rossetti's work. He was, for example, a fine draftsman, as the incomparable drawings of his wife amply demonstrate, or his Tennyson illustrations, or even his early reflections on Poe.[4] But his approach to drawing was abstract and decorative, not realistic. His human beings are typically clothed figures, with hands and faces the all but exclusive fleshly presences. Like the Japanese artists he came to admire, his human figures are most erotic because they appear in draped forms.

His lack of interest in anatomy was matched by his attitude toward perspective, which he clearly saw as an artistic problem rather than as a technical requirement. From the latter point of view, Rossetti's "quattrocentrism" was an effort to rethink the question of pictorial space. It began with his first two oils, continued through his watercolor experiments of the 1850s, and culminated in the decorative masterpieces of the 1860s and 1870s, which were produced by integrating the voluptuous decorative style of the Venetians into the abstract idealisms of his early primitive models.

But Rossetti's passages through primitive art were not solely or even primarily driven by technical concerns. Technique interested him only insofar as it could help to clarify and express his ideas. The great (and eloquent) paradox of Rossetti in 1849 is that he became the center and driving force of the PRB even though he was the youngest and far the least accomplished, in a technical sense, of its principal figures. Indeed, he willingly became the pupil of the others. Pupil though he was in one sense, he also knew that he was their master in another, even more important way. Hunt was every bit as programmatic an artist as Rossetti, which is why he later argued at such length about who was the intellectual center of the early PRB movement. But Hunt had nothing of Rossetti's breadth of mind or imaginative acuity. Though barely twenty years old, Rossetti's cultural and literary interests were broad, deep, and — most important — intense. For this reason he catalyzed the early Pre-Raphaelite movement, as everyone (except Hunt) understood.

Rossetti was drawn to pre-Renaissance art because of its peculiar spiritual character. From the secular vantage of his mid-Victorian world, Rossetti (like Hunt) was searching for an artistic method that would instantiate idealized states of being — an art of the soul and the soul's transcendental engagements. The early tale "Hand and Soul" describes his purposes — appositely enough, given Rossetti's ideas — in an imaginative form. It tells the story of an unknown artist, Chiaro dell' Erma, working just before the coming of Cimabue. He is, in art-historical terms, a failure, an all but completely forgotten figure. In Rossetti's tale, however, that failure is the badge of Chiaro's spiritual achievement. The story fashions a belated argument on behalf of Chiaro's primitivism, and the contemporary importance of his work lies in its sympathy with Chiaro's commitments. Chiaro's work held itself back from the illusions (and the "illusionism") of the Renaissance, with its "soulless self-reflections of man's skill," its humanist *superbia*. His success comes because of his modesty and his sincerity. These ideas enter Rossetti's story when Chiaro realizes, in a visionary dialogue with the emanation of his soul, that in order "to serve God" with human means he must follow this dictum: "Set thine hand and thy soul to serve man with God." In simplest terms, Chiaro's art must be primarily a devotional exercise, a sacramental rather than a representational act.

In this instance, however, the sacramental act involves the revelation of Chiaro's inner spiritual life. "Hand and Soul" is a distinctly "modern" tale. Chiaro's spiritual world appears as a portrait painting: "the figure of a woman, clad to the hands and feet with a green and grey raiment, chaste and early in its fashion." We see in the picture only "the face and hands" of this woman — a trademark of Rossetti's idealized portraits — and we are told that its "most absorbing wonder . . . was its literality. You knew that figure, when painted, had been seen; yet it was not a thing to be seen of men." The picture is important because, in a worldly point of view, it withholds itself, and even — as the story suggests — repels quotidian interests. The image it celebrates is from another order of reality — an image that has been seen, but not "of men," not through a glass darkly. Chiaro's painting is itself a dark glass, like every work of art. Its significance as art lies in its informing idea, its commitment to primal images and the supranatural order they define. It argues the existence and accessibility of that order by a kind of *ars negativa*. Chiaro's picture is a dark glass that has made its darkness — and ultimately "the darkness" — visible. The picture is a cloud of unknowing.

The story explains, and ultimately incarnates, the argument Rossetti makes in his two early paintings, and in nearly all of his best work. Chiaro is not simply a "failure" in art-historical terms, he is a failure in his own eyes — a weak vessel who, surveying his own work and career, is dismayed by its inadequacies. But the dialogue with his soul, and his single (and culminant) masterpiece, expose the resources of negative states. Chiaro (and Rossetti) are launched upon a program of antihumanistic art. It is an art not "for art's sake" but for the sake of a transnatural idea, a kind of antiart determined to abandon all hope in the proud displays of representational illusion. Hunt separated himself from Rossetti because he had little sympathy with the latter's antinomianism. From Rossetti's point of view, however, the only hope for morality in art was "to serve man with God." "Self reflections" for Rossetti enter artistic forms not as signs of "skill" but as elements of a devotional act, part of the revelation of the living soul's terrors and desires and all its "ideas of good and evil." Not without reason did Rossetti make himself the inheritor of William Blake or the chief English precursor of the Symbolist movement in art and literature.

Literality: Rossetti uses the word to try to define the special quality of the image Chiaro fashions as a *figura* for the transcendant image "seen . . . yet . . . not seen of men." He chooses the same word to describe a key feature of his translations of *The Early Italian Poets,* most of which were made in the late 1840s. There the word signifies Rossetti's decision

to pursue "metrical translations" that reconstitute the "beauty" of the
original poems. He explains his choice in this way: "Much has been said,
and in many respects justly, against the value of metrical translation. But
I think it would be admitted that the tributary art might find a not ille-
gitimate use in the case of poems which come down to us in such a form
as do these early Italian ones." "Literality" becomes a virtue when the obscurity of the original works has reached a critical state, as is the case with
these poems, whose original "corrupt dialect and imperfect expression"
has been exacerbated by succeeding "clumsy transcription and pedantic
superstructure." The effort in such cases is not "fidelity" but "literality,"
which for Rossetti means the execution of a poem — a "rhythmical translation" — that will stand in place of the original. The more "literal" these
are in relation to the physique of the primary texts, the better: not literal
as to "meaning" but literal as to "form."

The issues here are the same that Rossetti took up in "Hand and Soul"
and in his first two oil paintings. Through literality comes the evidence
of things not seen. We recognize the literality of Chiaro's painting because of the gap it dramatizes between the figure of the woman and the
ideal she represents. The painting incarnates not the ideal itself but the
absence that marks the force of Chiaro's belief and desire. The same
should be said of Rossetti's two paintings, his story, his translations of
the early Italian poets. The archaic and mannered qualities of all this
work, noted and deplored by Hunt, are cultivated by Rossetti. They are
the moves of a literalist style, the marks of perpetual longings and devotions: in religious terminology, the outward and visible signs of an inward and spiritual condition.

But for Rossetti these signs must function literally; to set them down
amounts to a magical act through which a "real presence" ensues. What
comes into presence is a form of beauty that is the equivalent of an inspiring premonition. Once again we see the relevance of his remarks on
translating the early Italian poets. The effort to recover those works is
pursued in aesthetic rather than conceptual terms. He moves through
various acts of "translation" because, he says, these involve "the neces-
sity of settling many points without discussion." He calls this procedure
"the most direct form of commentary." "Literal" translation is thus Rossetti's chief figure for the practice of art. It is a practice for turning ideas
into ideals, concepts into presences.

But while the object of that kind of action is devotional, its procedures are aesthetic. When critics describe Rossetti's work as the practice of a religion of beauty, they are responding to this structure in his work. But there is nothing loose or vague involved here. An imaginative discipline unfolds a system of symbols that stand for themselves. So in *The Girlhood of Mary Virgin,* the christological signs reference the economy of art, not the economy of grace. All the action in the picture proceeds literally. It leaves no room for references beyond itself—or rather, no room for references beyond its various symbolic forms, which mirror rather than reference each other. This kind of art is not the symbolic repetition of an original reality because it never admits such a distinction in the first place. This is why Rossetti's focus is on the "secondary" spiritual moment of the Middle Ages, and not the "primary" moment at the outset of the Christian era. The secondary moment — that is to say, the work of art — is the primal, defining event. Its power appears when and as it functions devotionally, renewing the economy of artistic signs the way the Mass renews the sacrifice of Jesus. Devotion is paid to the vitalizing and revelatory power of artistic practice. The fact that Rossetti chooses a legendary event in the Christian mythos underscores the point. But as *Ecce Ancilla Domini!* shows, Rossetti might as easily have chosen a scriptural event, for in his view the whole of Christian history appears as a poetic construction. To see it this way — which is precisely the way that Blake saw it — does not diminish its significance. On the contrary, in fact. Seeing it this way lays down a daunting, even a fearful, artistic imperative.

A magical act, this kind of art makes no appeal to external sources or authorities — for instance, to Nature, or to God. It appeals to something far more unbelievable — to Art. More unbelievable, but more real, because the work of the artist, the god of Art, is unfolding as the appeal being made. One thinks of André Breton's comments on the work of Tanguy: "Just what are these images? What shall we seek at these spiritual frontiers, where the mind rejects all external evidence, where man is determined to argue solely from his own existence?"[5] Rossetti's argument is especially appealing because it advertises itself at a discount. Flaunting its act of imitation, *The Girlhood of Mary Virgin* suggests pastiche, which is a genre Rossetti turns to remarkable account. The so-called "creative imagination" appears to have nothing to do with this startling

work. The same is even more plainly true of the sonnets attached to the
picture, which are written as if they were translations rather than original poems. Or consider "Hand and Soul" once again. So successful was
Rossetti in fashioning this story as a historical report rather than a work
of imagination that "more than one admirer of it . . . made enquiry in
Florence or Dresden after the pictures of Chiaro."⁶

The tale moves to an art beyond the reach of art. As a result, its source —
which is explicitly a certain ideal of Art — appears consumed within the
act of its immediate reconstitution. We see this result in the climax of the
tale — or, I should say, in the series of anticlimaxes that finish it off. These
begin at the apparent nadir of Chiaro's history, when he reflects on the
moral inconsequence of his work. "Fame failed me: faith failed me: and
now this also, — the hope that I nourished in this my generation of
men. . . . Am I not as a cloth drawn before the light, that the looker may
not be blinded? But which showeth thereby the grain of its own coarseness, so that the light seems defiled, and men say, 'We will not walk by
it.' Wherefore through me they shall be doubly accursed, seeing that
through me they reject the light. May one be a devil and not know it?"
Into this space of despair comes the visionary woman who declares herself "the image of thine own soul within thee," and she begins her discourse of consolation. The dynamic of the scene is clearly mystical, suggesting that Rossetti had an early acquaintance with works like *The Cloud
of Unknowing, The Interior Castle,* and *The Ascent of Mount Carmel* —
most likely through his sisters Christina and Maria. As in those works,
the consolation operates through what Hegel would term the "negation
of negation." The psychic peace that finally descends upon Chiaro comes
after he is urged to realize himself through acts of artistic renunciation.
The *via negativa* of the mystical tradition is translated by Rossetti into
artistic terms. If Chiaro's soul is "weak," as she says, she need not be imagined "a devil." St. Teresa will not renounce the poverty and weakness of
her soul, she will seek to be consumed by it, renouncing instead any last
pretensions of thought that she might have the power to overcome her
sinfulness. In Rossetti's translation Chiaro becomes an artistic ideal by
an act of renunciation, deliberately choosing "to serve man with God."

Literally that injunction refers to Chiaro's decision to work hence-
forth as a religious painter. The import of his choice becomes clear in the
final section of the story, where the narrative abruptly shifts from a mid-

thirteenth-century scene to "the spring of 1847 . . . at Florence." Here
Rossetti constructs a small modern parable — a distinctly Pre-Raphaelite
parable — about art history and the aesthetic values it pursues. The scene
is the Pitti Palace, the players a group of Continental art students, their
teacher, a museum archivist, and the (English) narrator. The moral of the
event pivots on the reactions of these characters to a pair of (imaginary)
paintings: on one hand, a magnificent Raphael, on the other a small
"Figura mistica di Chiaro dell' Erma." Art history has exalted the one and
forgotten the other, as we see in the behavior of everyone at the museum
except the (unnamed) English visitor. We are witnessing the historical
realization of Chiaro's final artistic decision, his inaugural failure. This
is not the failure of Browning's Andrea del Sarto, "the faultless painter."
It is the "mystical" failure of the artist whose "light seems defiled, and
men say, 'We will not walk by it.'" Chiaro's final decision is not to seek
the future glories promised to the path opened by Cimabue, Duccio, and
Giotto — according to the accounts scripted by the children of the
promise. "Hand and Soul" is in this respect a critique of Vasari, the first
of those official scriptures. In Rossetti's tale, primitive Italian art is undergoing a revisionary reading. Chiaro, the exponent of such work, is
being valued because he is refusing the promise of the coming of the glories of the Renaissance. An incarnation of what Trotsky was to call "the
privilege of historical backwardness," Chiaro becomes an imaginative resource because of his retrograde commitments — all those features that
would come to be judged crudities and incompetences by later art his-
torians, with their enlightened and progressivist myths of art. Chiaro's
work has two consummate virtues, according to Rossetti's parable: integrity of vision and spirituality. These emerge in the *selva oscura* of
Chiaro's decision to paint the truth of his soul in "the grain of its own
coarseness" and to make the work — not the art *object* but the *work* — a devotional offering to the ideal it can only ever seize by desire.

None of this argument implies a lack of interest in artistic technique
and method. Quite the contrary, as the "Hand" in the title of Rossetti's
story indicates. It does imply that skills of art, and not least the innovations achieved in the Renaissance, are not imagined as the source of artistic or imaginative vigor. Rossetti's thought here clearly recalls Blake, on
one hand, and anticipates the stance of Surrealism on the other. In this

perspective, imaginative vision and its technical means — soul and hand — emerge as a realization of the darkness. They develop the resources of the *selva oscura* as a field of intense desire.

Rossetti first entered that dark wood in 1848–1850 and spent the next decade exploring and meditating its energies. The greatness of his art in this period, early recognized and still apparent, comes through his work on paper — the watercolors and the drawings. Alastair Grieve has commented shrewdly on these productions. "Oils have been used traditionally to create illusionist effects of space and texture. Rossetti was happiest working on paper where medium and surface are integrated and there is no skin. His watercolours breathe and give off colour in a way that his oils do not. . . . Paper can also be cut, patched, and added to and many of Rossetti's watercolours and drawings have had drastic surgery done to them during their production. He also liked the scale of works on paper. His works demand to be picked up and examined minutely. . . . So they are akin to books but at the same time uncompromisingly visual as, say, Morris Louis's stain paintings."[7] Though focused on the watercolors, Grieve's comments also help to explain the revisionist ambitions of Rossetti's first two oil paintings. For all their remarkable qualities, however, both pictures demonstrate Rossetti's inability to exploit fully the medium's special demands (and limitations). Ten years of drawing and watercolor work developed his understanding of pictorial space and chromatic technique, so that when he did return to oil painting, the results were stunningly successful right from the start.

Whether working with oil or on paper, Rossetti succeeds when his work seems the vortex of a larger field of intense relationships that are intimated but unseen. A picture like *The Wedding of St. George and the Princess Sabra,* so minutely articulated, exhibits the visual conditions his pictures characteristically develop. Why should this legendary scene, where heroic victory is crowned with the emblems of love and marriage, appear in such a premonitory, even melancholic, key?[8] Such a question merely stands for any number of others we are drawn to ask by this haunting picture, so replete with the familiar and the strange. An impression is created that every detail of its thickened visual world supplies only glimpses of realities beyond, "seen . . . yet not seen of men." The subject matter, of course, is entirely apt for such treatment — a foundational but remote legend whose details, variously lapsed from memory, can be recovered only through an array of dispersed materials of different dates and media. Rossetti's medieval and Arthurian works regularly draw upon those highly suggestive cultural deposits, either to reinvent specifically recorded events or to enrich them with unimaginations.

Rossetti gravitates to this kind of material because it lets him develop the legends with his own improvisations — a method he called "allegorizing on one's own hook" when he spoke of the splendid illustrations he made for Tennyson's "The Palace of Art."[9] Though Tennyson professed never to have understood it, the *St. Cecilia* drawing is an exquisite response to the laureate's equally exquisite early text:

> Or in a clear-wall'd city on the sea,
>   Near gilded organ-pipes, her hair
> Wound with white roses, slept St. Cecily;
>   An angel look'd at her.

Rossetti's illustration is a drama of an imagination pursuing figural proofs of its own affected state. Once again details proliferate. The "city" and the "sea" become in the drawing remarkable constructions of many parts and relationships, none specified in Tennyson. There is a prominent soldier at the lower right, apparently a guard, and other figures stand or work in different places and at different tasks. Odd objects emerge in odd locations — a sundial, a striking tree placed at the drawing's golden mean, tiny windmills. Nothing is in perspective, but everything is meticulously arranged and, as in a dream, displacement appears repeatedly. Cecilia is not sleeping, she is in a trance, and her ecstasy seems to come partly from the music she is playing (she is not simply "near" the organ), and partly from the angel (who gives her more than a Tennysonian "look").

What distinguishes this kind of art is its imaginative vigor. But technique remains a pertinent concern. Rossetti was justifiably proud of the watercolor method he and Ford Madox Brown called "the dry brush style," an innovation he worked out and taught in the 1850s at the Working Men's College.[10] As he told Ernest Gambart in 1864, "I painted in the style which I originated, for years, when no works at all resembled mine but my own."[11] Martin Hardie defines that originality as an assumption of new technical licenses. "The central tradition of water-colour meant nothing to Rossetti," Hardie observes. "He started out to hack his way to expression," achieving "an unusual depth, glow, and translucency of colour."[12] He and Burne-Jones, his great student, "made free use of moist colours, rubbing and scrubbing them on the paper, with the most meagre intervention of water, as if they were oils." In such works one is struck, as Hardie is struck, by the drama of an artistic action rather than — as with Millais — a display of craftsmanship.

Many of Rossetti's pictures, in particular the oils, lack this kind of energy — *Sibylla Palmifera,* for example, or the later versions of those 1850s masterpieces *The Damsel of the San Graal* (1857/1874) and *The Salutation of Beatrice* (1859/1880–1881). It is probably wasted effort to seek to explain these things. Some used to argue that Rossetti damaged his art by making copies for people who admired certain works, and his brother was one of the first to say that Rossetti's reworkings often produced disastrous consequences. As in the late revisions by Henry James, however, the evidence here is ambiguous. Certain replicas and reimaginings are clearly successful, others are not. An obsessive artist, Rossetti makes "copies" with a will, if also sometimes with displeasure. Nor is money the only incentive. He cannot help revisiting and revising his subjects. The obsessive drawings of his wife Elizabeth constitute a body of work "stamped with immortality," as Madox Brown said.[13] A few are particular masterpieces, but the corpus has a special value and power, like Keats's odes, which as a group cancel out — even in a way exploit — the deficiencies of the individual poems.

Like St. John of the Cross or St. Teresa, Rossetti's desire is both fixated and insatiable, as his sister understood: the "one face [that] looks out from all his canvasses" is a queen, a nameless girl, a saint, an angel — all and none of these, a woman "not as she is, but as she fills his dream." His pursuit of models who might stimulate more intense and searching engagements with this imaginative ideal is famous.[14] The models are not the object of his devotions, but neither are the paintings. They inhabit a place Rossetti called "the spirit's Palestine," the divinity-charged locale that he searches out:

> Here with her face doth memory sit,
>   Meanwhile, and wait the day's decline,
> Till other eyes shall look from it,

Eyes of the spirit's Palestine,
Even than the old gaze tenderer:
While hopes and aims long lost with her
Stand round her image side by side,
Like tombs of pilgrims that have died
About the Holy Sepulchre.

These remarkable lines culminate an 1847 dramatic monologue titled "The Portrait." The speaker is a painter who is describing works in his studio—the central portrait of his dead beloved surrounded by other pictures he imagines as "tombs of pilgrims" who pursued (as it were) an *Imitatio Christi*. All these works are bereft, but their emptiness locates the vortex of the speaker's desire—in fact, the artist's desire, for the poem is an allegory about the spiritual dynamic of artistic work. It tells the same story as "Hand and Soul."

Beata Beatrix, The Blessed Damozel, Lady Lilith: all are either Holy Sepulchres or pilgrims' tombs, memorials of the *corpus mysticum* that is their object of devotion. As the geographical trope in "The Portrait" suggests, such works (they have numerous counterparts in Rossetti's *oeuvre*) locate regions of spiritual energy—Palestine in the Judaeo-Christian mythology, Glastonbury in Arthurian lore, Greece, Dante's Firenze, the London of Blake and Rossetti. Like Coleridge's Xanadu, these places are savage, holy, and enchanted. The gravity of their emblematic forms—that is, of the "Rossetti Women" looming through the portraits—is measured according to a scale of imaginative vigor, not moral eminence. That is why we are right to be so impressed by some of Rossetti's most disturbing and sinister pictures: *Lady Lilith, Monna Vanna, Veronica Veronese,* and of course the three final apocalyptic canvases, *Proserpine, Mnemosyne, Astarte Syriaca.* Repetitive? Rather, "exhaustless," which was Ruskin's word for Rossetti's powers of pictorial "invention."[15] Devoutly attended, the vision that stands beyond these imposing works— "seen . . . but not seen of men"—promises an art of consuming luxury, an antiaesthetic poised between imaginative profusion and waste.

The gallery of these images forms a romance tableau of the relation of art and eros. Each retells the story of a failed effort to see the god that generates the visionary effort in the first place. *Beata Beatrix* is particularly notable. Often read as a memorial to his wife Elizabeth, the work was in fact begun while she was still living. Indeed, it grows out of a primitive Dantean dream that enveloped Rossetti's imagination from an undatable early period and that he explored relentlessly in his poetry, his translations, his art. The oil, completed in 1870 and now in the Tate Gallery, was preceded not only by the usual preparatory drawings but by prevenient works from the early 1850s, studies for other pictures as well as finished drawings with no willful genetic relation to the Tate's version. More interesting still, that picture did not complete Rossetti's artistic pursuit, it simply recharged and expanded the work's affective field. Admirers saw the picture and wanted copies. Rossetti used these commissions to revisit the work again and again, returning like a widowed man to the grave of his lover.

The most famous is the first completed oil, the Tate picture, in which Beatrice appears marked with the features of the artist's wife. That double perspective, where details from nineteenth-century London are superimposed on thirteenth-century Florence, is subtly replicated in the urban scene before which the woman is posed in her trance. The river, the central figure, and the distant city might be seen as the Arno, Beatrice, and Florence, with the Ponte Vecchio and perhaps the Campanile also visible. But a shift of our affections brings to view the Thames and the Old Battersea Bridge, south London, and Elizabeth Siddal.

The symbolist technique encourages these kinds of duplicity, as is especially clear in the nonrealistic use of light. The placement of Beatrice's head turns what is formally a realistic moment (sunlight from the distant city) into an emblematic event. Beatrice's head is virtually in an aureole, as is the figure of Love at the left (and as Dante's, at the right, is not). The influence of stained-glass lighting is very clear in a painting like this, though Ruskin judged it characteristic of all Rossetti's work to the mid-1860s: "Its light is not the light of sunshine itself, but of sunshine diffused through coloured glass."[16] Most important, because the painting's inner golds connect to the outer, highly symbolic and decorative frame, the picture seems illuminated from within and not from some imagined realistic source of light. This integration of painting and frame via color and symbolic paraphernalia dramatizes the simplicity of the symbolical character of the color organization of the work — a "sombre harmony of gold and green and purple," as Waugh noted in distinctly Whistlerian terms.[17] The white underpainting, notable at the lower right and in Beatrice's sleeves, lends a strange luminosity to the largely darkened space dominated by the figure of Beatrice, and is an important element contributing to the work's power of spiritual suggestion.

Rossetti's patron William Graham was so moved by this picture that he begged the artist to undertake another. Reluctantly agreeing, Rossetti was soon unhappily involved in the new work. He complained constantly as it went on, but with the encouragement of Madox Brown he persisted, and in 1872 he broke through his frustrated attempt to reenter and reexplore his original dream. This is the oil version now in the Chicago Art Institute.

In all conceptual and iconographical matters the new painting differs very little from the first version, except that a predella thickens both the Dantean motifs and the autobiographical significance of the subject. Technically, however, the work is very different indeed, as one sees most readily if the background areas of the original are compared with this work. Here everything is articulated with greater precision: the figures of Dante and Eros; their respectively attendant symbolic accessories (the well, symbolizing rebirth and the New Life that Beatrice is dreaming toward; the Arbor Vitae ornamenting the backspace of Eros); and the distant cityscape architecture, which here is clearly Florence, not London.

In one sense the increased definition seems to give greater realism to the picture. But in another and even more telling way the symbolic resonance is increased. That effect comes about because of the way Rossetti has defined the presence of a field of golden light. In the original painting he gives Beatrice an aureole (like the figure of Love) via a witty manipulation of a gold color field that instantiates nature and supernature simultaneously. Here her glory spreads across the entire left two-thirds of the picture, and even appears to hollow out by the power of its lightening the otherwise planar structure of the background areas. The result is not at all to produce a kind of realistic depth recession, though it could be read that way; rather, the gold light comes to seem an extension of Beatrice's person, a flooding glory that rhymes with the darker gold flesh of her tranced face and folded hands.

So here Rossetti slightly alters the focus of the ideality he first pursued in the original work. In this painting the ideal is again centered in the face of Beatrice. But a remarkable transformation has overtaken that visage. In the Tate Gallery oil the face is clearly modeled from Rossetti's dead wife, Elizabeth. Repainting the picture for Graham, Rossetti dissolved that memory image into a synthetic *figura* in which we also discern the features of Alexa Wilding, Jane Morris, and perhaps others as well.

The Graham picture is a more dynamic work than the original, which is not to say a better work. The Tate oil distinctly looks back to the watercolors of the 1850s, as one sees in the chalky surface, the undefined contours, and what Gabriele Reithmiller calls "the subdued luminosity of the colors separated from each other in compact compartments to emphasize contrasting color fields."[18] That structure is not abandoned altogether in the replica, but it is clearly altered. This picture's energy runs along three clear disharmonic diagonals of force: the line defined by the ‑arm of the sundial, the line joining the dove to the figure of Love, and the line of Beatrice's right arm. In each case symbolic relations are being drawn in reds and golds. Furthermore, the formal balance between the main picture and the predella is shrewdly done: the three figures of the former have their mirror equivalents in the latter (with the train of Beatricean women introduced to rhyme with the figure of Love in the principal picture).

The difference between these two pictures and Rossetti's last oil replica is equally apparent, if less remarkable in an aesthetic sense. This work, another oil, was completed by Madox Brown after Rossetti's death. It is a nice picture but utterly different from the other two, which are strongly symbolistic oils. Here the location is unambiguously Florence, a gesture of facticity that is repeated everywhere. The messenger-dove in this version is white, not red, the poppies are red, not white; and the arbor vitae is replaced by a wall-niche with a crucifix — all shifts toward more realistic conventions that affect the whole compositional structure. Most telling is the altered light. Here it suffuses the area behind Beatrice from a source that is represented as natural (as the lines of light at the left emphasize).

The *Beata Beatrix* case is not unusual. Rossetti's works — writings and pictures alike — typically pass through transformations, often numerous and/or drastic. A work like *Lady Lilith* is especially useful in this context because it demonstrates how these changes emerge as it were from within the executed works, like extrusions from a volatile internal state. The conceptual treatment of the principal figure in *Lady Lilith,* made explicit in the choice of models, is riven with ambiguity. In the initial version of the painting the model was Fanny Cornforth, but in the repainted work the face of Lilith is Alexa Wilding. The importance of this change emerges when we remember that Wilding was used to model Lilith's antithesis, the figure enshrined as *Sibylla Palmifera*. From the great *Bocca Baciata* forward, however, Cornforth regularly appeared in pictures that sought to explore the ideal forms of what Rossetti called, in the companion sonnet to *Lady Lilith*, "Body's Beauty."

The conceptual significance of Wilding's features was initially defined in the pairing of *Lady Lilith* with *Sibylla Palmifera*. Rossetti used her features to explore an imagination of cool, even classic elegance, just as he used Cornforth's to study his idea of corporeality. Wallace Stevens later defined and pursued a similar dialectic as the beauty of innuendoes versus the beauty of inflections. As Rossetti undertook these imaginative studies, however, the initial pairing seems to mutate within the action of the pictures. *Sibylla Palmifera* is a peculiarly unsatisfactory work, but its legacy paintings are among Rossetti's best — works, that is, like *Monna Vanna*, in which Wilding's face becomes the focus of a great study of decorative luxuriance and commercial wealth. In a picture like this the Chiarian drive toward ideality is located not in the figure of the woman — her symbolic valence is clearly negative — but in the treatment of that figure. A conscious act of homage to Venetian art, as Rossetti said, the painting means to celebrate the power of the artistic imagination.

But Rossetti's dialectic of "Soul's Beauty" and "Body's Beauty," and ultimately the whole process of erotic idealization through art, lays itself open to regular revisionary shifts. The initial dialectic is unstable precisely because, as we saw in *The Girlhood of Mary Virgin*, Rossetti makes his own work part of his subject matter, which in his case means part of the problem of art. One recalls Chiaro worrying whether one might be a devil without knowing it, and comparing his work to "a cloth drawn across the light . . . which showeth thereby the grain of its own coarseness." *Monna Vanna* draws its power from that way of thinking about artistic practice, as the title itself emphasizes by alluding to Cavalcanti's mistress, the dream figure of his idealizing imagination. The greatness of his poetry can never be separated from its vanity, as Dante himself implicitly argues about his old friend in the *Commedia*.[19] Cavalcanti was a devil without knowing it.

But Rossetti's view—it may have been Dante's as well—is that Caval-canti's art knew what Cavalcanti did not. This happens because, ac-cording to Rossetti, art always adopts an inner standing point toward it-self. What that means for pictures like *Monna Vanna* or even *Beata Beatrix* and *The Blessed Damozel* can be clarified, I think, if we reflect for a moment on a poem like "Jenny."

Working from Browning's monologues and Poe's stories (especially the hoaxes), Rossetti here produces a portrait of the inner fantasy life of a contemporary young man, a bohemian artist. What is so remarkable about this work—so original, as Pater would insist—is the investment its reverie makes in realistic materials. The poem is littered with *things* of all kinds. It develops an imagination of the world of the imaginary as that world is, necessarily, a scene of desire materially reified and alien-ated to an extreme of facticity. The easy conversational manner is the work's principal index of that order of the ordinary. It carries a coded message, just as the poem is headed with a coded title. This is not a poem about "Jenny," a prostitute, but about a young man whose desire is drawn to her images—to her person, her imaginary self, and to the para-phernalia that constellate about her, like the ornaments that decorate portraitures, not least of all Rossetti's.

It is crucial to realize that we are led to see the whole from a Rosset-tian inner standing point, that is, from within the fantasy-space projected by the young man. It all appears to be a "real" scene, and is taken as real by the young man, as it must be: for these illusions, as a Marxian analy-sis would show, are precisely real. For the young man, or the poem, to see them more critically would be to break the spell of the images, to break the illusion that constitutes their reality. The man's sympathetic at-titude, including his self-ironies, are not critical moves, they are block-ing devices that serve to maintain the illusion of objectivity. And so it happens: unawakened from its dream of life, the poem draws the linea-ments of that supreme world of illusions we like to call "the objective world," the world as will and representation, "reality."

But to Rossetti's view—it follows Dante and Blake, two of his chief masters—reality is a set of illusionist projections. The function of art is to reveal the illusions, drawing their precise and various characters, and in the process instantiating their source (Energy, Eros). Even in the re-flexive realms of art there are always only inner standing points. "Jenny" is formally (and psychically, and socially) the same kind of work as *The Blessed Damozel,* poem and painting both: the passage on "my cousin Nell" defines how cousin and Jenny are mirror images, while the predella of the painting reminds us that both works are governed by a reverie form. Indeed, the poem differs only in minor ways from works like *Lady Lilith, Monna Vanna,* and *Proserpine,* where narrative structure, elaborated in "Jenny" and the early Marian works, is much more elliptical.

Modernist cultural ideology has sometimes found it convenient to compare Rossetti's fetishized women with, for example, Manet's *Olympia.* The comparisons propose a story of why Manet's picture is proto-Modernist, and why Rossetti's similar paintings linger in the benighted world of realist convention. The key difference lies in Manet's ironical treatment of his subject, a fact emphasized — not to say flaunted — in the lady's shoes. And it is clearly true that Rossetti's works, verbal as well as pictorial, almost always avoid those kinds of ironies. Instead of distance Rossetti cultivates involvement, the "inner standing point." The result is a self-consciousness quite different from what we see in *Olympia,* which puts on display not "the grain of its own coarseness" but its wit and (soulless?) skill. "And men [said]" — of Chiaro dell' Erma, of Rossetti — "'We will not walk by it.'" And so it happened. But now that the fault lines of Modernist enterprise are more clear to us, Rossetti's critique of that coming race may claim our attention. His skeptical view of Impressionism might be usefully recovered.

Not that Rossetti doesn't have his twentieth-century inheritors. His work's continuity is clearly preserved by the Surrealists, for example — which is no surprise given their evolution from Rossetti's immediate inheritors, the Symbolists. Other inheritors are various twentieth-century Romantics like Sutherland and Brangwyn, or the great Modern master Balthus, whose erotic portraits of young girls keep a divine vision in a time of trouble. That his incomparable works remain for many pornographic images and — in the easy terminology of Freudian puritanism — fetishistic, can help to explain the twentieth-century fate of Rossetti's work. Balthus's girls are of course nothing but pubescent madonnas, slightly disguised — like the parables of Jesus — for a secular world.

Rossetti's women are similar. Coming as fetish forms they come in judgment, driving a wedge between our enlightenment equations of pleasure and happiness, knowing and understanding. They are Buñuel's obscure objects of desire — disturbing, not to be controlled — whose nakedness appears as material luxuriance. Their adherence to old-fashioned forms should not deceive us about their complete modernity, in Baudelaire's sense of that term. As contemporary as the figures of Constantin Guys, they represent their ideological status even more directly. They are cultural signs all but literally rendered. If we turn from them, imagining an escape through a new and different language, we will find that they possess the power to return, like Mailer's armies of the night. For they are us, male and female alike. And their fetishism defines their truth.

6

VENUS SURROUNDED BY MIRRORS, REFLECTING HER IN DIFFERENT VIEWS

But, as he feels what he loves escaping, the painter or writer trembles from the cold of extreme want; vain efforts are expended to create pathways permitting the endless reattainment of that which flees. It is decisively important in this movement that the search, intellectually undertaken at the promptings of unsatisfied desire, has always preceded theory's delineation of the object sought. The belated intervention of discriminating intelligence certainly opened up a field of possibilities for empty error, whose extent became discouraging, but it is no less certain that an experience of this nature would not have been possible if some clairvoyant theory had tried to fix in advance its direction and its limits.

Georges Bataille, "The Sacred"

The Pre-Raphaelite Departure

Around 1870 Rossetti made the following notebook entry, the subject for a painting: "Venus surrounded by mirrors, reflecting her in different views".[1] Although he never executed that picture, the idea grew luxuriantly all around him, not least in his many remarkable portraits and drawings of women. When Christina Rossetti wrote in 1856 that "One face looks out from all his canvasses, / One selfsame figure sits or walks or leans," she was referring not to Elizabeth Siddal, as some have thought, but to the idea that Rossetti discovered in her and in many other women, real and imaginary.

Rossetti's unrealized painting of Venus names a classic allegorical topos. The subject of such a painting would be art itself, and especially pictorial art, where Beauty is reflexively presented in the form of visual images. Like many other artists, Rossetti painted multiple versions of this picture — paintings and drawings of women holding mirrors, standing before mirrors, looking into reflective pools. What is especially interesting about the notebook idea is Rossetti's desire to achieve multiple perspectives in a single picture. The thought seems more Modernist than Pre-Raphaelite.

In the context of Rossetti's world, however, the thought is exactly Rossettian, if not exactly Pre-Raphaelite. It constitutes a feature of his work that was noticed and deplored from the beginning. The first pictures exhibited by Rossetti and his early Pre-Raphaelite brothers were condemned not simply for their "errors in perspective" but for what was taken to be a programmatic pursuit of such error. "Pre-Raphaelite" meant (in part) a return to more primitive artistic styles, and hence — according to progressivist Victorian art critics — to pictorial methods based on sheer ignorance. Rossetti and his circle not only painted crude pictures, it was argued, they did so deliberately, systematically — theoretically.

But of course — we can now see this very clearly — the return to fourteenth- and fifteenth-century models was a practical move to study pictures that had certain estimable qualities. One of these was a treatment of color unhampered by the system of chiaroscuro, another the construction of pictures whose dominant feature would be line rather than volume. A third — it is closely related — involved perspective. In Cimabue, Duccio, and Giotto, in Dürer and the masters of medieval illumination, Rossetti discovered works where (so to speak) Venus appeared surrounded by mirrors, reflecting her in different views. The anti-illusionistic features of such works involved a way of seeing, an artistic method, he wanted to recover and adapt.

Let us look once again at Rossetti's two earliest works in oil, *The Girlhood of Mary Virgin* (1848–1849) and *Ecce Ancilla Domini!* (1849). In each case the linear perspective, classically announced in the flooring, is checked by the structure of horizontal planes and the uniform treatment of color and ornament, until it is finally scattered into isolated pictorial moments. As in Italian primitive masters, these moments are themselves nonuniform. Nothing in *Ecce Ancilla Domini!* is painted more scrupulously than the Virgin's loose strands of hair. This arbitrary point of focus establishes the painting's main argument, that anything here might be taken as a similar vortex of attention. The room and its contents are opening out from within. Walls, window, and floor make up a strange set of spaces that seem to lift the bed into verticality even as they run off into ambiguous angles to each other. Shadows (on the angel, on the bed) and reflections (from the angel's flaming feet) appear without the regulation of illusionistic method. In one perspective the angel stands in a plane slightly before the Virgin, but in another — signaled primarily by their haloes — they occupy the same plane. And the whiteness dominating all the planes and all the angles not only flattens the space remarkably, it defines a pictorial context where objects are measured by a value — color itself — that is and can only be internal to the pictorial space. This is a picture that means to be seen on its own terms, as it were, that refuses apprehension from that external point of understanding posited by linear perspective. It is also a picture in which the source of light has not been imagined in realistic terms. The domination of white, which would soon fire Whistler's attention, realizes the absolute value of color in the picture. The order of space here is not perspectival, the system of color is formal. True, Rossetti here does not exploit the symbolic potential of the window area, but even at this early stage of his work he knows enough to cancel the window's conventional realistic function and turn it to a formal coloristic moment.

The same approach dominates *The Girlhood of Mary Virgin*. Particularly noticeable here is the linear play orchestrated in the structure of the trellis, balustrade, curtain and curtain rod, and the potted lily tended by the angel. These lines draw various otherwise disparate planes into moments of convergence — for instance, the vortex pivoting around the topmost lily, which appears to rest simultaneously (inside) on its vertical stem and (outside) on the horizontal trelliswork. Furthermore, as with *Ecce Ancilla Domini!* light in this painting has no source point, it is diffused across the surface of the picture, where the colors themselves illuminate the world, as they do in the miniatures that inspired a work like this. Used in this way, color works to organize the structure of the picture, and to support the nonrealistic convergences developed in the picture's linear forms. So it is that the golden-haloed dove becomes an absolute moment in both linear and coloristic terms.

The equivalent of this moment in *Ecce Ancilla Domini!* is the depiction of the Virgin's hair. Both pictures arrest us with the appearance of a startling literalism, as it were: the realistic literalism of the Virgin's hair, the allegorical literality of the dove. That literalist approach defines the programmatic quality of these two early works. In each case a pictorial moment locates a style of expression (realist in one case, symbolic in the other). The consequence is that the action of the painting (or the argument of the painter) becomes the center of attention, and not some point of reference elsewhere.

Rossetti's picture works to make the dove (or the hair, or any of his other pictured elements) believable: believable not in doctrinal terms but in purely artistic and pictorial terms. In *Ecce Ancilla Domini!* the issue is joined, as we have seen, in the treatment of the Virgin's hair. The minutely rendered strands call attention to what can seem a grotesque stylistic contradiction in the picture. Indeed, Rossetti explicitly draws our attention to the contradiction by triangulating the hair with the allegorical flames scattering out from the angel's feet. When contemporary reviewers like Dickens attacked early Pre-Raphaelite work for mixing realistic detail, whether coarse or irrelevant, with the symbolic pictorial discourses traditional to devotional subjects, they were registering this stylistic collision. That it was an effect deliberately sought only compounded the error.

As with *Ecce Ancilla Domini!* Rossetti's aim in *The Girlhood of Mary Virgin* is to reconceptualize the language of artistic expression within the immediate pictorial event of the painting. The problem in this case comes because the doctrinal scheme invoked by the picture constructs a kind of language that stands ready to interpret — in fact, to *pre*interpret — the picture. In an entirely Blakean way Rossetti wants to reopen the viewer's doors of attention by short-circuiting the dead logic of the traditional discursive scheme. Rossetti himself underscored the presence of that interpretive scheme by writing a pair of sonnets to accompany the picture. This brilliant and paradoxical move created the first of Rossetti's many "double works of art," one of the signature innovations of his highly inventive career. A major function of these sonnets, which are written in a consciously constructed antique style, is to build a clear moment of aesthetic estrangement into the field of attention. In the sonnets, ideas come to us not in hermeneutic or conceptual forms but in ethnographic and documentary ones.

Let us look more closely at the picture. The haloed dove locates a vortex, an "inner standing point," that tries our visual understandings. A small decorative moment in the pictorial scheme, the dove is conceptually (in several senses) a center for all the actions represented in the picture. As a traditional *figura* for the Holy Spirit, through whom Jesus was "conceived," the bird represents God's real presence in this scene. The dove locates God's view of the events — the events that are explicitly represented here, as well as the events that these representations foretell (most notably, the birth of Jesus forecast in the child-angel, the death of Jesus signaled in the trellis-cross that centers the picture). Rossetti realizes that transcendental point of view in purely pictorial terms. More to the point, he locates it obliquely, in a minor key as it were.

The bird's halo is the defining golden moment in the picture. As such, it is the gravitational center of that delicate vortex of golds and yellows, not least of all seen in the rain of tiny gold flecks playing through the green of the curtain and Saint Anne's drapery. But this color of heaven does not dominate the painting, as it often does in the primitive models Rossetti has been influenced by (paintings as well as miniatures), and as it clearly does in some of Rossetti's own works, most spectacularly in the Tate Gallery's *Sancta Lilias*. *The Girlhood of Mary Virgin* is a picture of reds, blues, and greens — Rossetti's primal colors. And of course, gold. Gold is a regular presence in Rossetti's work, and it regularly stands for an infusing transcendental order.

But Rossetti's picture lets us know that this is an order we do not understand. Doctrine is not understanding, it is merely language: doctrine of faith (the Holy Ghost), doctrine of art-criticism (the symbolic value of gold). We can take only mortal views of divine orders. Consequently, in Rossetti's picture the dove appears in the most literal kind of way — just another small moment in the picture, almost an embellishment, like the vase and oil lamp nearby. There is great pictorial wit here — realizing in a startling and inventive way how, in the nineteenth century's disappearance of God, one may continue to apprehend the evidence of things not seen.

Rossetti's conceptual management of color moves in the closest relation to the linear composition we've already noticed. The ambiguous pictorial placement of the dove is a visible sign that divine presence will not be regulated by material orders, or by the artistic regulations for those orders (the illusions of perspective). One of the sonnets he wrote to accompany the painting registers the ambiguity that plays within the picture. Recollecting a doctrinal narrative, Rossetti explains why the dove is perched on the trellis: "The Holy One / Abides without" the house of the Virgin "until the end be full" (lines 11–12). But the pictorial ambiguity cuts across that idea, as if the picture were arguing (against the idea, not against the sonnet) that in some sense the end *is* full. In purely historical terms the "end," the birth of Jesus, has happened. But this painting does not exist to justify such an idea of fulfillment. Indeed, the dove's pictorial position argues, in another sense, that the end is *not* full, whatever the historical events. Thus the picture's ambiguous treatment of the Holy Ghost realizes the event of the painting as yet a further perspective on the idea of fulfillment. The Holy Spirit abides not "without" but within *The Girlhood of Mary Virgin* as a figural form, at once determinate and ambiguous.

Rossetti in Perspective

Ambiguous spaces and pictorial moments recur throughout Rossetti's work. His renegade treatment of linear perspective, like the odd anatomical appearances in his oil pictures, has been wrongly viewed as technical failures. It is true, of course, that he lacked the technical facility of (say) Millais, and that he had no aptitude for linear perspective. He could easily have brought his pictures into "correct perspective" had he taken the trouble to do so, and as Ruskin urged him to do. The system is mechanical and can be produced with mechanical devices. But as his brother William Michael pointed out very early, Rossetti was well aware that correct perspective was "required in order to make a picture conformable to" accepted standards, but "the fact is that he *preferred* the tone of mind which governed the treatment of such elements of the subject in olden art."[2] This was a programmatic preference that his early friend and mentor Holman Hunt noted and deplored. "To induce him to put the perspective right was . . . a business needing constant argument," Hunt observed, because of Rossetti's admiration for "the childlike immaturities and limitations of the German and Italian quattrocentrists." So Rossetti "denounced the science [of perspective], and objected strongly to each result of its application, declaring that what it proved to be wrong was obviously better."[3] Fifty years later Rossetti's views on this matter helped to launch some of the most important lines of Modernist art.

Perspective alternately bored and frustrated Rossetti, and in the end could only be worked with (not worked within). So we see in all his pictures, as we see in the Italian primitives he admired, recurrent *moments* of perspective that play alongside moments that develop contradictory perspectives, or moments that refuse perspective altogether. Some of his greatest works — the Tennyson drawings, for instance, or *Mary Magdalene at the Door of Simon the Pharisee,* or almost any of the 1850s watercolors, or *Lady Lilith* — manipulate linear perspective in systematically contradictory ways. The notorious *Found,* at which he worked recurrently over many years but never finished, has been conceived as the emblem of a technical incompetence. The moral of the story has been that he couldn't finish the picture because he could never figure out the lines of perspective. There is no doubt that Rossetti did not complete the picture's composition, and that issues of perspective were part of the problem. But this clear fact does not mean that the picture would have been finished, would have "succeeded," if only its parts could all have been arranged in correct linear perspective. Indeed, the finished drawing of *Found* in the British Museum exhibits impeccable perspective. If we are to judge from Rossetti's practice in his other work, what the picture needed more than anything was a clear imagination not of how to rationalize the composition but of how to disarrange and multiply his painting's internal structure and lines of sight. It seems likely that the contemporaneity of the subject matter blocked him from treating the picture as freely as he did his Dantean and Arthurian materials.

Or his Christological materials. A drawing like *Mary Magdalene at the Door of Simon the Pharisee* (1853/1858) defines Rossetti's views in especially clear terms. The picture makes itself an illustration of its argument against the authority of perspective. The conceptual (though not the emotional) center of the drawing is the head of Christ, which enters the picture as an iconic form. This form locates a key moment of pictorial contradiction. Abutting the right limit of the picture, and wholly framed within the window space, the form will be seen at the level of the picture plane itself. But it occupies a fundamentally ambiguous position, and we are also invited to see the form more realistically, as a head in a window that opens into a room with other figures, or, finally, as an artistic image like a religious icon. In this last view the image of Christ is placed on the forward plane defined by the exterior wall of Simon's house, as if it were hung there like a picture. In the left and center areas of the drawing, however, Rossetti builds an illusionistic space in standard perspectival terms. (Those are the terms inviting us to see Christ's head in a window, as part of the drawing's illusion of, and allusion to, "realistic" space.)

The drawing recalls Rossetti's admiration of primitive style and the alternative it offered to perspectivist rationality. The latter becomes here the technical exponent of an art committed to "soulless self-reflections of man's skill." In practical terms Rossetti represents worldliness as space organized according to lines of perspective. This is the recessive area of street, procession, high road, and the distant river. These elements, which form one of the three structural units composing the picture, constitute an integral symbolic narrative about the order of worldliness.

As in nearly all of Rossetti's work, the drawing is arranged as a structure of different areas, each of which forms a center of attention in its own right. Perspective does not organize these pictorial areas; rather, it becomes itself a figural event in one of them, a way of imagining and representing pictorial space. Rossetti thus makes space function as part of an argument about spiritual and aesthetic values. He said that the drawing "represents two houses opposite each other," by which he literally meant the opposition between the house of feasting (worldliness) and the house of Christ and Simon (spirituality).[4] But he meant something more, for spatial recession is made an emblem of the former, while an icon of the head of Jesus is the emblem of the latter. In that view, the two pictorial areas also represent two procedures of artistic representation.

That stylistic opposition locates the programmatic character of the drawing, which argues for a more catholic way of thinking about pictorial space than either the Albertian inheritance authorized in the academy or the doctrinal/moralistic approach favored (for instance) by Holman Hunt and the tradition of Victorian narrative art. In this picture Rossetti's appropriation and translation of these two traditions gets located in the third structural area: the field dominated by the grazing faun. In a formal sense the animal joins the "two houses opposite each other." Its spatial field accomplishes the jointure, just as its technical treatment replicates the effect. As to the latter, we register the minute realism of the drawing, on one hand, and the animal's symbolic value on the other. (To an initiated religious mind, the beast is a figural representation of the eucharist with its biblical source in Psalms 42:1.) But the painting treats both of these symbolic systems so elaborately that the faun assumes a grotesque, surreal appearance. It centers a moment of pictorial excess, literally foregrounded, where the authority of art as an order of independent and deliberate creation is being represented. The "two houses" of the picture, whether interpreted in moral or in stylistic terms, are joined together under that authority.

The sonnet that Rossetti wrote to accompany the picture replicates this dynamic. The "two houses" reemerge through the division between octave and sestet: the former is spoken by the Magdalene's worldly lover, calling her back; the latter by the Magdalene, who longs for Christ. The sonnet as a unit joins these two parts, and the "double work" of picture and sonnet dramatizes the presence of art as the authoritative agency in the entire field of action. In that respect one wants to note an important moment in the sonnet, for the Magdalene's desire receives a remarkable form of expression when she speaks of "my Bridegroom's face / That draws me to him" (9–10). Playing on the word *draws,* Rossetti makes an arresting claim for the drawing discussed by the sonnet. The words lie open to various readings, but all assert the spiritual authority of a certain kind of art — and of this picture particularly.

That authority was something quite different from the religious and ethical claims implicit in the work of the other early Pre-Raphaelites, and of Hunt's work in particular. All the early PRB claimed to favor "truth to nature," and all found inspiration in the linear clarity and purity of colors of the Italian primitives. But Rossetti was also fascinated by the devotional power of these painters. Their vibrant and intense colors seemed possessed by vital signifying forces that Rossetti sought to recover in his own work. Similarly, he saw a meaning in the nonillusionistic symbolic techniques of dugento and trecento primitive art. The depth of his response is clear in the elaborately programmatic quality of a picture like *The Girlhood of Mary Virgin,* as we have seen. Even more revealing, however, is that painting's immediate successor and companion work, the *Ecce Ancilla Domini!* — a more provocative work that we must examine still further.

If looked at from the perspective of Cimabue or even Giotto, the sight lines of the picture present no difficulty. On the other hand, if studied through the illusionistic conventions of Albertian perspective, the painting will appear hopelessly confused, and will produce a comment like Waugh's, that Rossetti "knew nothing of perspective."[5] But in a painting like this, as in so many primitive pictures, recessive space and volume are constructed in distinct areas of the work. These areas are not forced to cohere into a single, systematically organized spatial illusion. So we are drawn into the painting at different angles. The discrete spatial moments focusing our attention shift and change in Rossetti's picture, and when these shifts occur our sense of the general organization of the picture also shifts.

Look again at the lily held by the angel. The stem defines the strongest diagonal in the picture, and the stemmed flower is carefully located at the picture's golden mean. Because of the peculiar arrangement of the planes and sightlines, however, an arresting ambiguity appears at this crucial location: in one view the stem is pointing toward the womb of the seated Virgin, but in another it lies athwart her, with the lower part of the stem set forward of the upper. That central ambiguity indexes all the other estranged sightlines and localized compositional areas. The stand holding the embroidered lily, like the angel's lily, functions in two perspectives simultaneously: one along the lily's disharmonic diagonal, the other along the sightlines defined by the floor. The window's recess draws both window aperture and back wall out of perspective with the floor lines and the bed, but with a clear symbolic intent: to set the outer blue "sky" along the lily's diagonal, thus angling that sky toward the Virgin; and (in a very different spatial arrangement) to put angel and Virgin in parallel planes with parallel blue backgrounds.[6]

The dominance of white and white shadings in virtually all the planes further erodes the sense of spatial recession. There is clear volume in the picture, but as the angel's lily so dramatically shows, the volume is ambiguous and finally abstract, a nonrealistic space for arranging various kinds of symbolic relations. Rossetti was quite aware that Whistler's later, famous "white paintings" took their inspiration from this picture's formal experiment with the color white.

Like *The Girlhood of Mary Virgin,* this picture is therefore another polemical work. In point of expressive force, however, it goes well beyond Rossetti's first oil painting, which seems formal and brainy beside

Ecce Ancilla Domini! Two things in *Ecce Ancilla Domini!* lift the painting past its strictly conceptual goals. First, we get a distinct sense of the catastrophic effect of a divine intervention in nature in the contrast between the hieratic figure of the angel and the contorted body of the Virgin, with her brooding and haunted eyes. Second, the painting's strange series of white variations seems oddly obsessional, suggesting the presence of inexplicable yet plainly purposive agency.

Those qualities in the painting connect it to some of Rossetti's most important later works. The Tate Gallery *Beata Beatrix* (1864–1870), for example, as Gabriele Reithmiller has observed, is structured "in compact compartments . . . to emphasize contrasting color fields" rather than to support realistic representation.[7] The composition is by planes. Foreground and background are organized not by perspective but by emblematic relations. Indeed, Rossetti deliberately sought an organization after the manner of what he called "the old Italian painters" (in his letter to Ellen Heaton of 19 May 1863) when he took up his work on the picture after he had set it aside.[8] His symbolist technique, so unlike those masters in so many ways, should not obscure that Rossetti sought compositional models in primitive art.

Some of Rossetti's work—*Dantis Amor* (1859), for instance, or *Astarte Syriaca* (1877)—take Rossetti's anti-illusionism to remarkable extremes. These pictures are not so much dispersed into alternate lines of sight—Venus seen from many points of view—as thrown into a kind of reverse perspective. They are works treating wholly visionary realities. They project an iconic or totemic quality, as if they had nothing to do with representations or the idea of representation. Radically surfaced at every point, *Dantis Amor* nonetheless seems held before us by some gravitational field whose vortex lies at the center of the image we see, but far back, "behind" the picture. The overlapping gold and white discs at the top of *Astarte Syriaca* crown Astarte's head in some unimagined barbaric halo. We have no language for such a vision, where Albertian geometries are clearly beside the point. It is a disturbing, perhaps even a frightening picture. Lacking the erotic argument of Rossetti's late work, *Dantis Amor* does not threaten its viewer. Nonetheless, it stands in a similar posture of absolute refusal toward illusionistic lines of sight.

The equivalences that connect these two pictures are important for understanding the imaginative coherence of Rossetti's work in general.

They stand on either side of a famous watershed in his life, 1860, when he completed *Bocca Baciata,* which he had begun the previous summer on commission for George Boyce. The picture inaugurated his effort to incorporate into his work the procedures of sixteenth-century Venetian painting, especially Titian and Veronese. It marks as well his growing inclination to return to oil after ten years' concentration on drawing and watercolor.

The time had been well spent. Indeed, many regard it as the period when he produced his greatest pictorial work. With the encouragement of Ruskin and Madox Brown in particular, Rossetti developed — as he well knew and as later scholars have acknowledged — his highly original style with watercolor, at once ideal and aggressively physical. But the medium set a limit to what he could do along these lines, so when *Bocca Baciata* appeared, its breakthrough character was apparent. Five years later, after Rossetti had been pursuing his new line through a series of pictures in both oil and watercolor *(Fair Rosamund, Fazio's Mistress, Lucrezia Borgia),* he and Ruskin suffered through their painful falling-out over the latest of these new works, the *Venus Verticordia.* Ruskin's disapproval repeats more or less exactly what Hunt said of *Bocca Baciata* when he saw the painting just after it had been finished early in 1860. In a letter to Thomas Combe, Hunt wrote: "Most people admire it very much and speak to me of it as a triumph of our school. I have strong prejudices and may be influenced by them in this respect so dont let my opinion prevent you from looking at it attentively to judge it justly. After which caution I will not scruple to say that it impresses me as very remarkable in power of execution — but still more remarkable for gross sensuality of a revolting kind. . . . Rossetti is advocating as a principle mere gratification of the eye and if any passion at all — the animal passion to be the aim of Art."[9] Hunt's reaction to Rossetti's new work exposes their sharply divergent views about art. These differences always existed despite their common involvement with Pre-Raphaelitism and their public association with a particular "school" of work.

What looked like coarseness and sensuality to Hunt and Ruskin, however, was to Rossetti the index of an idea (and an ideal) that had possessed him since the mid-1840s, and that received its classic expression in the synthetic idea of the union of soul, body, lover, artist, and God. The best-known formulation of that idea came in the 1871 sonnet "Heart's

Hope." But two years before, Rossetti fashioned an interesting variant of the same thought. It comes as the climactic line in his poem "Love-Lily": "Whose speech Truth knows not from her thought, / Nor Love her body from her soul" (ll. 23–24). In this case the synthetic event incorporates key linguistic and intellectual elements.

The passage is perhaps an even more telling one because of the poem in which it occurs. It opens with this stanza:

> Between the hands, between the brows,
>   Between the lips of Love-Lily,
> A spirit is born whose birth endows
>   My blood with fire to burn through me;
> Who breathes upon my gazing eyes,
>   Who laughs and murmurs in mine ear,
> At whose least touch my colour flies,
>   And whom my life grows faint to hear.

A pair of oblique allusions runs through this text — one to the stilnovista preoccupation with the mechanics of the soul's experience of love, which Dante exploits throughout the *Vita Nuova* in particular; and the other to the great symbolistic tale of love by E. T. A. Hoffman, "Der Goldene Topf," where a Fire Lily presides over a love initiation that is at once completely sensual and completely ideal. Rossetti's Love-Lily is a reimagination of Hoffman's Fire Lily. The Blessed Damozel of 1847 incarnates the same imagination, as the damozel's prayer to "Christ the Lord" makes very clear:

> Only to live as once on earth
>   With Love, — only to be,
> As then awhile, for ever now
>   Together, I and he. (129–132)

A text like that shows why *Bocca Baciata* does not mark Rossetti's turn from "monastic sentiment to Epicureanism," as Hunt later declared.[10] Its ideas grow out of a long-standing set of Rossettian preoccupations. But a shift has taken place that is glossed in the title of that painting, which quotes a part of a significant Boccaccian text: "A kissed mouth loses none of its freshness; it rather renews itself, like the moon." Two things are notable here. First, the allusion glosses the title of the picture, whose wordplay signals its purely aesthetic significance through its doubled homage to Boccaccio and (as we saw earlier) Titian. Second, the Boccaccian proverb truncated in the title culminates Tale 7 of Day 2 of the *Decameron*, the story of Alatiel and her numerous lovers. Far from being punished or even criticized for her promiscuity, Alatiel emerges as a figure of ideal love-permanence in a world riven by the conflicts of male desire. Here was suggestive allegory indeed for a man who never thought of "sensuality" except in ideal terms. What "loses none of its freshness" are works of art like Hoffman's, Titian's, Boccaccio's; and their vitality, as well as their intellectual force, rests in their sustained physical power.

Intellectual Beauties

From about 1860 Rossetti began to explore how this embodied condition of soul functions as the engine of the spirit's life and development. The characteristic form of this move came in the series of obsessional portraits of women that preoccupied him for the rest of his life. Whereas his earlier figures of women typically appear at full length, in compositions organized by simple geometric forms and with space to show the color fields — that is, the compositional structure — in the clearest way, from 1860 the pictorial space gets exhausted in a face or bust or half-length figure. As the focus grows tighter, the pictures seem to invite more local dynamic forms. Composition by color field is not abandoned, however, and the new more complex shapes are still organized hieratically. Neither does the symbolistic apparatus cast about Rossetti's early pictures disappear. In the later work it thickens into spreading draperies and engulfing floral ornament. Through it all looms the face and upper torso of Lady Beauty, Lady Lilith, and her numerous avatars.

How are we to read these imposing forms? An acute remark by Robert Rosenblum about Carstens's work is helpful. In *The Heroes in the Tent of Achilles,* he observes, "the figures are placed [in] an idea of space, rather than an illusion of space."[11] Nothing could be more true of Rossetti's work in general, but it carries special force in the case of the portraits (most of which are in fact portraits only in a formal sense). Like Alfred Hitchcock with his actors, Rossetti chooses models for specific intellectual ends. They are stimuli to lead him to see the visionary forms of his desire with greater precision. This is why forms of nature in Rossetti's work are never pursued for their own sake. His object is always what Shelley called Intellectual Beauty. This is also why critics regularly say that he is most interesting for his ideas — including his purely technical and pictorial ideas — than for his execution, as Martin Hardie remarks. (And here the contrast with Millais — a virtually brainless artist, though a shrewd technician — is all but complete.) On the other hand, Rossetti's intellectual qualities have little in common with those of artists like Poussin or David. His precursors — Flaxman, Fuseli, Blake — underscore the romanticism of his ideas, which lead him to undertake artistic procedures of an essentially magical kind. When critics speak of the fetishist structure of Rossetti's work, they implicitly acknowledge this thaumaturgy. And of course Rossetti himself often emphasizes his own spiritual commitments, not least openly in the late sonnet that names his "Astarte Syriaca" an "amulet, talisman, and oracle." The Syrian Venus performs a cultic service, opening doors of perception to a world of otherwise inaccessible yet primary realities. In the case of this painting, the figure of Jane Morris — Rossetti's model — performs a related, more immediate function for Rossetti as he tries to communicate the idea of magical Being, the idea of this kind of magical event.[12]

Rossetti's portraits are thus revelations of embodied soul, "reflecting her in different views." The multiplicity is important. Critics sometimes map the exaltation of these pictures along a goddess/whore dialectic, or perhaps within the more mythic and Blakean Jerusalem/Babylon dichotomy. Such moves, as we know, are licensed by Rossetti's famous pair of double works *Sibylla Palmifera* and *Lady Lilith,* sometimes referenced through their sonnets' latest titles, "Soul's Beauty" and "Body's Beauty." Useful for certain general critical purposes, these dichotomies can also obscure essential features of the actual works. The two "beauties" do not represent moral ideas, for example, as they would for Hunt, although in Rossetti they can and do draw moral problems into intellectual presence, as we see so clearly in a poem like "Jenny." To appreciate how Rossetti works in and through such forms of thought we shouldn't attentuate his "ideas" — his imaginative works — into conceptual categories. Doubtless Turner's storms could be usefully classified, but the pictures would remain to be seen. So if we observe Rossetti exploring (and hence acknowledging) such a cultural formation, we might judge that he found it a scene of wonderment, inexhaustibly interesting. The dialectic points toward a question rather than an answer. One thinks perhaps of Wordsworth, who himself imagined his masterpiece *The Prelude* within a dialectic of Beauty and Fear. But Wordsworth's dialectic is no more an explanation of *The Prelude* than are the glosses to "The Rime of the Ancient Mariner" or Rossetti's sonnets for his different pictures. All such materials have been summoned into larger imaginative conceptions. Rossetti's "portraits," like Turner's storms, must be searched for their integrities.

To paint a picture like *Astarte Syriaca* is to approach what the accompanying sonnet calls "Mystery." The purpose, at once erotic and Faustian, governs Rossetti's work, but can be traced with particular clarity in his Venetian oils. These pictures initiate Rossetti's deepened exploration of the great subject he first took up through Dante. With Titian and Veronese, however, Rossetti discovered new vocabularies for the contradictions he was pursuing. Ruskin endured this new line of work for several years, but when he saw *Venus Verticordia* in 1865, he revolted at what he called its "coarseness." Recognizing the "enormous power" of this new style, Ruskin deplores its general tendency and purpose: "Certain conditions of non-sentiment . . . underlie all you are doing — now — and . . . make your work, compared to what it used to be, what Fanny's face is to Lizzie's."[13] The final comparison could not be more telling. In fact, the model for the picture was not Fanny Cornforth but a woman Rossetti met by chance in the street, a "beautiful cook."[14] Nonetheless, Ruskin's reaction was entirely correct, for the woman was "beautiful" in the Fanny mode, "Body's Beauty." And "non-sentiment" typifies the picture because Rossetti is using it to reimagine the traditional moral value of its signs. Setting the head of Venus in a Christian glory forces one to reconsider its entire symbology. So in this picture the elaborate floral decorations do not easily translate either through realistic or iconographical filters. These are flowers culled from a place unknown alike to corporeal eye and rational mind — a place Rossetti called the "bower of unimagined flower and tree" ("Love's Lovers," 11). They are drawn from the coverts of the bird placed — Chagall-blue, and posed in motion — in the upper right corner of the picture.

Though by no means one of his great works, *Venus Verticordia* is without question one of his most interesting exactly because of the ambiguities by which it is so clearly riven. Rossetti made several versions of the painting, and in each case he used a different model. Much to his brother's disappointment, he painted out the face of the cook and substituted Alexa Wilding, a model he regularly used to idealize the sexuality of his imaginary portraits. Another version used the voluptuous Fanny Cornforth, and the wife of Walter Knewstub, Rossetti's assistant in 1864, sat for a third — now untraced — picture. These changes testify to one of Rossetti's most characteristic patterns of behavior: using his work as a means to explore its own meanings.

These pictorial shape-changings occur as well throughout his written work. *Venus Verticordia* is one of Rossetti's double works, and the accompanying sonnet replicates the contradictions we've been tracing through the picture. When Rossetti was preparing to republish the sonnet in his 1870 *Poems,* his brother suggested that he might want to alter the title. William Michael pointed out that according to the lexicographer John Lemprière, *Verticordia* signified a Venus who "could turn the hearts of women to cultivate chastity. If this is at all correct [she is] just the contrary sort of Venus from the one you contemplate."[15] Rossetti changed the title of the sonnet to the more neutral "Venus" in the 1870 *Poems.* But that was not the end of the matter. When he re-collected the sonnet, in the 1881 *Poems,* he changed the title back to its original.

The point is that Rossetti is searching for a picture, or rather for a pictorial method, that will open itself to "different views." He wants to paint the *idea* of Venus, just as Chiaro dell' Erma wanted to paint an image of his soul. Such a picture would incarnate simultaneously all the reflected forms of the primal goddess, would evoke her presence under every name by which she has been named. Nor is Rossetti meaning to range only across the dialectical space we measure between the Pandemian and the Uranian Venus. His haloed goddess is a syncretic figure, as Jewish as she is pagan, as modern as ancient. Not without reason do we see through the design of this picture a witty and perhaps disturbing reference to conventional representations of the Enthroned Virgin. For this being is indeed the Queen of Heaven, though the heaven she knows has scarcely been imagined.

It is a heaven we glimpse in the ambiguities of Rossetti's sonnet, a labyrinth of suggestions triggered in the opening lines:

> She hath the apple in her hand for thee,
> Yet almost in her heart would hold it back;
> She muses, with her eyes upon the track
> Of that which in their spirit they can see.

The general context of this scene is a pagan one, as the sestet emphasizes and the picture shows. The offered apple, consequently, recalls the apple of discord. But Rossetti supplies that "view" of the matter and then torques it. By representing his Venus-figure offering the apple — in this case to the reader/viewer of the double work — Rossetti associates the apple of discord, which Paris awarded to Venus, with the apple of the Tree of Knowledge, which Eve offered to Adam. This move, conflating the Judaeo-Christian ethos with its pagan antecedents, explodes the traditional signification of the apple. The emblem of pleasure and beauty is returned to us as an emblem of secret, perhaps still forbidden, knowledge.

The rhetorical structure of Rossetti's work directly addresses, and addresses itself to, the reader/viewer. The work thereby makes its own action a central subject. In that context, the syncretic treatment of the mythic materials implicitly supplies what Plato called for in the *Republic:* an argument for the relation between beauty and knowledge. Plato wanted a rational argument, but Rossetti insists that the argument must be executed in an aesthetic form and medium, as it is here.

We track this argument largely through Rossetti's darkly shifting figural forms. The sonnet gives premonitions of social catastrophe, and the picture too troubles, like Pater's *Mona Lisa,* eroding the Burkean distinction between the sublime and the beautiful. William Sharp's contemporary description of the painting — which probably reflects Rossetti's own views — is much to the point: "The Venus of this picture is no Aphrodite, fresh and white and jubilant from the foam of Idalian seas, nor is she Love incarnate or human passion; but she is a queen of Love who loves not herself, a desire that is unsatiable and remorseless, absolute, supreme."[16] Fascinating and mysterious, this Venus is born of these imaginative particulars as they double and redouble themselves in this double work of art. The argument doesn't ask us to decide, from the experience of this work, that this Venus is a *figura* of Art. It asks us instead to recognize an Idea of Venus because she has been raised up through an imaginative action, and *as* she has been raised. The sensuous forms of text and picture carry us to a knowledge, a realm of Idea, that escapes the limits of the mind's conceptual and thematic forms.

This work is not just "Venus surrounded by mirrors, reflecting her in different views." It gathers itself into an idea of what such a work must be. Indeed, it becomes that idea because, like Chiaro's soul-picture, it fleshes itself out, because it individuates itself through a Scotist-like *haecceitas*.

Rossetti's numerous abstractions ("Vain Virtues," "Lost Days") and allegorical forms ("Love, Life, and Death") are thus to be understood as instances of what philosophers call universals. To make them intelligible ideas (rather than simply conceptual categories) Rossetti engulfs them with particulars, hurling them into the realm of desire (or what Scotus calls the Will). Consequently, the famous Rossetti Woman, so-called, is a critical abstraction that distills, and usually distorts, the Idea that Rossetti has recurrently in view and that the abstraction itself means to locate. The distortion comes about when we forget that the "Idea" of The Rossetti Woman can be known *as Idea* only when she assumes intelligible — that is to say, intuitive and apparitional — form. Engaged at an abstract extreme she appears in flight, a Dantean figure in Botticellian drapery:

> This is that Lady Beauty, in whose praise
>   Thy voice and hand shake still — long known to thee
>   By flying hair and fluttering hem — the beat
>   Following her daily on thy heart and feet,
> How passionately and irretrievably,
> In what fond flight, how many ways and days!
>   ("Soul's Beauty," 9–14)

But she is no less magnificently present in "Lady Lilith," "Monna Vanna," "Veronica Veronese," "Fazio's Mistress," although in these cases the "views" are more worldly ones. Like Lady Lilith, all remain "young, while the world is old," even as they come to us in the decadent forms their eternities do not disdain.

Monna Vanna, for example, appears the very emblem of voluptuous modernity, as Rossetti and his critical surrogate, F. G. Stephens, both point out.[17] Tellingly, the painting passed through three different titles, and the received one wasn't Rossetti's final choice. The first title, *Venus Veneta*, was specifically chosen to make a contrast with *Venus Verticordia* — the latter, as Rossetti remarks, set dominantly with "classical" accoutrements, the former meant to suggest "the Venetian ideal of female beauty."[18] In this perspective the painting is, like *Veronica Veronese*, a symbol — or rather a Peircean index — of a specific kind of artistic practice. This initial imagination of the picture is important for throwing into relief the fluidity of Rossettian dialectics. Imagined wholly within itself, *Venus Verticordia* plays its classicism off against its more recessive biblical elements within an ethnomythological context. Paired with *Venus Veneta*, however, the entire frame of reference shifts to the historical, aesthetic, and economic.

When Rossetti titled the picture *Monna Vanna*, he was partly thinking of Cavalcanti, and partly of the association to the idea of "vanity" that he could evoke, in a contemporary context, from the abbreviated name of Cavalcanti's mistress. But when his brother pointed out that such a title would undermine the picture's central concern with art and modernity, Rossetti agreed and changed the title once again, this time to *Belcolore*, fair color. This word virtually labels the painting's programmatic character, as Rossetti's comment on it shows: "Belcolore had served as a female name in Venice."[19] The new title has exactly the same character as the title of *Veronica Veronese*, which translates as "true Veronesian image." In each case Rossetti turns his picture into a visual metaphor for art itself by drawing an equivalence between a painting style and a figural representation.

These changes of title help to elucidate Rossetti's remarkable ability to carry out an argument with images and purely pictorial materials. If we think only about *Monna Vanna*'s color composition, for example, we can follow one thread of this argument and even come to realize some of its larger implications. In this painting white and gold — dominant colors — become disassociated from the spiritualized values they so often possess in Rossetti's work — for example, in *Sancta Lilias* or his two early oils. Here we want to read the colors in relation, for example, to a picture like *Lucrezia Borgia*, which is similarly dynamic and worldly (where *Sancta Lilias* and pictures like it are hieratic and transcendental). These differentials point up a signal quality of Rossetti's pictures in general: that the moral value, in a referential sense, of any pictorial element

The Girlhood of Mary Virgin (oil on canvas, 1849; 32¾ × 25¾ in.: Tate
Gallery). Frederick Hollyer photographic reproduction (ca. 1880–85) of
the original oil. Reproduced with permission, Delaware Art Museum,
Samuel and Mary R. Bancroft Memorial.

Fazio's Mistress (oil on canvas, 1863; 17 × 15 in.: Tate Gallery). Frederick Hollyer mezzotint reproduction (ca. 1880–85) of the original watercolor. Reproduced with permission, Delaware Art Museum, Samuel and Mary R. Bancroft Memorial.

Bocca Baciata (oil on canvas, 1859; 13¼ × 12 in.: Boston Museum of Fine Arts). Reproduced with permission, Museum of Fine Arts, Boston.

Monna Vanna (oil on canvas, 1866; 35 × 34 in.: Tate Gallery). Reproduced with permission, Tate Gallery, London.

Lady Lilith (watercolor, 1867; 20 × 16⅞ in.: Metropolitan Museum of Art, New York). Reproduced from the Medici Society colored engraving (ca. 1905) with permission, Delaware Art Museum, Samuel and Mary R. Bancroft Memorial.

Beata Beatrix (oil on canvas, 1864; 34 × 26 in.: Tate Gallery). Reproduced with permission, Tate Gallery, London.

The Blessed Damozel (oil on canvas, 1875–78; 68½ × 37 in.: Fogg Museum, Harvard University). Reproduced with permission, Harvard University Art Museums, Fogg Art Museum, Bequest of Grenville L. Winthrop.

The Damsel of the San Graal, early version (watercolor, 1857; 13⅞ × 4⅝ in.: Tate Gallery). Frederick Hollyer mezzotint reproduction (ca. 1880–85) of the original watercolor. Reproduced with permission, Delaware Art Museum, Samuel and Mary R. Bancroft Memorial.

The Blue Closet (watercolor, 1857; 13½ × 9¾ in.: Tate Gallery). Frederick Hollyer mezzotint reproduction (ca. 1880–85) of the original watercolor. Reproduced with permission, Delaware Art Museum, Samuel and Mary R. Bancroft Memorial.

The Tune of Seven Towers (watercolor, 1857; 12⅜ × 14⅜ in.: Tate Gallery). Frederick Hollyer mezzotint reproduction (ca. 1880–85) of the original watercolor. Reproduced with permission, Delaware Art Museum, Samuel and Mary R. Bancroft Memorial.

Sancta Lilias (oil on panel, 1874; 19 × 18 in.: Tate Gallery). Reproduced with permission, Tate Gallery, London.

Ecce Ancilla Domini! (oil on canvas mounted on panel, 1850; 28⅝ × 16½ in.: Tate Gallery). Reproduced from the Medici Society colored engraving (ca. 1905) with permission, Delaware Art Museum, Samuel and Mary R. Bancroft Memorial.

The Wedding of St. George and the Princess Sabra (watercolor, 1857; 13½ × 13½ in.: Tate Gallery). Frederick Hollyer mezzotint reproduction (ca. 1880–85) of the original watercolor. Reproduced with permission, Delaware Art Museum, Samuel and Mary R. Bancroft Memorial.

Astarte Syriaca (oil on canvas, 1877; 72 × 42 in.: Manchester City Art Galleries). Reproduced with permission, Manchester City Art Galleries.

Dantis Amor (oil on panel, 1860; 29½ × 32 in.: Tate Gallery). Reproduced with permission, Tate Gallery, London.

Lucrezia Borgia (watercolor, 1860–61; 17 × 9¾ in.: Tate Gallery). Frederick Hollyer mezzotint reproduction (ca. 1880–85) of the original watercolor. Reproduced with permission, Delaware Art Museum, Samuel and Mary R. Bancroft Memorial.

Venus Verticordia (oil on canvas, 1864–68; 38⅝ × 27½ in.: Russell-Cotes Art Gallery, Bournemouth.) Reproduced with permission, Russell-Cotes Art Gallery and Museum, and the Bridgeman Art Library.

How They Met Themselves (watercolor, 1860; 10½ × 8¼ in.: Fitzwilliam Museum). Frederick Hollyer mezzotint reproduction (ca. 1880–85) of the original watercolor. Reproduced with permission, Delaware Art Museum, Samuel and Mary R. Bancroft Memorial.

lies open to an indefinite series of variations, including variations of contradiction; and that all pictorial elements, in an aesthetic sense, maintain a reference to an ideal order, no matter what the reference may be perceived to be from a moral or historical point of view.

"Chinese Puzzles and Japanese Monsters"

Rossetti's turn to Venetian models overlaps the period of his involvement with Whistler and his discovery of Japanese art.[20] The linearity of Japanese art, its intimate style, and its close relation to the book arts suggest connections to Rossetti's earlier work rather than to his growing involvement with oils and the development of his monumental fantasy portraits. The Japanese influence is important, however, because it helps us to understand the relation between these two phases of Rossetti's work, and to explain why the Venetians interested him in the first place.

When Rossetti began studying art, the Venetian school had a particular academic valence. Its work was infamous, particularly in English readings of art history, as decorative and intellectually superficial, an art purely (or impurely) for the eye. Hunt's revulsion from *Bocca Baciata* replicates that general way of thinking. Ruskin's critique, more academically measured, is even more revealing; for Ruskin had become a key figure in arguing against the prevailing view of the Venetians. He warned Rossetti in no uncertain terms that he didn't understand Venetian painting, either its virtues or its faults, and that consequently he was leading himself into bad practices. Rossetti, he charged, was following not nature but "sensational purposes."[21]

Already disapproving of Whistler, Ruskin connected these purposes with Rossetti's recent fascination for Japanese art, an interest he picked up from his new American friend. We glimpse Ruskin's view in a letter he wrote to Rossetti at the height of their 1865 collision. Trying to defuse the situation, he invited Rossetti to dinner, "and, when you come, we'll look at things that we both like. You shall bar Parma [Correggio], and I, Japan; and we'll look at Titian, John Bellini, Albert Dürer, and Edward Jones."[22] It was a sweet letter, but it came too late, in all respects. When he subsequently came to reflect on Rossetti's career after the artist's death, Ruskin remembered this period as the beginning of Rossetti's artistic debasement. But instead of associating Rossetti's faults with the

Venetian art they both admired — Ruskin's admiration being, of course, the "correct" one — he shifted the blame to the Far East. After the wonderful 1850s watercolors, inspired by stained glass and those missals Rossetti had borrowed from Ruskin, the artist has "willfully perverted and lacerated his powers of conception with Chinese puzzles and Japanese monsters . . . fit for nothing but a fire screen."[23] In short, Rossetti had turned from painting after nature to painting as decoration. Indeed, he had approached Venetian art not as another model of painting after nature, but as if it *were* "merely" decorative.

"Draw only what you see," Rossetti used to tell his pupils at the Working Men's College in the mid-1850s — what they saw either with or through their eyes. Like Blake, however, his principal object was to see through rather than with. Stained glass, quattrocentro art, illuminated books were passports to imagination, not to nature, as well as practical guides for rendering transnatural forms in articulate ways. The foundation of Rossetti's visionary watercolors is purely decorative and nonrepresentational. This is not to say that they are abstract, however, except in a formal sense. Rossetti's decorative style, as Pater understood, is absorbed in a symbolist (but not a symbolic) *gout de l'infini*. Speaking for the artist, Stephens described *The Blue Closet* as "an exercise intended to symbolize the association of colour with music."[24] Rossetti himself often spoke of his work in similarly Aesthetic terms (as when he called *Fazio's Mistress* "chiefly a piece of colour").

The fantasy watercolors of the 1850s, in particular the famous medieval pictures, are nothing more (or less) than meditations on composition by fields of pure colors. When the subject is completely recondite — for instance, in pictures like *The Blue Closet* or *The Tune of Seven Towers* — the colors and their formal relations come to seem the scripts of an uncanny language, as if such works indexed a system of communication whose residues we glimpse in heraldic devices. This effect is gained precisely by not choosing to organize the pictures abstractly but by constructing instead a determinate narrative organization, an eventual scene so precisely articulated that (we believe) it must be true, somewhere, somehow. The fact that such pictures record (as it were) unknown events — one thinks of Blake's similarly bizarre prophetic narratives — is exactly the point. They thereby become for us transports to a world where colors and their relations seem the elements of a language.

These pictures implicitly argue that ornamental forms possess secret meanings and a power of nonconceptual communication. Largely reserving the subjects of these pictures to a Christian horizon, however legendary, Rossetti intimates an ideal or spiritual character for their meanings. With the appearance of *Bocca Baciata* the horizon expands to include subjects and materials of very different kinds — secular and even pagan materials, "coarse," commercial, voluptuous. But these worldly and sensuous, not to say sensual, faces and forms come to us radiant with the same kind of surface energies Rossetti developed in his 1850s watercolors. As early as 1851, in the *Lucrezia Borgia* watercolor, we see forecasts of the Venetian work he will take up so resolutely nine years later. The *Lucrezia Borgia* is particularly notable because it involved a deliberate study of the expressive power of decoration — in this case, of the Borgia's rich dress, which Rossetti modeled after a dress of the fifteenth-century Comptesse de Cellant that he knew from Bonnard's book of *Costumes*. Rossetti often used Bonnard as a source for his decorative representations.[25]

The dispute about Venetian art between Ruskin and Rossetti goes to a foundational difference between the way the two men saw nature, artistic practice, and their relation. Ruskin held firmly to a representational position. Empirical reality — Nature — called the artist to disciplines of imaginative precision. Art's function was to reveal the wonders of Great Creating Nature. Rossetti, by contrast, took a decidedly Blakean line. Nature for him is a set of imaginative constructions — "a fire screen" in two senses: both a form of artistic practice and a Neoplatonic philosophical conception of what Blake called "our mortal & perishing nature."[26] So where Ruskin saw "puzzles and monsters" — artistic and decorative forms intervening, as it were, between the viewer and the empirical truth underlying the images — Rossetti perceived elementary acts of imagination: a "seeing through the eye" in the full sense of that splendid Blakean pun.

We are not sure precisely which Chinese or Japanese works Rossetti cried up to Ruskin. But some of the devices characteristic of Eastern graphic art can be readily seen in Blake's illuminated books. When Rossetti worked on the Gilchrist *Life of William Blake* (1863, 1880), for example, he helped Mrs. Gilchrist choose the decorative illustrations for the two volumes. Among these are some striking puzzles and monsters.

Plate 7 of *America* is paradigmatic.[27] The balance at the left makes a kind of frame for the lettering. The problem is that the image leaves open two possibilities of vision: either to see the balance beams at a level with each other, and hence pictorially foreshortened, or to see them as radically unbalanced, and hence drawn on the plane of the lettered text. The whole composition of this plate shifts into different arrangements depending on how we choose to see this elementary relation. That the visual ambiguity is central to the subject of this plate, and of *America* in general, hardly needs to be pointed out, any more than we have to emphasize Blake's shrewdly imaginative choice of the image of the balance to make its statement about how one perceives and measures perception. The plate could easily be read as a gloss on the famous proverb of Hell: "Bring out number weight & measure in a year of dearth."

This way of proceeding treats representational forms in a decorative mode. To Ruskin's mind it ends up as puzzles and those monstrous, unnam'd forms that populate all of Blake's work. But to Rossetti it demonstrated another way of breaking the referential spell of images, replicating what he learned from the anti-illusionist art of the quattrocentro. A decorative style makes a self-display of an artistic practice, turning its work to an example of an idea-that-is-an-action.

Rossetti's turn to Venetian models, then, involves an act of extreme artistic self-consciousness. Just because he had always been a decorative artist, this move forced him to think deeply about the epistemological status of artistic images. In the great fantasy pictures of the 1850s Rossetti could, so to speak, play in the fields of the Lord. The question of their representational status could be set aside. The same was not possible when he plunged into that stronghold of representational art, portraiture, via the sensational work of the Venetians. No one should be surprised that his pictures in this new mode were labyrinths of self-reflection from the start.

One of the earliest, *Fazio's Mistress* (1863), is in part an allegory of his own artistic progress and preoccupations. As we have seen, the painting incorporates, or calls out, three different worlds: modernity, sixteenth-century Venice, and the thirteenth-century Florence of Dante. The original frame for the picture, designed by Rossetti, had been inscribed with part of the famous canzone that Fazio degli Uberti wrote and that Rossetti turned to brilliant translation in his 1861 volume *The Early Italian*

Poets. These three points of reference map the world of Rossetti's imaginative interests.

As usual with Rossetti, the choice of subject for such a picture was not casual, and two matters are particularly important. First, Uberti occupied a significant place in Rossetti's conception of the world of Dante and his circle. The canzone referenced by Rossetti's painting was so admired that scholars sometimes attributed it to Dante. But the poem's "style . . . is more particularizing than accords with the practise of Dante," Rossetti observes in his notes to *The Early Italian Poets*, and in this respect "its manner is quite his" — that is to say, quite like the author of Uberti's most ambitious work, the *Dittamondo*, or "The Song of the World." Rossetti spends some time discussing this work, whose technical faults weaken its "conception, which is a grand one": "In scheme it was intended as an earthly parallel to Dante's Sacred Poem, doing for this world what he did for the other. At Fazio's death it remained unfinished. . . . The whole earth (or rather all that was then known of it) is traversed, — its surface and its history, — ending with the Holy Land, and thus bringing Man's world as near as may be to God's; that is, to the point at which Dante's office begins. No conception could well be nobler" (*Works* [1911], 420). Uberti's "Mistress," a Veronese lady, stands in the same relation to his highest imaginative desires as Beatrice did to Dante's. Whatever she may have been in historical fact, Rossetti will also have seen her as a Neoplatonic figural form. In this case, however, as Rossetti's comments on the *Dittamondo* show, she is being cast as a figure of Body's Beauty, the counterpart of Dante's Beatrice, or what Rossetti called Soul's Beauty.

This frame of reference exposes the slightly disguised significance that the subject of "Fazio's Mistress" had for Rossetti. If we had such a "Portrait" as Fazio imagines in (and as) his canzone — if Fazio had made such a picture — it would have looked more like Titian's *Young Woman at Her Toilette* than like a Venus of Botticelli. That is Rossetti's argument in his painting, where it comes in the most literal way. For *Fazio's Mistress* was in fact consciously modeled after Titian's picture, which Rossetti had seen at least twice in Paris. And of course Titian, along with Venetian art in general, represented for Rossetti an Ubertian "Song of the World," fashioned in due time and in painterly terms.

This highly nuanced relation that Rossetti draws between Fazio and Titian takes us to a second topic of even greater significance. It centers

in the puzzles that Rossetti's double works tend to develop by playing at
the border of two forms of art. *Fazio's Mistress* supplies a remarkable example of what happens partly because the textuality of this double work
is a typical Rossettian translation. Reading the translation after the painting is like reading the poem of "The Blessed Damozel" after the paintings he subsequently executed under that title, or like reading the *Vita
Nuova* after seeing the *Beata Beatrix*. The pictures halt any inclination to
read the texts unequivocally. In the case of "His Portrait of His Lady, Angiola of Verona," we are held suspended forever between the duck of
Fazio's original and the rabbit of Rossetti's literalist reimagining. Often
unfaithful as translation, Rossetti's splendid poem discovers (literally) a
new life:

> I look at the crisp golden-threaded hair
>   Whereof, to thrall my heart, Love twists a net:
>   Using at times a string of pearls for bait,
>   And sometimes with a single rose therein.
> I look into her eyes which unaware
>   Through mine own eyes to my heart penetrate. . . . (1–6)

Is the text suggesting that it is itself the "Portrait" of the title, or are we
to imagine that it represents an actual painterly object? By Fazio? Surely
not. But by Rossetti? Perhaps, yes, at least partly. But once Rossetti has
been insinuated into this scene we are drawn within a Borgesian space of
flattened and overlapping planes of time. The vertigo redoubles when
the text enters the troubadour and stilnovista convention of psychic al-
legorization:

> Then my thought whispers: "Were thy body wound
>   Within those arms, as loving women's do,
>   In all thy veins were born a life made new
>   Which thou could find no language to declare.
>   Behold if any picture can compare
> With her just limbs, each fit in shape and size,
>   Or match her angel's colour like a pearl.
>   She is a gentle girl
> To see . . .

The text builds not uncertainties but multiplicities: multiple speakers, multiple subjects, multiple references. All are present simultaneously, as precisely articulated as the carved language, the sharp images that come and come again: .

> Soft as a peacock steps she, or as a stork
>   Straight on herself, taller and statelier:
>   'Tis a good sight how every limb doth stir
>   For ever in a womanly sweet way.
> "Open thy soul to see God's perfect work,"
>   (My thought begins afresh), "and look at her. . . . "

The figure of Fazio's mind is as determinately visible as the figure of Angiolina, or as the tropes that carry her presence to us. Even the general thought offered in the fourth line here gets affected by the "particularizing" style, as Rossetti aptly called it. But most remarkable is the way all these poetical forms seem suspended in a kind of shallow pictorial space, as in medieval miniatures, or primitive paintings, or—of course—in those Japanese prints Rossetti discovered years after he wrote this poem.

The same effect is gained in the accompanying picture, where three distinct levels of reference play together in the flattened space of the painting. The three levels might be named—in receding historical order—Fanny Cornforth, Titian, and a Song of the World. Each is a version of an ideal Rossetti named, more generically, Body's Beauty—three phases or ways of considering that form of the beautiful, three faces of Venus seen in different views. Taken together they constitute a kind of art that is at once puzzling and determinate, self-conscious yet monstrously fetishized. What is it that Rossetti is trying to do with these embrained and voluptuous constructions? Perhaps more important: why should we care?

Forbidden Knowledge

As we all know, the history of art after the death of Rossetti is dominated by various formalisms and methods of abstraction. I've tried to indicate how Rossetti's work contributed to these developments. But he shrinks back from the coming race in a number of important ways. His work is almost never ironical, for instance, which is surely one reason he did not like Manet. Even more significant, he was hostile to the professionalization of art. His attitude here is interesting and (therefore) ripe with paradox. For example, he clearly subscribes to romantic ideas about artistic inspiration. He is also extremely cash-conscious and markets his work assiduously. These complicated positions are further complicated by other, very different ideas. Most important is his lifelong passion for religious art, for an ideal of the *pictor ignotus* whose work knows nothing of that Renaissance pride in what Rossetti called the "soulless self-reflections of man's skill." The dazzling displays of that self-imagined second Renaissance we call Modernism — making it new and making sure that we all see how new it is — are already weighed and found wanting in Rossetti's severe balances. But as a religious artist Rossetti also appears — correctly, for in art all appearances are true — pagan, worldly, and fetishistic. In those respects we have no problem decoding his idealist and Neoplatonic forms through Freudian and Marxist models. Too easily, in fact. We want to remember, in this case particularly, that he cultivated an art of the inner standing point, where the acts of the artist — poet or painter — are as much the subject under study as any of its manifest, referential forms. Indeed, Rossetti makes the relation between these two phases or moments in the work of art one of his higher-order subjects. "Hand and Soul" makes this topic very clear, as it also shows how the subject necessarily brings forward the issue of imaginative failure in the most immediate and self-referencing way. For a man who could not draw or paint a convincing nude body, and who constructed labyrinthine obliquities, his work is startlingly naked and unguarded.

Negotiating these contradictions grew more and more difficult during the past one hundred or so years because of the rise of Modernism, and more particularly because of the coming to academic dominance of certain ways of thinking about imaginative works. On the other hand, should we desire to reimagine the cultural horizon framed by institutional Modernism, Rossetti becomes an interesting point of departure, as Moreau would be in a French connection. Both turned into forbidden subjects — not forbidden in any romantic sense, as Byron was once imagined "mad, bad and dangerous to know," but forbidden in a Neoclassical sense, as subjects unworthy of serious or informed interest. Subjects refused as Keats was famously refused by Lockhart in the *Quarterly Review*.

Think again about Rossetti's female portraits through the 1860s and 1870s. Emerging out of his early work with ornamental and surface forms, these figures discover their modernity by passing through Rossetti's Venice. They become what we behold — decorative objects, figures plucked from a society of the spectacle. But these images are not the Gibson and Vargas Girls fashioned by Renoir and Millais, they are the images Pater described in his famous Conclusion to *The Renaissance*, older than the rocks among which they sit, fully aware of their history and their hypocrite viewers. Lady Lilith is an image, a myth, a story — or what Ruskin thought she was, an imaginative monster. Not only (as has been said) a symbol of Art, she is an artifice, an artifact, she is *this* thing that Rossetti made as a painting and that he glossed in a companion sonnet, another image made in the image and likeness of an image:

> And still she sits, young while the earth is old,
>   And, subtly of herself contemplative,
>   Draws men to watch the bright web she can weave,
> Till heart and body and life are in its hold.

Rossetti holds nothing back from us, as the characteristic pun on the word *draws* makes so clear. *Lady Lilith* shows us a form of desire turned to a spectacle. But showing that — and showing it before a hermeneutics of suspicion thought to look for it — it shows more. This woman, image in paint and image in words, outstares our thought, "looking as if she were alive" in a demonic sense Browning would not have thought, nor dared, to represent. For if the duchess was a commodity to Browning's duke, she will become a thing of beauty, a joy forever, to everyone else, including Browning. Rossetti's uncanny gothic imagination sees its world very differently, sees itself projected through its world, standing within. So Rossetti brings out Lady Lilith the way Mary Shelley brings her monster out — self-aware and forcing a dialogue with the god who made her, Dr. Frankenstein, the man Baudelaire named "hypocrite lecteur."

Rossetti follows these forbidding thoughts by pursuing contradictions. This is why Ruskin defined Rossetti as a "grotesque" artist. Self-conscious about his contemporary situation as an artist, Rossetti identifies with retrograde models of artistic practice like Chiaro dell' Erma. He cleaves to certain forms of Realist illusion even as he pursues his decorative goals. These kinds of double allegiances give him the means for marking his images, including his portraits, as signs. The portraits are not signs of actual or even representative women — they are not strictly speaking portraits at all — but signs of "the image making faculty" itself and its erotic conventions. His poems about painting — like Fazio's "Portrait of His Lady" — literalize the argument, as we see through the sonnet "A Portrait," a poem with no correspondent picture.

> Lo! it is done. Above the enthroning throat
> The mouth's mould testifies of voice and kiss,
> The shadowed eyes remember and foresee.
> Her face is made her shrine. Let all men note
> That in all years (O Love, thy gift is this!)
> They that would look on her must come to me.

That is to say, to this sonnet, whose textual voice figures itself as an imaginary portrait. The clear celebratory mood of the sonnet participates deeply in its splendid deceptions, which are also represented (but now only secretly) as self-deceptions, to be exposed as such by the sequence of sonnets, "The House of Life," where the whole painful tale of the fragile gifts of Love gets unfolded.

In the paintings, as in the work of Renoir and Millais, the opulence of the images brings an implicit critique of what Marx at that very moment was calling "commodity fetishism." Rossetti's critique, though it comes in aesthetic forms, is no less explicit. So in its gloom — and Rossetti's loveliness is always haunted with gloom — a realm of gold gathers the light against itself, gutting the idea of the creative imagination, so called. But twentieth-century Modernist criticism will read Rossetti's double allegiance very differently. It became an emblem of his artistic failure, of his inability to shed a representational heritage and give himself completely to his abstract and intellectual impulses.[28] But failure is no threat to art in Rossetti, it is the promise of art, and the argument of

"Hand and Soul" now comes to appear a kind of prophecy. He divined what the later twentieth century came to understand: that Modernist elisions of illusion could turn art as cold and unaware of itself as the world it sought to distance or set aside or escape. So in our century we learned to look at art in air-conditioned museums—a metaphor as well as a fact—and to see Rossetti through unselfconscious tropes, speaking of his "hothouse" art, as if such a word, like the word *fetishist,* were all one had to say to understand it.

"To understand it": the thought bends toward a kind of knowledge anciently forbidden, or devoutly to be wished to be forbidden, by Jewish iconoclasts and that secular patriarch of Greece, Plato. These are the traditions that locate intelligibility in the semantics of language, whether oral (as in Plato) or written (as throughout our present liturgies). They are also the traditions that try to measure intelligibility by ethical or logical norms, or some combination of both. To an artistic understanding, however, intelligibility is a function of presence, or what Blake figured as cleansed doors of perception: the serial and rhythmic immediacies of music, the *Gestalten* of the visual arts, all playing out their thoughts as elemental events. Understanding is measured in those events, and if there are norms for such measures, they will have been known, perhaps, only to mystics and ecstatics. "The Argument" of *The Marriage of Heaven and Hell* is a free-verse travesty of a conventional piece of paratextual rhetoric—a summary of *The Marriage* only by analogy, for its thought is all pictorially developed, in that respect, perhaps, more a mirror than a summary because Blake's work performs its alternative kind of thinking as a collage of texts and images. Throughout the work, visibility— what Rossetti called literality—is more important than legibility. And like *Songs of Innocence and of Experience* or so many of Rossetti's textual and pictorial inventions, the parts of the collage can be set to different arrangements, as it were.[29]

The explicitly intellectual character of paintings like *The Girlhood of Mary Virgin, Fazio's Mistress,* or *Veronica Veronese* seems most apparent only because their principal subject is art itself, and (perhaps) because Rossetti casts his arguments in art-historical terms that academical persons like ourselves easily recognize. Not that *Bocca Baciata* or *The Blue Closet*—I choose these randomly from his clear masterpieces—are less intellectual or less interested in problems of art. For all his visionary qualities, Rossetti — like Blake and Dante once again — was almost never not programmatic in his work. In cases like these, however — and there are many — the arguments do not incorporate a recognized conceptual discourse into their apparitions. Yet both are discursive pictures — indeed, they are, like so much of Rossetti's work, "literary pictures." *Bocca Baciata*'s meditation on pleasure and the social taboos surrounding it glosses itself with its oblique reference to Boccaccio, just as it gets glossed by Hunt's acute, puritanical commentary. No specific precursors, textual or otherwise, stand behind *The Blue Closet*, which is a free meditation on medieval courtly materials. When Morris wrote his brilliant and equally enigmatic poem "on" the painting, he captured Rossetti's argument perfectly. He allegorized on his own hook, as Rossetti did with Tennyson. The fact that the poem develops only the most tenuous representational equivalences with the picture defines the critical intelligence of Morris's poem, exposing in that process the intelligibility of Rossetti's rich abstractions. But we are not accustomed to read poems — especially highly fantastical poems like this one — as critical or interpretive works until we recast their imaginative moves into rational or academic terms.

Textual and discursive as we are, Rossetti's methods may seem most clear when we follow them in his writing. His life's work along and across the borders of the sister arts led him to reciprocal moves in the impossible or forbidden zones of each. If intelligibility seems an unnatural vocation of the visual artist — ideas being normally imagined the province of language — textual constructions, we also regularly believe, cannot achieve the sensory immediacy of graphic forms. But these normative beliefs carry less authority — sometimes no authority at all — within nonnormative expressive systems. The intellectual beauties of an artist like Rossetti correspond to (and with) the physical immediacy coveted in his texts.

I am not speaking here of poetic images in the usual understanding of the term — the "speaking pictures" of the sonnets for pictures, the ekphrastic poems. I have in mind, rather, what Sigurd Burckhardt proposed forty years ago, "to release words in some measure from their bondage to meaning, . . . to give or restore to them the corporeality which a true medium needs."[30] What else is happening in a text like the following?

A Superscription

Look on my face; my name is Might-have-been;
  I am also called No-more, Too-late, Farewell;
  Unto thine ear I hold the dead-sea shell
Cast up thy life's foam-fretted feet between;
Unto thine eyes the glass where that is seen
    Which had Life's form and Love's, but by my spell
    Is now a shaken shadow intolerable,
Of ultimate things unuttered the frail screen.

Mark me, how still I am! But should there dart
    One moment through thy soul the soft surprise
    Of that winged Peace which lulls the breath of sighs —
Then shalt thou see me smile, and turn apart
Thy visage to mine ambush at thy heart
    Sleepless with cold commemorative eyes.

If a prose "meaning" can be reconstructed for this sonnet — as it can and has been done, by several readers for other readers — it will need to be reconstructed virtually every time the poem is read. For the text is a puzzle whose knotted syntaxes, off- and internal rhymes and echoing structures, inversions, and acquarian pronouns "drive a wedge between words and their meanings," as Burckhardt looked for poems to do. It is surely one of the most astonishing poetical works in our language — some would no doubt say one of the most perverse. But it is perverse only by the measures of normative meaning — Burckhardt calls them "prose" measures — which are always in "all too ready flight from [words as such] to the things they point to."

    Rossetti's texts, by contrast, tend to flee from meanings toward the words those meanings desire and need. Words are *prima materia,* symbols standing for themselves, and aspire to the condition of music. As in the famous case of the sonnets for *The Girlhood of Mary Virgin,* Rossetti moves to eliminate the distinction between symbols and their meanings. Not that "meanings" and references do not occur in the texts — they do, and even flaunt themselves in the allegorical forms that populate those early sonnets or "A Superscription." But Rossetti's meanings and references get severely localized by the allegorical forms to which he relegates them.

There is little doubt that he learned to write this way by studying Dante and other early Italian poets. More especially, by trying to recast that work into literal translation. The project led him to discover an effective poetic device for neutralizing language's prose urgencies: complicate the text's system of first-person address by turning its lyrical focus into a theater of different voices and points of view. The elaborated forms of Dante's shorter poems, especially his canzone, illustrate the method. The famous "Donne ch'avete intelletto d'amore," for example, turns Dante to one voice among various voices, one creature among many, including the poem itself, whose independent being is figured (imaged) through the complex allegorized exchanges. The more sensuous particulars of the Fazio degli Uberti poem we already looked at succeed in Dante to meticulous mental forms of many kinds and scales. The poems address themselves in a dialogue of their emergent creatures, with Dante himself situated at an inner standing point of the process, at once author and participant.

> An Angel, of his blessed knowledge, saith
>   To God: — "Lord, in the world that Thou hast made,
>   A miracle in action is display'd,
>   By reason of a soul whose splendours fare
>   Even hither: and since Heaven requireth
>   Nought saving her, for her it prayeth Thee,
>   Thy Saints crying aloud continually."
>   Yet Pity still defends our earthly share
>   In that sweet soul; God answering thus the prayer:
>   "My well-belovéd suffer that in peace
>   Your hope remain, while so My pleasure is,
>   There where one dwells who dreads the loss of her:
>   And who in Hell unto the doomed shall say,
>   'I have looked on that for which God's chosen pray.'"

This is a poetry of distinct figures and images, a poetry of human types. Every figure gets precisely defined, starting with the "ladies" addressed by the poem. It does not matter that they never speak here, they are as immediately present, as clearly vital, as the emergent textual forms — as we see in the opening and closing stanzas of the canzone.

Ladies that have intelligence in love,
   Of mine own lady I would speak with you;
   Not that I hope to count her praises through,
     But telling what I may, to ease my mind.
And I declare that when I speak thereof
Love sheds such perfect sweetness over me
That if my courage failed not, certainly
   To him my listeners must be all resign'd.
   Wherefore I will not speak in such large kind
That mine own speech should foil me, which were base;
But only will discourse of her high grace
   In these poor words, the best that I can find,
With you alone, dear dames and damozels:
'Twere ill to speak thereof with any else. . . .

Dear Song, I know thou wilt hold gentle speech
   With many ladies, when I send thee forth:
   Wherefore (being mindful that thou hadst thy birth
     From Love, and art a modest, simple child),
Whomso thou meetest, say thou this to each:
"Give me good speed! To her I wend along
In whose much strength my weakness is made strong."
   And if, i' the end, thou wouldst not be beguiled
   Of all thy labour, seek not the defiled
And common sort; but rather choose to be
Where man and woman dwell in courtesy.
   So to the road thou shalt be reconciled,
And find the lady, and with the lady, Love.
Commend thou me to each, as doth behove.

How brilliantly the last stanza preserves the presence of the "dames and damozels" of the first, as well as the precision of the complex interchange. Everything entering the space of the poem comes to articulate the intelligence of Love, even the impersonal forms anatomized in the prose commentaries Dante sets down after each of the poems in the *Vita Nuova*. "This poem, that it may be better understood, I will divide more subtly than the others preceding; and therefore I will make three parts of it. The first part is a proem to the words following. The second is the matter treated of. The third is, as it were, a handmaid to the preceding words.

The second begins here, 'An Angel'; the third here, 'Dear Song, I know.' The first part is divided into four. In the first I say to whom I mean to speak of my Lady, and wherefore I will so speak." And so forth, in amazingly elaborated detail. These rhetorical distinctions further generate, and therefore clarify, the confederacy of imaginative forms. For Love's intelligence follows prolific measures. Metrical and rhyming networks enter the poetry as vital physical things, quantitatively determinate, as Dante's descriptions indicate. Distinctions can be made, can be made again and again, can be traced in endless detail. At certain levels of perception everything in the texts gravitates toward an elementary phonemic and morphemic status. Personifications, ideas, images; rhetorical and metrical units; rhythms, sonic structures, vocabulary, syntax: all move, like the *Paradiso*'s culminant sun and the stars, at an equivalent signifying level, like images in the flat space of the primitive art Rossetti also loved.

In this kind of system, as "A Superscription" shows, any unit may leap at any moment into surprising and apparently arbitrary prominence, scattering the reader's focus into unexpected and perhaps even unwanted directions. One recalls Merleau-Ponty's critique of Albertian perspective: "It is the invention of a world dominated and possessed through and through by an instantaneous synthesis, which is at best roughed out by our glance when it vainly tries to hold together all these things seeking individually to monopolize it."[31] Here we are witnessing a revolt against equivalent textual urgencies. Rossetti's notorious fondness for archaic and unusual words defines his procedure. When a text follows these kinds of inclination, conceptual forms turn spatial, rebuilding traditional structures of meaning as arrays of detail, some iconic, many not. The arbitrary rules of meter and rhyme introduce abstract, secondary forms that hold prevenient images, which grow more mysterious in being sustained by such alien constructions. The sestet of Rossetti's sonnet on Ingres's *Ruggiero and Angelica* gives a clear illustration of the result.

> The sky is harsh, and the sea shrewd and salt:
>   Under his lord the griffin-horse ramps blind
>   With rigid wings and tail. The spear's lithe stem
>   Thrills in the roaring of those jaws: behind,
> That evil length of body chafes at fault.
>   She doth not hear or see — she knows of them.

The archaic usages—for instance, the words *shrewd* and *thrills*—signal Rossetti's method. Their obsolete meanings ("bitter" and "to penetrate") perform real if residual functions. They are meanings that have to be consciously recovered. Forced to do that, we are led to rethink the presence of such words in the text—their peculiar sonic relationships, their power to introduce modern (psychological) machinery into the geophysical details and other paraphernalia. And drawn to those textual moves, we are urged to others. Certain letters grow uncanny—here, the l's, r's and s's among the consonants, and among the vowels, the a's and the i's especially. They seem poised within some ordering and significant patterns that we can see and hear but that escape conceptual formulation. What the poem finally makes us see more clearly is not the painting by Ingres but its concrete textual elements—the words, the letters, their striking arrangements and relationships. And borne along by these seeings and hearings are our fascinated minds, whose rational procedures are thrown into bewilderment.

That superb rationalist Murray Krieger, himself fascinated with Sigurd Burckhardt's views on poetry, finally warns us not to take "his claims too literally, since to do so would allow us to charge him with mystifying poems and their behavior" (184). But of course Krieger's view assumes Plato's position toward art. Works of imagination will be let into the city if they can justify themselves—that is to say, if they can explain themselves in critical terms. But artists understand by other forms of thought and argument, as Rossetti's work shows—and argues—so clearly and so repeatedly. Systems of ethical and rational norms stand back from or fall short of the imagination's norms, which will be "mystifying" by definition to the former.

Especially will this be the case for an artist and writer like Rossetti, whose life's work was an argument for the independence and rigor of mystified—that is to say, aesthetic—intelligence. Rossetti's work covets the irrational, but not the vague. Reading him we would do well to think through analogies with religious ceremonials, which have no tolerance at all for failures of discipline or deliberateness. Rossetti founded his work on the model of devotional images and their elemental laws of form: laws that draw out their distinctions as forms of desire and, reciprocally, laws for executing desire as the elementary form of knowledge. Plato of course understood these matters very well, certainly when he wrote the *Symposium;* but when he came to think philosophy might be better pursued as a fascist politics rather than an art, he left the *Symposium* behind and headed for the *Republic* and, worse yet, for those final dismal *Laws.*

St. Teresa and St. John of the Cross — Dante as well, of course — developed their texts and their arguments within philosophical traditions that assumed the primacy of transrational intelligence. It was called Love, Desire, Eros even by the great Christian philosophers, Dionysius the Areopagite, Thomas Aquinas. By Rossetti's day the authority of secular reason had replaced those mystified earlier authorities with what we now scrutinize, perhaps, as the ideology of enlightenment. Those great historical shifts help to explain, on one hand, why Rossetti undertook to develop his argument for the intelligence of desire in the first place, and, on the other, why we might now be inclined to attend those arguments again.

7

SINKING STAR

Yet all experience is an arch wherethro'
Gleams that untravell'd world whose margin fades
For ever and for ever when I move.

Tennyson, "Ulysses"

Imagine the desperation of knowing something, of seeing
something with your own eyes, that is absolutely impossible
to communicate . . . — the feeling, vague at first but eventually overwhelming, that you are not really experiencing the
life you are living, and that your senses and thoughts are per-
versely filtered by precisely that which removes their essence.

Tony Robbin, Fourfield

Just about one hundred years ago Ford Madox Ford — writing under his
nineteenth-century birth name Hueffer — began the process of making
Rossetti safe for modernity. Unlike later derivative treatments of his subject, Ford's critical assessment, anchored in an inner standing point of
personal knowledge, mixes sympathy and condescension, shrewd intelligence and blank misgivings. From the vantage of his modernist works,
fictional and otherwise, *Rossetti* now seems the very emblem of Ford's
transitional cultural identity. The book is the first in a famous set of retrospective works that Ford wrote partly to define and partly to negotiate
a rite of historical passage. Rossetti must be come to terms with because
Rossetti — as much for Ford as for Ruskin and Pater — is an epitome of
the last fifty years of the nineteenth century.

Intimidated by the wonder of Rossetti, the man who had been king,
Ford is determined not to be intimidated. So his study broadcasts authoritative pronouncements on Rossetti's work, judging, praising, and
dismissing with equal ease and measure. All of this, as problematic as it is
informed, culminates in some brilliant final pages of general assessment

where Ford takes up the question "What then is to be the lot of Rossetti's fame and influence?" Picking up on a remark by Whistler, Ford judges that Rossetti will come to emblemize artistic failure: "'an amateur who failed in two Arts.' It is true. Yet it hardly harms Rossetti or touches his standing. On the contrary it defines both very brilliantly. . . . The small word 'failed' is a small word and little more to artists who are for ever going on until they give over a game that must be lost. Every artist when confronted by the immensities of Art which is Life must confess to failure. And failure is a thing very relative" (Ford, 82, 83). Ford is playing with the word *failure*. On one hand he means to judge critically an "amateur" lack of interest in "technique": in Rossetti's art these would include "failures" of composition, of perspective, of anatomical knowledge; in writing, his fussiness, obscurantism, lack of discipline and restraint. On the other hand Ford sees that "a future tired of professionals who succeed in . . . art" may "call again out of the depths" a figure like Rossetti, a "prodigal" artist for whom "Art . . . is Life" and whose method — if such it can be called — is expenditure. Ford weaves his study of Rossetti's works with anecdotes of his life because he understands that for Rossetti both were part of a single pursuit: "His mode of living was self-indulgent and irregular; he sat up very late at nights and in no way 'took care of' himself. He had no essential feeling for the value of exercise. He 'spent' his life in fact with no idea of husbanding it" (71). And that way of living mirrored, Ford says, a correspondently unmethodical practice of art: "He never really mastered the theory of either of his arts; because he never really and clearly recognized his limits or systematically put his great powers to their best uses and to these uses alone. He was not cold-blooded enough to be self-conscious, self-analytical enough to be other than prodigal. He wasted his gifts as he wasted his life with a fine unconsciousness" (84).

A contemporary apologist for Rossetti might object, with a good deal of justice, that Ford's judgments are not really accurate. We know that Rossetti was an immensely self-conscious artist; that he worked programmatically, often took a deep interest in "technique," and that he made a number of signal artistic innovations, most especially in watercolor, in graphics, and in book design. Rossetti the poet occupies a similarly innovative position, as Pater was the first to show. *The Early Italian Poets* kept him at a painstaking and difficult set of technical verse exercises for almost thirty years.

But these kinds of response, though important to make, ultimately skirt what seems both deeply right and deeply wrong with Ford's judgments as we weigh them from a late twentieth-century perspective. That vantage leaps to attention, however, if we simply speak the name Georges Bataille. For Rossetti's work is prodigal and spendthrift in a fully Bataillian sense. Rossetti's revelation of a culture of luxury and waste gains its authority and power from its inner standing point. It develops no "imitation of life," as if pointing to a world elsewhere. That style of art, enlightened and ultimately (neo)classical, is anathema to him, who regularly, not to say remorselessly, *involves* himself and his audience in what he is doing.

Ford's sympathy with Rossetti's work is slightly but decisively distanced, like Henry Adams's sympathy for Swinburne. In each case the sympathy is fastidious, partly wonderment, partly distaste. The differential leads Ford to this interesting judgment: "Rossetti left a large body of original poetry of a kind that stands alone in English literature. It has a great luxuriance, an impulse, a great importance. Its appearance may be said to have altered the aspect of the modern literary field — to have enlarged its bounds. It is, as a whole, almost purely sensual — as opposed to purely intellectual" (77). This is Ford's translation of Pater on Rossetti, but if he has had the experience of Pater's thought, he has missed its meaning, as his concluding distinction shows. For Pater, Rossetti's importance and originality lay exactly in the "intellectual" character of his "sensuality."

Pater's view of Rossetti is elaborated in a pair of essays, "Aesthetic Poetry" and "Dante Gabriel Rossetti," and in the famous Conclusion to *The Renaissance*, which originally formed part of the essay he later retitled "Aesthetic Poetry." Rossetti is "understood to belong to, and to be indeed the leader, of a new school" of artists who work in both the literary and the visual arts. Rossetti's doubled pursuit of poetry and painting becomes for Pater an emblem of this "new school" of artistic practice, the Aesthetics, whose leading idea was to overthrow the "Manichean opposition of spirit and matter." "As with Dante," Pater says, in Rossetti "the material and the spiritual are fused and blent" (Pater1, 236). That attitude, realized as an artistic practice, exposes the truth of "modern philosophy" and its "relation . . . to the desire of beauty" (Pater3, 272).

Rossetti and the works of his "new school" come to instantiate Pater's

philosophy of experience. Pater's "Winkelmann" essay (1866) forecasts
the argument he was to elaborate two years later in relation to the work
of the new "Aesthetic" school: "But a taste for metaphysics may be one
of those things which we must renounce, if we mean to mould our lives
to artistic perfection. Philosophy serves culture, not by the fancied gift
of absolute or transcendental knowledge, but by suggesting questions
which help one to detect the passion, and strangeness, and dramatic contrasts of life" (Pater3, 183–184). That thought became the crux of Pater's
appreciation of Rossetti and his Aesthetic inheritors:

> *Philosophiren,* says Novalis, *ist dephlegmatisiren, vivificiren.* The
> service of philosophy, or speculative culture, towards the hu-
> man spirit, is to rouse, to startle it to a life of constant and ea-
> ger observation. . . . Not the fruit of experience, but experi-
> ence itself, is the end. A counted number of pulses only is
> given to us of a variegated, dramatic life. How may we see in
> them all that is to be seen in them by the finest senses? . . .
> What we have to do is to be for ever curiously testing new
> opinions and courting new impressions, never acquiescing in
> a facile orthodoxy of Compte, or of Hegel, or of our own.
> Philosophical theories or ideas, as points of view, instruments
> of criticism, may help us to gather up what might otherwise
> pass unregarded by us. (Pater3, 188–189)

We must not forget that Pater originally wrote all this to explain the relation of art and philosophy, and to suggest how the work of Rossetti's
"new school" had renovated the understanding of that relation. Making
the poet Novalis his point of departure, Pater underscores the fundamental idea: that philosophy will serve culture to the extent that it can
function as art.

These central Paterian texts show how well he understood the importance — for philosophy as well as for art — of working from what
Rossetti called "an inner standing point." Pater's "philosophy of experience" is a conceptual translation, more or less "purely intellectual," of
Rossetti's artistic practice. The Paterian view encompasses a scene of
endless transfiguration because the view is imagined to be wholly experiential, engulfed in the phenomena it registers. To maintain awareness

of the "strange, perpetual, weaving and unweaving" (Pater3, 188) that constitutes "experience," and to do so with no end or object in view that overgoes the experience itself, is to possess — or perhaps to be possessed by — a philosophic mind.

Pater saw that mind operating in Rossetti's works, and especially in his poetical works. Rossetti's startling wordplays, as we have seen, focus the operation at an atomic level, torquing the poems for odd associations, unexpected meanings, bizarre or seemingly random suggestions. But the process runs like a cancer through the whole body of his work and at all levels. There is endless rewriting and revision, and even when the elementary texts preserve linguistic stability, the poems shift into new arrangements and relations as they suffer alteration of the time, place, and circumstances of their appearance. Exactly the same dynamic functions in the pictorial work. "The Rossetti Woman," so called, is as metamorphic as her numerous individual representations, which seem always lying in wait for dissolution and translation, "driven," as Pater writes, "in many currents." How many versions of *Proserpine* did Rossetti execute? No one is sure. Pictures are constantly replicated and reworked, sometimes in such extreme ways as to lose their "identity." And when Rossetti's texts invade his pictures, or vice versa, a constant occurrence, all the vehicular forms surge toward yet other transformations.

Rossetti and his new school are special because their work seems not to represent but to undergo these successive translations. That would be Pater's view, though *we* might perhaps be inclined to say that they develop conventions of expression for managing such an illusion. What is most remarkable — and for Pater, "philosophical" — about the work is how it appears to operate as it were objectively and absolutely. "Rossetti" seems as immersed in its turnings and shiftings as any of his "characters" or visible *figurae,* any of his viewers or readers. Poems that seem evidently intimate and personal — so many of "The House of Life" sonnets, for instance — are almost invariably haunted by other possible voicings, as we have seen. This is a stylistic procedure for scattering the text with multiple points of view and setting the reader within "a drift of momentary acts of sight and passion and thought" (Pater3, 187), none invested with firm identity. Everything, including the poet, seems caught up in a supervening poetic energy. Martin Hardie's comments register the same process in the pictorial work: "Neither oil nor water-colour were pliant and malleable materials in [Rossetti's] hands. He was wrestling with refractory substances, and perhaps for that very reason his work has the intensity and inner glow so often lacking in the painter who attains a surface of superficial ease. Rossetti impregnates our imagination not only with his subject but with his fight to achieve an impassioned result."[1] Such poems and pictures are less integral "works of art" than dynamic fields of embodied and sensuous awareness — as we see so clearly in that extraordinary and haunting "bogie picture" *How They Met Themselves*. As often as not the works will tell stories about such experiences and then instantiate the moral of the tale in the act of telling it. "Hand and Soul" is perhaps the clearest textual example of this kind of work, while "The House of Life" is surely the most vertiginous.

Hardie's acute reading of Rossetti's pictures leads one to realize why aesthetic judgments about the "quality" of individual works might be a secondary concern. No one doubts that *Bocca Baciata,* for example, or several of the 1850s watercolors, or the Tennyson illustrations, or various drawings of Lizzie are "stamped with immortality," as Brown said of the latter; and few would argue that these objects, considered simply as integral things, surpass well-known paintings like any of the versions of *Beata Beatrix* or *The Blessed Damozel* or *Lady Lilith*. But in these last three cases — they are paradigmatic — we are dealing not so much with integral works as with scenes of artistic adventure. Here the example of Duchamp, and in particular of his *Green Box,* is most apt. As often as not these Rossettian scenes are crowded with verbal and pictorial objects, all undergoing investigation and change, all impinging on each other in harmonic, conflicted, or random ways. They offer opportunities of discovery and revelation. And while these opportunities are always being implicated with aesthetic and technical judgments — Rossetti's in the first instance, ours in the last — they need not and probably cannot find fulfillment in such judgments.

So we understand why Rossetti's best work is so often not easily, or uneasily, finished. It feeds on its own drive and intellectual restlessness. He will become impassioned of an idea — say, "Giotto Painting the Portrait of Dante" — or by a subject ("Found," say) — or by a strange dream or vision ("The Orchard Pit"). The idea will then run away with him, take him to wondrous or terrible places, but, as likely as not, finally abandon him. Experiences of these kinds of journey descend to us as a mastering corpus of fragments, studies, and unended works; as the obsessive drawings of Lizzie; as Rossetti's lifelong quest to enter the gone world of Dante and his circle. "Finishedness" is a deeply ambiguous idea for Rossetti, as much a threat as a promise. *Fazio's Mistress* begins in a reading of an obscure fourteenth-century poem, turns aside to a translation of that text, and culminates — momentarily — in a splendid painting completed fifteen or more years after he first read Uberti. In that painting Rossetti will attempt to record the pilgrimage of his mind between about 1845 and 1863. Ten years pass and Rossetti returns to the picture to rethink it, rework it, finally even give it a new name. It makes a considerable difference whether we encounter this work as *Aurélia,* which was the new name, or as *Fazio's Mistress*. Both titles hyperlink to a common relation with Dante's Beatrice, but the one travels by a contemporary road marked out by Gérard de Nerval, the other along a route almost five centuries old. It makes an even greater difference if we engage the work — as Rossetti would have been the first to do — with all of its network of relations held clearly in view. In his eye's mind.

Pater responded to this fluxion in Rossetti's work. It exhibited the processes extolled in the Conclusion to *The Renaissance* as "a perpetual motion of . . . waste and repairing," cycles of dissolution and renewal, rusting iron and ripening corn (Pater3, 186). But true as this congruence is between Pater's criticism and Rossetti's work, a gulf finally separates the two. The problem is that a Bataillian *notion de dépense* — what Ford saw as Rossetti's failure — is inadmissible, except in theory, to Pater. Because waste and corruption enter Pater's field only as ideated terms, they get cleansed and recuperated. We glimpse the difference in Pater's essay on Wordsworth, in which experiential processes come to us under the sign of "contemplation." The "tremulous wisp constantly reforming itself on the stream" (Pater3, 188) of experience gets its apotheosis in *Plato and Platonism* as Darwinian nature, Heraclitean fire, and the Victorian Age of Improvement fold into each other: "The entire modern theory of 'development,' — what is it but old Heracliteanism awake once more in a new world, and grown to full proportions. . . . It is the burden of Hegel on the one hand . . . and on the other of Darwin and Darwinism, for which 'type' itself properly *is* not but is only always *becoming*" (Pa-

ter2, 13–14). Passages like this explain why the intramural Pater will take
us only so far toward appreciating a sensibility like Rossetti, the *flaneur*
of London's late night demiworld whose early Dantean dreams ran on
to the wastage of the "chloralized years," as his brother called them. "As
if it were possible to spend and be spent without getting dirty, as if
dépense could be thoroughly presentable, spending energy without pol-
luting, shamelessly, nothing repugnant about it."[2] In this crucial respect
Madox Ford, who was after all there, understood Rossetti's art as Pater
never could. For Rossetti's works are littered with disastered things—
not merely stories of disaster, like the incomparable "Sister Helen" or
"The Orchard Pit," or exquisite images of corruption like *Monna Vanna;*
but all those nearly unreadable texts, like "Hero's Lamp," and the pictures
we can scarcely endure the sight of—say, *A Vision of Fiammetta.*

Why do such works appear so repellent? Because by the measures of
traditional aesthetics, neoclassical as well as romantic, they constitute a
peculiar, proto-modern "ready made" object: "Beauty" that has not undergone its obligatory passage through a skill we would admire or an
imagination that courts our sense of wonder. "This is that Lady Beauty"
corrupted before our eyes by the ideas of commerce and capitalism. Her
kissed mouth loses none of its freshness precisely, paradoxically, because
it has escaped infection by the idea and the ideal of original innocence.
Such an art aspires to cure us of the sickness of our old passion for transcendence.

Pictures and texts like these pile up during the 1870s. Their mon-
strosities are paradoxical, however, for they come with a panoply of aesthetic attention and self-consciousness. In fact, Rossetti grew increasingly possessed by the idea of the finished and masterful work. The
"Sixteen Sonnets" published in *The Fortnightly Review* in 1869 prolifer-
ated rapidly, growing in 1870 to the "Sonnets and Songs, Towards a Work
to be Called 'The House of Life,'" and in 1871–1873 pushing out a whole
new set of growths that momentarily organized themselves as "The
Kelmscott Love Sonnets." At some point this amazing process finally
metastasized, becoming, in 1881, Rossetti's consummate "House of Life."
But in truth that "Work" is but a simulacrum of finishedness and completion. Vital and known elements are missing: "Nuptial Sleep," most famously, but also all the "Songs" printed in 1870. Individual sonnets and
groups of sonnets, some of these, like "The Kelmscott Love Sonnets,"

substantial, have been transformed and reborn, which is also to say that part of their lives have, like the years, passed away. The 1881 "House of Life," seeking to defy those abandonments, merely consumes them. They go on to live their secret life in the sequence according to a darker working, whose power is only augmented by the Work's textual losses, its acts of bad faith, and all those flaunted poeticizings that Rossetti might call — half expecting us, and himself, to believe him — "fundamental brainwork." The truth of the sequence is so much better than it tries to be because so much worse than it seems.

"The House of Life" is thus one more work uneasily finished. Rossetti's best readers have liked to praise particular sonnets and passages rather than the whole lumbering edifice, whose "structure" is only too imperative, insisting that we pay attention to it and assent to its importance. But its overall form and local finish are "important" quite in the way of so many of Rossetti's paintings of the 1870s. Several of the best known — *Mnemosyne, Proserpine, Astarte Syriaca* — are self-consciously repulsive pictures, but many simply seem appalling — "bad art" in the most traditional evaluative sense. We shrink back the more from works like *A Sea Spell* or *La Bella Mano* exactly because they insist upon being engaged within the discourse of High Art. These things are monumental and they tell us so. They will be expensive. They are about being expensive.

They are — in every sense, if only from one point of view — immensely vulgar. So Pater will have nothing to say of them, for Pater's idea of art, like his idea of philosophy, flees from just these vulgar forms of modernity — as Rossetti himself fled during the first part of his career, between 1848 and 1860. But even the worst of these late Rossetti works often exude a vitality lacking in many of the best works of Millais, that gifted man. The "intensity and inner glow" that Hardie and others rightly see in the watercolors have not left Rossetti's late painted ladies. They are infected as ever — more than ever — with his life, dreadful forms arising in a series of final wasted struggles. No less of these visionary emanations of morbid luxury should it be written: "This is that Lady Beauty, in whose praise / Thy voice and hand shake still" ("Soul's Beauty," 9–10).

"I loved thee ere I loved a woman, Love" (*Works* [1911], 240): that is how Rossetti summarized his passion for art. It possessed and consumed him, as St. Teresa and St. John were spent with their passion for God. But Rossetti's passion, if equally intense, carries no such transcendental license. Its visionary pursuits are worldly altogether — erotic and "fleshly," of course, but driven as well by commercial ends and a determination to be successful in the most quotidian terms. These clear inflections explain why his late works, naked and shameful as they are, might be usefully submitted to Marxist or psychoanalytic enlightenment, much as Paterian enlightenment falls usefully upon so much of Rossetti's other work.

But in truth the understanding we can gain by such lights seems bloodless and pale compared to what is offered through the original works themselves. This result happens because second-order cultural interpretation and critique regularly observes its subjects from without, or (worse yet) from above. The "inner standing point" that Rossetti adopted and learned to prize so early — in the 1840s — is very different, and it discovers both its greatest power and worst fate in those final monumental works, where Rossetti's early dreams turn traumatic. These pictures are commentaries, often (like *Lady Lilith* and *Monna Vanna*) explicit commentaries, on the artistic transmission of culture (as opposed to other principal forms of cultural transmission like education, science, religion). As such the pictures are self-commentaries, poised at an inner standing point and lit darkly from within.

The figures in these paintings typically stare out toward their viewers, looking indifferently at or away from our returning looks. Patently allegorical figures of instituted Beauty, they fix a label to the pictures, naming them Mirrors of Art, with ourselves before them. Their pictures simultaneously observe and execute themselves as vehicles of cultural transmission, and they foresee us in our places in the drama they are staging.

And I speak of these pictures "as if," like Browning's last duchess, they "were alive" for the same reason that Marx rightly spoke of fetishized commodities as living creatures. But whereas the latter were created to seduce us from awareness, the pictures are fearfully self-conscious. They are Medusan pictures, a last gallery of dark "stunners." They don't arrive denying the art of the earlier Beatricean drawings and paintings, which come graceful before us, even now, exactly as Chiaro's soul appeared to him. But they do come to fill out the story of the whole truth of Art as Rossetti knew it and lived it.

This is why they are so troubling to the secondary enlightenment of criticism. These pictures have gone too far and know too much. They know themselves from dream to nightmare; and they know themselves not at a distance — not by what they might be taken to mean — but from within, by what they have in fact undertaken to do, which is to engage in acts of self-exposure at a time and in a vantage that many artists would find too terrible to put on display. Informed criticism may well find them repellent, for they stand before it as more than signs or ideas. They are instances of the kind of knowledge that philosophy, criticism, and science can never have. And perhaps *should* never have.

But these works deserve One Word More, for like Ahab they have their humanities. We glimpse it when we look carefully at the faces of the women and try to abstract away from our awareness all the luxurious paraphernalia weighing them down. The crass and barbaric accoutrements that work to dehumanize these figures make us want to remember something else about them, something that they *appear* to have forgotten: that the paintings signal more than the cult objects of secular culture, museum bound. They are also portraits.

The human face haunts Rossetti's work, perhaps because his imperial world obscured and defaced its magical lineaments. His favorite and most loved faces were familiar and vulgar — in the terms of one of his most famous poems, Jenny and his cousin Nell, the same person in the end, as the poet in the poem all but says. Longing to see that face, to see it again and again, he studied the great discourses of desire: dream, nightmare, art, poetry. Like that stormiest vision of all, the great "dream of life," all swept him away in their engulfing erotic surge. And he surrendered to them all — or rather, he chose to surrender. The choice drew him far out to sea, plunging along further fading margins into deeper confusions and fantasmal worlds, "lower than the tide of dreams." But it seemed the only possible way.

Once he described the rhythm of that way in entirely benevolent terms, in a sonnet of great erotic truth and innocence. It is a sonnet about making love, very simple. To some of his contemporaries "Nuptial Sleep" seemed as revolting as *Bocca Baciata* was to Hunt, or as *Venus Verticordia* seemed to Ruskin, or as *Astarte Syriaca* or other of the late Rossetti works have been for so many in the twentieth century.

At length their long kiss severed, with sweet smart:
      And as the last slow sudden drops are shed
      From sparkling eaves when all the storm has fled,
So singly flagged the pulses of each heart.
Their bosoms sundered, with the opening start
      Of married flowers to either side outspread
      From the knit stem; yet still their mouths, burnt red,
Fawned on each other where they lay apart.

Sleep sank them lower than the tide of dreams,
      And their dreams watched them sink, and slid away.
Slowly their souls swam up again, through gleams
      Of watered light and dull drowned waifs of day;
Till from some wonder of new woods and streams
      He woke, and wondered more: for there she lay.

Think about the structure of experience described and relived in that text. It is a model, even an exegesis, of what happens in Rossetti's portraits, where human faces rise out of the erotic swirl of dream and nightmare: Fanny Cornforth from *Bocca Baciata;* from the *Venus* Ruskin hated, a beautiful cook he met by chance on a London street; and in *Astarte Syriaca,* Jane Morris.

In those unforgotten, unforgettable faces, so appealing in several senses, a disturbing male gaze turns to look back at itself, at us, men and women both. The event seems the more significant and moving exactly because it has hardly been recognized or translated as an important moment in the history of art. Through the distorted lens of Rossetti's erotic fantasies, through the programmatic goals and ideas that announce themselves in these images, we yet perceive loved and lovable forms of a human world that these fantasies and ideas, and this art itself, has at once baffled and pursued. The candor of this game of loss is Rossetti's preserve of knowledge and its broken remains.

At several points in this study I suggest that we might approach Rossetti's work through a consideration of Duchamp's programmatic practices. We would do this exactly because the analogy and critical relation initially appears so inapt. Rossetti's paintings have none of Duchamp's ironical attitudes, and he would have shrunk from the kind of public exhibition of his intellectual goals that Duchamp cultivated. But before we make a final reconsideration of these differences and their implications, let us briefly reflect on what the men have in common.

First of all is the double work of art, which Duchamp pursues in ways that certainly recall Rossetti. *A l'infinitif* and *The Green Box* comprise far more than random sets of notes recording Duchamp's ideas about *The Large Glass* and other of his visual works. In fact, presented as randomly collected pieces of text, these works turn that formal gesture into an argument about art as a space of exploratory intellectual practices.

Duchamp's texts and visual objects are mirror images of each other in a very special and important sense, and one that is anticipated by Rossetti's double works.[3] When Duchamp (so to speak) looked into the mirror he discovered a two-dimensional medium for engaging higher dimensional forms. The dimensional nonequivalence between the mirror image and the form it reflects provides Duchamp, as it had many others, with a practical *figura* for how one can represent nonillusionistic forms and spatial relations. Rossetti's double works function in exactly the same way. Their power as mirrors — as what Duchamp would later call the "appearances" of "apparitions" — is a direct function of the differentials they call to attention.[4] As in Duchamp, when Rossetti figures and then refigures sets of mirror apparitions, the doubled work exposes the illusory character of a world of appearances.

Sharing such ideas (they are really artistic practices), both treat art as a quasi-magical instrument for exploring transrational and irreal orders of being. Rossetti seems to have had little interest in the kinds of philosophy and philosophical mathematics that were a regular part of Duchamp's reading and conversation. Nonetheless, he certainly wanted to access what philosophers and mathematicians from the mid-nineteenth century onward called "n-dimensional" space — the space defined, that is, through his Venus surrounded by mirrors. His proto-Modernist critique of illusionist art and perspective was central to that goal.

In this connection I would draw a comparison between a signature work by each man: *The Blessed Damozel* and *The Large Glass*. Both are conscious reworkings of the *figura* of the Enthroned Madonna.[5] More interesting yet, both works divide themselves into separate spatial areas, the upper being reserved for the Ideal object (Rossetti's Damozel and Duchamp's Bride), the lower representing a nontranscendental space

(Rossetti's reclining artist, Duchamp's Bachelors). In each case the artist introduces in the most self-conscious way a distinction between a lower world that has been illusionistically ordered and an upper world of iconic forms. That is to say, the lower worlds deploy conventions of perspective that are forbidden in their respective upper worlds. Like Duchamp's Bride, the Damozel is not the appearance of a realistic (illusory) form, she is the appearance of an apparition. She is a figure of what Shelley called Intellectual Beauty, as well as her work's chief "figure," in a rhetorical sense, of what the whole of it is proposing to us. Though "realistic" forms and even perspective make *appearances* in Rossetti's painting, the picture itself is transcendental and abstract, a brainwork.

Like Duchamp—for that matter, like Blake, like Dante—Rossetti's whole career was an effort to put the artist's work "at the service of mind."[6] Rossetti's famous portraits of ladies are mirrors of a transcendental Venus and of the higher order she embodies: *alma Venus genetrix,* which in this cases means *poiesis.* And like any programmatic artist, certainly like Duchamp, Rossetti understood that this kind of "fundamental brainwork" ought to be achieved through stylistic means. *The Blessed Damozel* is hardly the only picture Rossetti created in which he used contrasting representations of space both to make an argument about the intelligence of art and to fashion a form of transcendental belief. In this respect *The Blessed Damozel* and *Mary Magdalene at the Door of Simon the Pharisee* are closely equivalent works.

Within these equivalences, however, a crucial difference between the two men remains. It comes into relief when we read a comment like the following, which Duchamp made to Pierre Cabanne by way of explaining his work with *The Large Glass:* "Since I found that one could make a cast shadow from a three-dimensional thing . . . I thought that, by simple intellectual analogy, the fourth dimension could project an object of three dimensions, or, to put it another way, any three-dimensional object, which we see dispassionately, is a projection of something four-dimensional, something we're not familiar with" (Cabanne, 40). This language of things, objects, and dispassion is far removed from Rossetti, whose Intellectual Beauties turn in vortices of passion and unfulfillable desire.[7] This happens because an intellectual life for Rossetti is grounded in affect. "Ladies . . . have Intelligence in Love," not in the cold discourse of ideas, which for Rossetti, as for nearly all his contemporaries, is a discourse gendered male. In the discourse of art, however, which Rossetti imagined to be gender-neutral, Rossetti's (male) artist may project dreams of escape to the transrational order of love's intelligence.

They *are* dreams, however, or what Duchamp called apparitions. Forms of desire in which the artist and his work move through an indeterminate set of inner standing points. As a result, Rossetti's apparitions are always simultaneously dissolving back into their appearances. His works, verbal as well as visual, disallow an objective vantage or stable ground, all is subjective or simulacral or both. By contrast, Duchamp has a deep commitment to enlightenment and neoclassical goals. The Rossettian equivalent of these were his medieval and Dantean dreams of order, which he cherished until the early 1860s. To that point Rossetti, like Duchamp, dreamed that he knew what he was doing or that he might one day come to know. The later Rossetti dreams he never will. The later dream of Intelligence in Love was perhaps most completely realized in the astonishing *Astarte Syriaca,* a dream of knowledge that would be open, shameless, and — consequently — forbidden.

Notes

1. A Dynamic of Reflection

1. According to Ford Madox Ford, when Whistler on his deathbed heard Rossetti being disparaged, he opened his eyes and said: "You must not say anything against Rossetti. Rossetti was a king" (Ford1, 33).

2. For an excellent (psychoanalytic) critique of narrow, and ultimately moralized, treatments of the nexus death/woman/art in the Romantic tradition, see Bronfen, 59–60, 72–73.

3. I have in mind here the antithetical Modernist attitude famously expressed in Auden's "In Memory of W. B. Yeats": "poetry makes nothing happen."

4. "Passion and Worship" is the title of one of "The House of Life" sonnets.

5. Quoted in Sulman, 549.

6. This is the heading he chose for a group of writings he proposed to develop in 1847. He finished at least one, "Mater Pulchrae Delectionis" (later changed and titled "Ave"), and he seems to have planned the group to accompany his early devotional pictures, especially the Marian paintings like *The Girlhood of Mary Virgin* and *Ecce Ancilla Domini!*

7. "Fundamental brainwork": see Caine, 249.

8. Certain notable scholarly exceptions stand out: William E. Fredeman, of course, who kept Rossetti's vision through its recent times of trouble; other notable students of Rossetti include D. M. R. Bentley, Susan Casteras, Alicia Faxon, Alastair Grieve, David Riede, Richard Stein.

9. He jotted this in a notebook — it was to be the subject for a painting. The painting was not executed but a study for it survives. The text is printed in the 1911 *Works,* 615. For the pencil study see Fredeman4, no. 23.

10. In the first volume of *Capital.*

11. He used this phrase twice, once in a prose note to the poem "Ave" and again in his rejoinder to Buchanan, the essay "The Stealthy School of Criticism."

12. In Johnson, 138.

13. Ibid., 129.
14. Commentators from William Michael Rossetti to Paull Baum have puzzled over the phrase "soul-sequestered." "Immemorable" is perhaps equally enigmatic since it swings between the antithetical poles of its customary meaning ("not worthy of remembrance") and its (here, clearly invoked) obsolete meaning ("immemorial, ancient beyond record or memory").
15. The concept of the "double work" is crucial for understanding Rossetti. For a useful introduction see Ainsworth.
16. See Allen for a good discussion of Rossetti's Lilith work. Ponsonby Lyons, a contemporary of Rossetti's, explicitly told the artist of his view that Lilith was a figure of the Emancipated Woman.
17. Swinburne's description is one of three he wrote for his part of the *Notes on the Royal Society Exhibition, 1868;* see Swinburne.
18. Whereas the Cornforth Lilith is a voluptuous image, the Wilding is ophidian (a colleague always refers to the latter as the "Lizard Lilith").
19. See Bentley4. In this respect older critics like Pater and Hearn are more reliable guides to Rossetti's work.
20. *Letters* 2: 850.
21. WMRossetti1, 69.
22. See Surtees 1: 92.
23. The allusion is to Nerval's 1855 tale "Aurélia," which is the author's version of Rossetti's "Hand and Soul" (both tales deriving more or less explicitly from Dante's *Vita Nuova*).
24. Rossetti's interest in spiritualism was intense, and the relation between his artistic practice — verbal as well as pictorial — and magical practices is as unmistakable as it is in Picasso and Breton. I borrow the phrase "artifice of absorption" from Charles Bernstein's *ars poetica* of the same title. See Bernstein.
25. Morris's pair of poems appeared first in his seminal Pre-Raphaelite volume *The Defence of Guenevere and Other Poems* (1858).
26. For Merleau-Ponty's key writings on these matters see above, note 12. The most pertinent text by Derrida is *The Truth in Painting,* from which the epigraph for this chapter is taken (trans. Geoff Bennington and Ian McLeod [Chicago: University of Chicago Press, 1987]).
27. See *Letters* 2: 726–727.
28. *The Blessed Damozel* is by no means the only work that multiplies into many versions, verbal as well as pictorial. *Beata Beatrix* and *Proserpine* are two other notable examples, but there are many.

2. Intelligence in Love

1. Richard Stein calls this formality Rossetti's "ritual of interpretation." That shrewd phrase calls attention to the pictorial formality of Rossetti's paintings and poems, especially in the works of the first half of his career. See Stein, 130–143, where he discusses Rossetti's "Sonnets for Pictures." In *The Girlhood of Mary Virgin,* for example, the compositional structure is sharp and clean: it is organized around the trellis at which St. Joachim is working. More crucially, the trellis itself is constructed upon a central crucifix design.

2. The critique is in Welland, 27, where he also quotes the Ruskin passage.

3. See *The Early Italian Poets,* viii.

4. Pound wrote that "in the matter of these translations and of my knowledge of Tuscan poetry, Rossetti is my father and my mother" (6).

5. Perhaps the best treatment of Rossetti's translation project is by Edwards.

6. Gitter, 355.

7. Gray, 45, 52.

8. For a somewhat different approach to Rossetti's appropriation of Dante see Goff, especially pp. 102–105.

9. Rossetti does not "literally" render Dante's third line ("in cio che mi re-scrivan suo parvente"); in particular, he introduces the term *interpretation,* which is nowhere in Dante, and he leaves out the literality of *writing back.* The move is so effective because it displays — indeed, it enacts — Rossetti's understanding that interpretation is or ought to be an active event, more a rewriting than a reading. Dante's friends are poets, they interpret his poetry by writing other poems. For Rossetti, this is being faithful to the original poetic impulse. His own method of translation is a similar act of faithfulness, rather than literality. For a more general consideration of this kind of "deformative" interpretation see Samuels and McGann.

10. Quoted in Buckley, 489.

11. In England this tradition of a poetics of opacity is specifically born in the Pre-Raphaelite movement: see McGann, especially chapter 1 ("Thing to Mind: The Materialist Aesthetic of William Morris"); and see also Drucker.

3. Dante and Rossetti

1. All quotations from the poetry are taken from *The Complete Writings and Pictures of Dante Gabriel Rossetti: A Hypermedia Research Archive.*

The standard edition hitherto has been the 1911 *Works*, edited by William Michael Rossetti, which may be consulted for most of the writings quoted in this essay.

2. This note appears in several of Rossetti's surviving manuscripts and proofs.

3. See *Letters* 2: 821.

4. That is to say, whereas Gabriele Rossetti searched the texts for coded political references, his son was attentive partly to hidden biographical connections, and partly to mythic and quasi-philosophical patterns that were involved with the biographical details. When people refer to Rossetti's interest in spiritualism and "superstition," and when scholars track lines of "mystical" and "spiritual" ideas in his work, they are registering matters that connect to his characteristic way of reading as well.

5. The practice of writing from an "inner standing point" represents one of the key features of Rossetti's work. He formulated the idea early, in a note he attached to the poem "Ave," and he adverted to it again much later in "The Stealthy School of Criticism," his critical reply to Buchanan's notorious attack.

6. Specifically, the argument with Freud about the direction, as it were, of libidinal desire. Breton argues that it is not primarily memorial but, rather, prophetic. See Breton1.

7. See "The House of Life," 115.

8. See Samuels, 2.

9. A crude translation would be:

> Weeping with my soul bewildered,
> saying to myself: she has already gone to heaven,
> she whom men call by the name Blessed One,
> alas, when and how will I be able to see you in a visible form
> so that I might have the power to make you
> a living presence? So do I comfort my life?
> Then listen to me because I speak on purpose
> of love and refrain from sighs.
>
> And indeed she speaks of all her grace.
>
> And all you who are now sanctified,
> and who contemplate in heaven where
> your heart resides, love her through whom
> he who has painted such a blessed face
> has been torn within himself.

10. On the verso of the single surviving manuscript of this work Rossetti has a series of notes, including a reference to Abbate Luigi Rigoli's *Saggio di rime di diversi buoni autori . . . dal 14. Fino al 18 secolo*. This book, published in Florence in 1825, was one of Rossetti's sources for his translations. He lists others at the end of his Introduction to *The Early Italian Poets*.

11. This work was published only recently; see Slayton.

12. See, for example, *Jerusalem* 4:5.

13. See William Michael Rossetti's notes on the event in his 1911 edition of his brother's *Works*, 673–674n.

14. The first was initially published in WMRossetti6, the second in his edition of 1911.

4. The Iconic Page

1. But see Bornstein and Williams, Drucker, Grigely, Hoagwood, McGann1, McGann3, McKenzie. Also, various essays by Randall McLeod, which have not been collected, are unfailingly stimulating, even inspirational.

2. See Hardie 3: 119.

3. Ruskin was the first to see that Rossetti's early color studies were propelled by his interest in stained glass. When he began to study Venetian painting in the early 1860s, both Ruskin and Hunt were dismayed and consequently judged the work of his last two decades as largely a failure. See Ruskin1, 394, and W. Hunt (1905) 2: 363.

4. See Grieve6 and *From Realism to Symbolism*. For a good study of Rossetti and the Venetians see Macleod.

5. The best study of this aspect of Rossetti's work is Grieve1. But see also Lottes and Fredeman2. Rossetti's innovative use of picture frames was surely influenced greatly by Ford Madox Brown's work; see especially the frame of Madox Brown's *Wycliffe Reading His Translation of the Bible to John of Gaunt* (1847–1848), a work that influenced Rossetti in a number of ways, as one sees clearly by comparing it to Rossetti's *The Girlhood of Mary Virgin*.

6. Although some later critics minimize the influence of Japanese art on Rossetti, to Ruskin the influence was apparent, and baleful. For Ruskin, Rossetti "lacerated his powers of conception with Chinese puzzles and Japanese monsters" (Ruskin1, 394). See Tanita, Watanabi1, Watanabi2.

7. See Fredeman6, Fredeman2, and Barber.

8. The story of Rossetti's involvement is best found in his letters of 1869–1870; see *Letters* 2: 686–853 passim. See also McGann2.

9. See his letters through 1861 (and especially *Letters* 2: 389, 393, 398).

10. In addition to the death of Rossetti's wife in 1862, the crucial event is the onset of his passion for Jane Morris (date uncertain, though it was certainly active by 1868).

11. See, e.g., McGann3, 60–75.

12. An attempt at such a "super" version was made in the 1890s by the American publishers Copeland and Day, who issued a splendid edition containing all the published sonnets as well as all the published "songs."

13. This love-gift to Jane Morris was first published in 1954 (see *The Kelmscott Love Sonnets*).

14. That is to say, Rossetti writes "For *The House of Life*" below or beside the title of a great many manuscript sonnets that he is writing in the 1870s. The notations are only rarely added subsequent to the scripting of the text itself.

15. The manuscript titled "Three Songs" is in the British Library and can be dated confidently to this period.

16. See especially Fredeman2 and the poems "On the 'Vita Nuova' of Dante" and "Dantis Tenebrae" in the 1870 volume.

17. The note is inserted in the set of "A Proofs" housed in the Troxell Collection, Firestone Library, Princeton University.

18. The essay appears in Davies's collection *Signage* (New York: Roof, 1987), 70–74.

19. See Coleridge's prose preface to "Kubla Khan," published with the poem in 1816.

20. See Ruskin1, 395.

21. The lines are from the sonnets "For Our Lady of the Rocks by Leonardo da Vinci" and the "Sonnet [on the Sonnet]," respectively.

22. This is the title Rossetti gives to his translation of the canzone in *The Early Italian Poets*.

23. See Surtees, nos. 168, 212, 372.

24. See Surtees, no. 244. *Sancta Lilias* (now in the Tate Gallery) is a cut-down version of the more famous painting. It represents the head of the damozel against a gold field.

25. William Michael Rossetti inaugurated this line of criticism in his early study *Designer and Writer* (WMRossetti1), which includes a paraphrase of each of the sonnets in "The House of Life." The other crucial instance is Paull Baum's edition of the sonnet sequence, which regularly gives paraphrases of Rossetti's poems.

26. See Drucker and McGann3.
27. See Breton1.

5. Ars Negativa

1. Hunt 2: 354, 357.
2. Ibid., 2: 354–355.
3. But see Smith1, 86–87, and Smith2, 2–3. Smith studies what she regularly calls "the elusive depth of field" (Smith1, 96) in various Pre-Raphaelite works — an anti-illusionist visual space that Smith argues is a function of the influence of stereoscopic visuality on Ruskinian and Pre-Raphaelite approaches to pictorial representation. Smith's discussion of Millais's *The Woodman's Daughter* (1850–1851) argues for an "infinitely problematic depth of field" (Smith1, 95) in the painting, and the argument has wide applicability — as Smith shows — to the work of the PRB, and not least of all to Rossetti's work. It is my view that only Rossetti, of the original group of PRB artists, made a programmatic commitment to creating that kind of spatial complexity.
4. Most of the Siddal drawings are listed in Surtees nos. 457–515; the Tennyson illustrations are listed in Surtees nos. 83–86, where the Poe illustrations are nos. 19, 29, 30.
5. Breton3, 44.
6. As Rossetti's brother pointed out in his 1911 edition of his brother's *Works,* 679n.
7. Grieve3, 3.
8. I do not pose the question as if seeking for an interpretive answer (an answer, for instance, that might "read" the picture as a critical reflection on the illusions of certain central Victorian ideas and attitudes). The question means only to locate the psychological tone of the picture, which can be missed because of the power of its surface effects.
9. *Letters* 1: 239.
10. Sulman, 549.
11. Hardie 3: 120.
12. Ibid., 3: 117.
13. Brown, 101, 148.
14. "I loved thee ere I loved a woman, Love": that telling notation appears in one of Rossetti's notebooks. (See the 1911 edition of his *Works,* 240, where William Michael Rossetti gives it the title "To Art.")
15. Ruskin3, 12: 162.
16. Ibid., 33: 271.

17. Waugh, 122.
18. Reithmiller's notes on the picture, unpublished, are preserved in the files of the Tate Gallery library.
19. Cavalcanti's influence on Dante's style and ideas was very great, but eventually Dante grew critical of his friend's views. See the *Inferno* Canto 10, in which his critique appears in a displaced form.

6. Venus Surrounded by Mirrors, Reflecting Her in Different Views

1. See the 1911 edition of *Works,* 615.
2. WMRossetti2, 1: 159–160.
3. Hunt (1914) 1: 83–85. Hunt's condescension here, which reflects the judgments of the early reviewers, is a retrospective one, and partly reflects his belated effort to define Pre-Raphaelitism in relation to himself and Millais rather than Rossetti and Burne-Jones.
4. See Surtees 1: 62 (letter to Mrs. Clapham of July 1862).
5. Waugh, 22.
6. It is difficult not to think that the word *lily* and its many cognate forms, as well as the image of the lily, possess a virtually magical authority in Rossetti's work. His treatment of the pictorial figure of the lily in his two first oil pictures is extremely suggestive.
7. See Chapter 5, note 18.
8. Quoted in Surtees 1: 94.
9. Quoted in Surtees 1: 69.
10. Hunt (1914) 2: 111.
11. Rosenblum1, 96.
12. The analogy to Picasso is difficult to resist. See Gasman for a thorough treatment of Picasso, magic, and Surrealism.
13. This letter, first published in WMRossetti4, 135, is reproduced more fully in Angeli, 92, which is the source of the present text.
14. So William Michael Rossetti has told us: see Surtees 1: 99.
15. WMRossetti5, 220–221.
16. Sharp, 206.
17. Stephens, 70.
18. See Rossetti's letter to John Mitchell, 27 September 1866 (*Letters* 2: 606).
19. WMRossetti1, 69.
20. Rossetti's interest would have begun around 1862–1863, partly through Whistler, whose intimacy with Rossetti began early in the decade, and

partly in the wake of the International Exhibition of 1862. William Michael Rossetti was collecting Japanese woodcuts by 1863, and it is likely that Dante Gabriel was as well. In any case, the brothers were on intimate terms and would have been sharing this new and exciting aesthetic source. See the studies by Toshio Watanabe.

21. WMRossetti4, 136.
22. WMRossetti4, 138.
23. Ruskin1, 394.
24. Stephens, 41.
25. Grieve3, 15, 45.
26. It was a favorite expression of Blake's: see his "Annotations to the Works of Sir Joshua Reynolds" and his *Descriptive Catalogue*.
27. This plate is reproduced in Gilchrist 1: 122, facing page. See also the plate from *Europe* reproduced facing p. 129.
28. This was Roger Fry's argument, which became normative.
29. No two copies of Blake's *Songs* are identical.
30. See Burckhardt, 24.
31. Merleau-Ponty, "Indirect Language and the Voices of Silence," in Johnson, 87.

7. Sinking Star

1. Hardie 3: 119.
2. Hollier, xiv.
3. See Henderson, 137–157, where she has an illuminating discussion of Duchamp's use of mirroring.
4. See *A l'infinitif* in Sanouillet, 84–85.
5. Duchamp's horizontal Madonna underscores his witty conflation of the sacred and the profane. His bride recalls a reposing Venus, even an odalisque. Rossetti's conflation of the two orders has none of that kind of irony.
6. Sweeney, 20.
7. One of Rossetti's characteristic geometries in his pictorial work is the spiral, which can run simultaneously clockwise and counterclockwise. He introduced a spiral brooch of pearls mounted in silver in a number of his Venusian portraits (see, for example, *Monna Vanna*).

BIBLIOGRAPHY

Works by D. G. Rossetti

Note: Unless otherwise indicated, citations of the poetry and prose are made to *The Complete Writings and Pictures of Dante Gabriel Rossetti: A Hypermedia Research Archive,* ed. Jerome McGann (Ann Arbor: University of Michigan Press, online, 2000).

The Early Italian Poets, from Ciullo d'Alcamo to Dante Alighieri (1100–1200–1300 . . .). London: Smith, Elder, 1861.

The House of Life, Being now for the First Time Given in Its Full Text. Boston: Copeland and Day, 1894.

Dante Gabriel Rossetti: His Family Letters, with a Memoir, ed. William Michael Rossetti. 2 vols. London: Ellis, 1895.

The Works of Dante Gabriel Rossetti, ed. William Michael Rossetti. London: Ellis, 1911.

The House of Life: A Sonnet Sequence, ed. Paull Franklin Baum. Cambridge: Harvard University Press, 1928.

The Kelmscott Love Sonnets of Dante Gabriel Rossetti, ed. John Robert Wahl. Cape Town: A. A. Balkema, 1954.

The Letters of Dante Gabriel Rossetti, ed. Oswald Doughty and John Robert Wahl. 4 vols. Oxford: Clarendon, 1965.

Dante Gabriel Rossetti and Jane Morris, Their Correspondence, ed. John Bryson and Janet Camp Troxell. Oxford: Clarendon, 1976.

The Rossetti-Leyland Letters, ed. Francis L. Fennell Jr. Athens: Ohio University Press, 1978.

Secondary Sources

Ainsworth, Maryan Wynn, ed. *Dante Gabriel Rossetti and the Double Work of Art.* New Haven: Yale University Art Gallery, 1976.

Alighieri, Dante. *Vita Nuova,* ed. Eduardo Sanguineti. 4th ed. Milan: Garzanti, 1984.

Allen, Virginia M. "'One Strangling Golden Hair': Dante Gabriel Rossetti's *Lady Lilith,*" *Art Bulletin* 66 (1984): 285–295.

Angeli, Helen Rossetti. *Dante Gabriel Rossetti: His Friends and Enemies.* London: Hamilton, 1949.

Banerjee, Ron D. K. "Dante Through the Looking Glass: Rossetti, Pound, and Eliot," *Comparative Literature* 24 (1972): 136–149.

Barber, Giles. "Rossetti, Ricketts, and Some English Publishers' Bindings of the Nineties," *The Library*, 5th ser., 25 (1970): 314–330.

Barthes, Roland. *Writing Degree Zero on Elements of Semiology,* trans. Annette Lavers and Colin Smith. Boston: Beacon, 1970.

Bataille, Georges. *Inner Experience,* trans. Leslie Anne Boldt. New York: SUNY Press, 1988. [Bataille1]

———. *Visions of Excess: Selected Writings, 1927–1939,* ed. Allan Stoekl. Theory and History of Literature vol. 14. Minneapolis: University of Minnesota Press, 1985. [Bataille2]

Belting, Hans. *Likeness and Presence: A History of the Image before the Era of Art.* Chicago: University of Chicago Press, 1994.

Benjamin, Walter. *Charles Baudelaire: A Lyric Poet in the Era of High Capitalism,* trans. Harry Zohn. London: Verso, 1973.

Bentley, D. M. R. "Rossetti and the *Hypnerotomachia Poliphili,*" *English Language Notes* 14 (1977): 279–283. [Bentley1]

———. "Rossetti's 'Ave' and Related Pictures," *Victorian Poetry* 15 (1977): 21–35. [Bentley2]

———. "Rossetti's 'Hand and Soul,'" *English Studies in Canada* 3 (1977): 445–457. [Bentley3]

———. "Rossetti's Pre-Raphaelite Manifesto: The 'Old and New Art' Sonnets," *English Language Notes* 15 (1978): 197–203. [Bentley4]

Bernstein, Charles. *A Poetics.* Cambridge: Harvard University Press, 1992.

Bois, Yves-Alain, and Rosalind E. Krauss. *Formless: A User's Guide.* New York: Zone, 1997.

Bornstein, George, and Ralph G. Williams, eds. *Palimpsest: Editorial Theory in the Humanities.* Ann Arbor: University of Michigan Press, 1993.

Breton, André. *Communicating Vessels,* trans. Mary Ann Caws and Geoffrey T. Harris. Lincoln: University of Nebraska Press, 1990. [Breton1]

———. *Mad Love,* trans. Mary Ann Caws. Lincoln: University of Nebraska Press, 1987. [Breton2]

———. *Surrealism and Painting,* trans. Simon Watson Taylor. New York: Harper and Row, 1972. [Breton3]

Bronfen, Elizabeth. *Over Her Dead Body: Death, Femininity, and the Aesthetic.* Manchester: Manchester University Press, 1992.

Brown, Ford Madox. *The Diary of Ford Madox Brown,* ed. Virginia Surtees. New Haven: Yale University Press, 1981.

[Buchanan, Robert] Thomas Maitland. "The Fleshly School of Poetry: Mr. D. G. Rossetti," *Contemporary Review* 18 (October 1871): 334–350.

Buckley, Jerome H. *The Pre-Raphaelites.* New York: Modern Library, 1968.

Burckhardt, Sigurd. "The Poet as Fool and Priest: A Discourse on Method," in *Shakespearean Meanings.* Princeton: Princeton University Press, 1968.

Butterworth, Walter. *Dante Gabriel Rossetti in Relation to Dante Alighieri*. London: Sheratt and Hughes, 1912.

Cabanne, Pierre. *Dialogues with Marcel Duchamp*, trans. Ron Padgett. New York: Viking, 1971.

Caine, T. Hall. *Recollections of Dante Gabriel Rossetti*. New York: Roberts, 1883.

Casteras, Susan P. *English Pre-Raphaelitism and Its Reception in America in the Nineteenth Century*. Rutherford, N.J.: Fairleigh Dickinson University Press, 1990. [Casteras1]

————, ed. *Pre-Raphaelite Art in Its European Context*. Rutherford, N.J.: Fairleigh Dickinson University Press, 1995. [Casteras2]

Christ, Carol T. *Victorian and Modern Poetics*. Chicago: University of Chicago Press, 1984.

Crary, Jonathan. *Techniques of the Observer: On Vision and Modernity in the Nineteenth Century*. Cambridge: MIT Press, 1990.

Davies, J. L., ed. *The Working Men's College, 1854–1904*. London: Macmillan, 1904.

Dickens, Charles. *Household Words*. Leipzig: Tauchnitz, 1851.

Doughty, Oswald. *A Victorian Romantic: Dante Gabriel Rossetti*. 2d ed. London: Oxford University Press, 1960.

Drucker, Johanna. *The Visible Word: Experimental Typography and Modern Art, 1909–1923*. Chicago: University of Chicago Press, 1994.

Edwards, Robert R. "Guinizelli's Readers and the Strategies of Historicism," *Philological Quarterly* 71 (1992): 419–436.

Eliot, T. S. *The Sacred Wood: Essays on Poetry and Criticism*. London: Methuen, 1920. [Eliot1]

————. *Selected Essays, 1917–1932*. London: Faber and Faber, 1932. [Eliot2]

————. "Ulysses, Order, and Myth," *Dial* 75 (1923): 480–483. [Eliot3]

————. *The Use of Poetry and the Use of Criticism: Studies in the Relation of Criticism to Poetry in England*. London: Faber and Faber, 1933. [Eliot4]

Elkins, James. *The Poetics of Perspective*. Ithaca: Cornell University Press, 1994.

Ezell, Margaret J. M., and Katherine O'Brien O'Keefe, eds. *Cultural Artifacts and the Production of Meaning: The Page, The Image, and The Body*. Ann Arbor: University of Michigan Press, 1994.

Faxon, Alicia Craig. *Dante Gabriel Rossetti*. New York: Abbeville, 1989.

Fennell, Francis L., Jr. *Dante Gabriel Rossetti: An Annotated Bibliography*. New York: Garland, 1982.

[Ford] Hueffer, Ford Madox. *Memories and Impressions: A Study in Atmospheres*. New York: Harper, 1911. [Ford1]

————. *Rossetti: A Critical Essay on His Art*. Chicago: Rand, McNally, 1915, rpt. from 1896 Longman's ed. [Ford2]

Foster, Hal, ed. *The Anti-Aesthetic: Essays on Postmodern Culture*. Port Town-
send, Wash.: Bay Press, 1983.

——. *Compulsive Beauty*. Cambridge: MIT Press, 1995.

Fredeman, William E., ed. *The P.R.B. Journal . . .* Oxford: Clarendon, 1975.
[Fredeman1]

——. "The Pre-Raphaelite Literary Art of Dante Gabriel Rossetti," *Journal of Pre-Raphaelite and Literary Studies*, N.S. 1 (1988): 55–74. [Frede-
man2]

——. *Pre-Raphaelitism: A Bibliocritical Study*. Cambridge: Harvard University Press, 1965. [Fredeman3]

——. *A Rossetti Cabinet: A Portfolio of Drawings by Dante Gabriel Rossetti*.
Stroud, Glouchestershire: Ian Hodgkins, 1991. [Fredeman4]

——. "Rossetti's 'In Memoriam': An Elegiac Reading of *The House of
Life*," *Bulletin of the John Rylands Library* 47 (1965): 298–341. [Frede-
man5]

——. "'Woodman, Spare That Block': Published and Unpublished Illustrations and Book Designs of Dante Gabriel Rossetti," *Journal of Pre-
Raphaelite Studies*, N.S. 5 (1996): 7–41. [Fredeman6]

——, ed. *Centennial Essays on Dante Gabriel Rossetti*. Special issue of *Victorian Poetry*, 20, nos. 3–4 (1982). [Fredeman7]

From Realism to Symbolism: Whistler and His World. New York: Wildenstein
Gallery, 1971.

Fry, Roger. "Rossetti's Water Colours of 1857," *Burlington Magazine* 29
(June 1916): 100–109.

Gasman, Lydia. "Mystery, Magic, and Love in Picasso, 1925–1938: Picasso
and the Surrealist Poets." Ph.D. diss., Columbia University, 1981.

Gilchrist, Alexander. *Life of William Blake*. 2 vols. London: Macmillan,
1863.

Gitter, Elizabeth J. "Rossetti's Translations of Early Italian Lyrics," *Victorian
Poetry* 12 (1974): 351–362.

Goff, Barbara Munson. "Dante's *La Vita Nuova* and Two Pre-Raphaelite
Beatrices," *Journal of Pre-Raphaelite Studies* 4, no. 2 (1984): 100–116.

Gray, Nicolette. *Rossetti, Dante, and Ourselves*. London: Faber and Faber,
1947.

Grieve, A. I. "The Applied Art of D. G. Rossetti: 1. His Picture Frames,"
Burlington Magazine 115 (1973): 16–24. [Grieve1]

——. *The Art of Dante Gabriel Rossetti: The Pre-Raphaelite Period*. Hing-
ham, England: Real World, 1973. [Grieve2]

——. *The Art of Dante Gabriel Rossetti: The Watercolours and Drawings of
1850–1855*. Norwich: Real World, 1978. [Grieve3]

——. *The Art of Dante Gabriel Rossetti: 1. Found; 2. The Pre-Raphaelite Modern Subject*. Norwich, England: Real World, 1976. [Grieve4]

———. "Rossetti's Applied Art Designs: 2. Book Bindings," *Burlington Magazine* 115 (1973): 79–83. [Grieve5]

———. "Whistler and the Pre-Raphaelites," *Art Quarterly* 34 (1971): 219–228. [Grieve6]

Grigely, Joseph. *Textualterity: Art, Theory, and Textual Criticism.* Ann Arbor: University of Michigan Press, 1995.

Hardie, Martin. *Water-colour Painting in Britain,* ed. Dudley Snelgrove with Jonathan Mayne and Basil Taylor. 3 vols. New York: Barnes and Noble, 1966–1968.

Hearn, Lafcadio. *Pre-Raphaelite and Other Poets: Lectures.* New York: Dodd, Mead, 1922.

Henderson, Linda Dalrymple. *The Fourth Dimension and Non-Euclidean Geometry in Modernism.* Princeton: Princeton University Press, 1983.

Hoagwood, Terence Alan. *Politics, Philosophy, and the Production of Romantic Texts.* De Kalb: Northern Illinois University Press, 1996.

Hollier, Denis. *Against Architecture: The Writings of Georges Bataille,* trans. Betsy Wing. Cambridge: MIT Press, 1989.

Hunt, John Dixon. *The Pre-Raphaelite Imagination, 1848–1900.* Lincoln: University of Nebraska Press, 1968.

Hunt, William Holman. *Pre-Raphaelitism and the Pre-Raphaelite Brotherhood.* 2 vols. London: Macmillan, 1905, rev. ed. Chapman and Hall, 1913.

James, William. *Principles of Psychology.* 2 vols. New York: Holt, 1890.

Johnson, Galen A., ed. *The Merleau-Ponty Aesthetics Reader: Philosophy and Painting,* trans. Michael B. Smith. Evanston: Northwestern University Press, 1993.

Kandinsky, Wassily. *Concerning the Spiritual in Art,* trans. M. T. H. Sadler. New York: Dover, 1977.

Krieger, Murray. *Ekphrasis: The Illusion of the Natural Sign.* Baltimore: Johns Hopkins University Press, 1992.

Lakoff, George, and Mark Johnson. *Philosophy in the Flesh: the Embodied Mind and Its Challenge to Western Thought.* New York: Basic, 1999.

Landow, George P. "Life Touching Lips with Immortality: Rossetti's Typological Structures," *Studies in Romanticism* 17 (1978): 247–266.

Leavis, F. R. *Revaluation: Tradition and Development in English Poetry.* London: Chatto and Windus, 1936.

Lottes, Wolfgang. "'Take Out the Picture and Frame the Sonnet': Rossetti's Sonnets and Verses for His Own Works of Art," *Anglia* 96 (1978): 108–135.

Macleod, Diane Sachko. "Dante Gabriel Rossetti and Titian," *Apollo* 121 (1985): 36–39.

Manganiello, Dominic. *T. S. Eliot and Dante.* Basingstoke, England: Macmillan, 1989.

Marillier, Henry Currie. *Dante Gabriel Rossetti: An Illustrated Memorial of His Art and Life*. London: Bell, 1899.

Marti, Mario. *Storia dello Stil Nuovo*. 2 Vols. Lecce, Italy: Milella, 1972.

Maturana, Humberto, and Francisco Varela. *Autopoiesis and Cognition: The Realization of the Living*. With a preface by Sir Stafford Beer. Boston: Reidel, 1980.

McGann, Jerome. *Black Riders: The Visible Language of Modernism*. Princeton: Princeton University Press, 1993. [McGann1]

———. "Dante Gabriel Rossetti and the Betrayal of Truth," *Victorian Poetry* 26 (1988): 339–361. [McGann2]

———. *The Textual Condition*. Princeton: Princeton University Press, 1991. [McGann3]

McKenzie, D. F. *Bibliography and the Sociology of Texts*. The Panizzi Lectures, 1985. London: British Library, 1986.

McLean, Ruari. *Victorian Book Design and Colour Printing*. Rev. ed. London: Faber and Faber, 1972.

McLeod, Randall. "Information on Information," in *TEXT* 5, ed. D. C. Greetham and W. Speed Hill, 241–284. New York: AMS, 1991.

Morse, B. J. "Dante Gabriel Rossetti and Dante Alighieri," *Englische Studien* 68 (1933–1934): 227–248.

Paolucci, Anne. "Ezra Pound and Dante Gabriel Rossetti as Translators of Guido Cavalcanti," *Romantic Review* 51 (1960): 256–267.

Panofsky, Erwin. *Perspective as Symbolic Form,* trans. Christopher Wood. New York: Zone, 1991.

Pater, Walter. *Appreciations*. London: Macmillan, 1889. [Pater1]

———. *Plato and Platonism: A Series of Lectures*. London: Macmillan, 1893. [Pater2]

———. *The Renaissance: Studies in Art and Poetry,* ed. Donald L. Hill. Berkeley: University of California Press, 1980. [Pater3]

Plato. *Collected Dialogues,* ed. Edith Hamilton and Huntington Cairns. Princeton: Bollingen Foundation, 1961.

Pound, Ezra. *Sonnets and Ballate of Guido Cavalcanti*. London: Stephen Swift, 1912.

Rees, Joan. *The Poetry of Dante Gabriel Rossetti: Modes of Self-Expression*. Cambridge: Cambridge University Press, 1981.

Riede, David, ed. *Critical Essays on Dante Gabriel Rossetti*. New York: Hall, 1992. [Riede1]

———. *Dante Gabriel Rossetti and the Limits of Victorian Vision*. Ithaca: Cornell University Press, 1983. [Riede2]

———. *Dante Gabriel Rossetti Revisited*. New York: Twayne, 1992. [Riede3]

Robbin, Tony. *Fourfield: Computers, Art, and the 4th Dimension*. Boston: Little, Brown, 1992.

Ray, Gordon N. *The Illustrator and the Book in England from 1790 to 1914*. New York: Pierpont Morgan Library, 1976.

Rosenblum, Robert. *The International Style of 1800: A Study in Linear Abstraction*. New York: Garland, 1976. [Rosenblum1]

———. *Modern Painting in the Northern Romantic Tradition: Friedrich to Rothko*. New York: Harper and Row, 1975. [Rosenblum2]

Rossetti, William Michael. *Dante Gabriel Rossetti as Designer and Writer*. London: Cassell, 1889. [WMRossetti1]

———, ed. *Dante Gabriel Rossetti: His Family Letters with a Memoir*. 2 vols. London: Ellis and Elvey, 1895. [WMRossetti2]

———, ed. *Ruskin: Rossetti: Pre-Raphaelitism*. London: Allen, 1899. [WMRossetti3]

———, ed. *Rossetti Papers, 1862 to 1870*. London: Sands, 1903. [WMRossetti4]

———. *Selected Letters of William Michael Rossetti*, ed. Roger W. Peattie. State College: Pennsylvania State University Press, 1990. [WMRossetti5]

———. "Some Scraps of Verse and Prose by Dante Gabriel Rossetti," *Pall Mall Magazine* 16 (1898): 480–496. [WMRossetti6]

Ruskin, John. *The Art Criticism of John Ruskin*, ed. Robert L. Herbert. Glouchester, Mass.: Peter Smith, 1969. [Ruskin1]

———. *Modern Painters*. 6 Vols. London: George Allen, 1897. [Ruskin2]

———. *The Works of John Ruskin*, ed. Edward T. Cook and Alexander D. O. Wedderburn. 39 vols. London: Longmans, Green, 1902–1912. [Ruskin3]

Samuels, Lisa. "Introduction to Poetry and the Problem of Beauty," *Modern Language Studies* 27 (1997): 2–7.

Samuels, Lisa, and Jerome McGann. "Deformance and Interpretation," *New Literary History* 30 (1999): 25–56.

Sanouillet, Michel, and Elmer Peterson, eds. *Salt Seller: The Writings of Marcel Duchamp*. New York: Oxford University Press, 1973.

Sharp, William. *Dante Gabriel Rossetti: A Record and a Study*. London: Macmillan, 1882.

Shaw, James Eustace. *Essays on the Vita Nuova*. Elliott Monographs in the Romance Languages and Literature, ed. Edward C. Armstrong, no. 25. Princeton: Princeton University Press; Paris: Les Presses Universitaires de France, 1929.

Shields, Frederic. "A Note Upon Rossetti's Method of Drawing in Crayons," *Century Guild Hobby Horse* 5 (1890): 70–73. [Shields1]

———. "Some Notes on D. G. Rossetti," *Century Guild Hobby Horse* 1 (1886): 140–154. [Shields2]

Slayton, William T. "'Roderick and Rosalba': D. G. Rossetti's First Juvenile Work," *Victorians Institute Journal* 17 (1989): 181–191.

Smith, Lindsay. "Stereoscopy and the Pre-Raphaelites," in *Pre-Raphaelites Re-viewed,* ed. Marcia Pointon, 83–99. Manchester: Manchester University Press, 1989. [Smith1]

———. *Victorian Photography, Painting, and Poetry: The Enigma of Visibility in Ruskin, Morris, and the Pre-Raphaelites.* Cambridge: Cambridge University Press, 1995. [Smith2]

Stein, Richard L. *The Ritual of Interpretation: The Fine Arts as Literature in Ruskin, Rossetti, and Pater.* Cambridge: Harvard University Press, 1975.

Stephens, Frederic G. *Dante Gabriel Rossetti.* London: Seeley, 1894.

Sulman, Thomas. "A Memorable Art Class," *Good Words* 38 (1897): 547–551.

Surtees, Virginia. *The Paintings and Drawings of Dante Gabriel Rossetti, 1828–1882.* Catalogue raisonné. 2 vols. Oxford: Clarendon, 1971.

Sweeney, James Johnson. "Eleven Europeans in America: Marcel Duchamp," *The Museum of Modern Art Bulletin* 13 (1946): 19-21.

Swinburne, A. C. "Part II," in *Notes on the Royal Academy Exhibition, 1868.* London: Hotten, 1868.

Tanita, Hiroyuki. "W. M. Rossetti's 'Hoxai,'" *Journal of Pre-Raphaelite Studies* 7, no. 1 (1986): 89–91.

Troxell, Janet Camp. "The 'Trial Books' of Dante Gabriel Rossetti," rpt. from *The Colophon* (1938) in *The Princeton University Library Chronicle* 33, no. 3 (1972): 177–192.

Vasari, Giorgio. *Lives of Seventy of the Most Eminent Painters, Sculptors, and Architects,* ed. E. H. Blashfield et al., trans. Mrs. Jonathan Foster. 4 vols. London: G. Bell, 1897.

Vincent, E. R. *Gabriele Rossetti in England.* Oxford: Clarendon, 1936.

Vitale, Murizio. *Poeti della Prima Scuola.* Arona, Italy: Paideia, 1951.

Watanabi, Toshio. *High Victorian Japonisme.* Swiss Asian Studies. Research Studies vol. 10. Bern: Peter Lang, 1991. [Watanabi1]

———. "Pre-Raphaelite *Japonisme?* Enthusiasm for and Ambivalence Toward a New Culture," *Journal of Pre-Raphaelite Studies,* N.S. 3, no. 2 (1994): 2–7. [Watanabi2]

Waugh, Evelyn. *Rossetti: His Life and Works.* London: Duckworth, 1928.

Welland, D. S. R., ed. *The Pre-Raphaelites in Literature and Art.* London: Harrap, 1953.

Williams, Charles. *The Figure of Beatrice: A Study in Dante.* London: Faber and Faber, 1943.

INDEX

A l'infinitif (Duchamp), 155
abstraction, 3, 7, 32, 136; art history
   and, 131; Rossetti Woman as, 123
Adams, Henry, 145
Aesthetic Movement, 3, 28, 145–
   146
allegory, 105–106, 108, 123, 128, 130,
   136, 152
"Another Love" (D. G. Rossetti),
   63
Aquinas, St. Thomas, xv, 142
Arnold, Matthew, 60
art: anti-illusionism and, 67, 102,
   106, 107, 115, 128, 135, 155, 165n3;
   of the body, 27; conceptual, 7,
   48; "failure" and, 89; knowledge
   and, 37; literature and, xvi; magic
   and, 59, 65, 119, 160n24; "materialist," 77; meaning and, 22, 30, 121;
   mission of, xvii, xviii; morality
   in, 89; nature and, 13; perspective
   and, 110–118; pictorial genres,
   81; portraiture and, xvii, 26;
   professionalization of, 132; as
   revelation, 4, 31–32, 84–97;
   science and, xiv, xvii; total work
   of, 67, 71, 76; transcendence and,
   62, 88, 150; truth-functions of,
   15–16, 45; v. philosophy, xv,
   xvii, 20, 21–23, 142; as vehicle
   of ideas, 20, 72
Art Catholic, 5, 30, 45
art for art's sake, 6, 89
Arthurian lore, 97, 111
Arts and Crafts Movement, 71

Astarte Syriaca (D. G. Rossetti), 3, 8,
   97, 120, 151; anti-illusionism in,
   115; eroticism of, 153, 154; forbidden knowledge and, 157
Atalanta in Calydon (Swinburne),
   70, 71
Aurélia (D. G. Rossetti), and Nerval,
   Gérard de. See *Fazio's Mistress*
"Autumn Idleness" (D. G. Rossetti),
   56
"Ave" (D. G. Rossetti), 61
Awakening Conscience, The (Hunt),
   31, 32

Ballads and Sonnets (1881), 80
Balthus, 1, 103
Barthes, Roland, xiii–xiv, xvi
Bataille, Georges, 1, 105, 145
Baudelaire, Charles, xiii, 104, 133
Baum, Paull, 57
Beata Beatrix (D. G. Rossetti), 18, 19,
   20, 79, 102, 148; relation between
   art and eros in, 97–98; structure
   of, 115; *Vita Nuova* (Dante) and,
   130
Beatrice, 3, 36, 40, 48–49, 149; as
   Dante's guiding focus, 60; death
   of, 56; Fazio's mistress and, 129;
   refusal of salutation to Dante, 53;
   in Rossetti's *Beata Beatrix* paint-
   ing, 98–99
"Belcolore" (D. G. Rossetti), 74
Bella Mano, La (D. G. Rossetti), 151
"Belle-buona" (D. G. Rossetti), 74
Bentley, D. M. R., 16